Fostering Skills in Cameroon

DIRECTIONS IN DEVELOPMENT
Human Development

Fostering Skills in Cameroon

Inclusive Workforce Development, Competitiveness, and Growth

Shobhana Sosale and Kirsten Majgaard

WORLD BANK GROUP

Contents

Boxes

Figures

Tables

Acknowledgments

The team is grateful to officials from the Cameroon Ministry of Economy, Planning and Regional Integration (MINEPAT), Ministry of Finance (MINFI), Ministry of Employment, Vocational Education and Training (MINEFOP), Ministry of Basic Education (MINEDUB), Ministry of Higher Education (MINESUP), Ministry of Youth (MINEJEUNE), Ministry of Science and Innovation (MINRESI), the National Institute of Statistics, and the Association of the Private Sector for sharing valuable data and information at various phases of the preparation and completion of this report. The team is also grateful to the Youth Group leaders and their constituents in Cameroon for their valuable inputs for the preparation of the study.

This report is a product of collaboration between a Government of Cameroon multi-sectoral team, the World Bank Central Africa Education, Poverty Reduction and Education, and Finance and Private Sector Development Global Practices teams. The work was led, and the report was prepared by Shobhana Sosale with contributions from Kirsten Majgaard. Ramahatra Mamy Rakotomalala and Samira Halabi were key contributors at the concept note stage of the study. The peer reviewers at concept note stage were Amit Dar, Xiaoyan Liang, Dena Ringold, and Taye Alemu Mengistae. The Advisory Committee for the study at concept stage comprised Emanuela di Gropello, John Giles, Patrick Premand, and Jee-Peng Tan. The final draft report has benefited with inputs from peer reviewers Souleymane Coulibaly, Venkatesh Sundararaman, John Giles, Gilberto de Barros, Alphonsus Tji Achomuma, and Birger Fredriksen (external reviewer). Overall guidance was provided by Gregor Binkert and Peter Nicolas Materu.

Jee-Peng Tan, Viviana Gomez Venegas, Ryan Peter Flynn, Judith Lewetchou, and Eleni Papakosta were instrumental in all stages of client training, data collection, and data scoring for the SABER-Workforce Development tool. The team is grateful to Kristen Himelein and Rose Mungai for their timely support with data. The multi-sectoral Government team comprising staff from ministries of education & training, youth, agriculture, forestry, industry and mining, *Groupement Inter-patronal du Cameroun* (GICAM) provided valuable inputs and guidance for the preparation of the workforce development analysis. Short background papers based on extensive consultations with the Government multi-sectoral team on public sector employees, youth leaders and constituent groups and information about ongoing programs and projects from secondary data/literature review for the note were prepared by consultants Judith Lewetchou Efouefack,

Eleni Papakosta, Monica Chavez, and Vincent Perrot. The team acknowledges the support for logistics for the numerous consultations from integral team members Natalie Tchoumba Bitnga, Rose-Claire Pakabomba, and Laurence Hougue Bouguen, and to Francine le Touzé for the French translation of the document. The report was edited by Paul Holtz, from Next Partners, and Sandra Gain, consultant, Publishing and Knowledge Unit, ECRPK at the World Bank.

The report has benefited from the deliberations of the Program for Applied Sciences, Engineering and Technology (PASET) workshop that took place from June 10-12, 2014 in Dakar, Senegal. Pre-workshop consultations with the Cameroon Ministry of Employment, Vocational Education and Training (MINEFOP), Ministry of Higher Education (MINESUP), and Ministry for Science and Innovation (MINRESI) added value to the document.

The initial versions of the skills analysis, policies and institutions for workforce development and the background papers were progressively presented during the preparation phase of the study to the Government multi-ministry team officials, GICAM, and public and private sector education and training stakeholders in Cameroon.

Executive Summary

Vision 2035 describes the Government of Cameroon's goals for the country's growth and development—the main goal being for Cameroon to become an emerging economy by 2035. The vision includes medium-term objectives, with a focus on alleviating poverty, becoming a middle-income country, becoming a newly industrialized country, and consolidating democracy and national unity while respecting the country's diversity. Vision 2035 also serves as the long-term anchor for the government's recently updated poverty reduction strategy, which puts employment at center stage.

The vision, officially known as the Strategy for Growth and Employment (DSCE), was finalized in 2010. Among other aspects, the DSCE identifies unemployment and weak productivity as key challenges for the country's development.[1] Thus, the vision seeks to:

- Develop more robust formal and informal employment opportunities by strengthening human development
- Increase productivity in agriculture, mining, and key value chains (timber, tourism, and information and communications technology)
- Stimulate growth through investments in critical infrastructure (notably energy, roads, port infrastructure, and water supply and sanitation) and through improvements in the business climate and regional integration.

The DSCE sets an ambitious target of reducing underemployment from 76 percent of the workforce to 50 percent by 2020, by creating tens of thousands of formal jobs. But based on the results from the first two years of its implementation, the DSCE is far from achieving that target.

This report is intended to support Cameroon's efforts to augment the skills of its workforce to increase labor productivity and competitiveness and to create jobs—while recognizing that many factors other than skills can inhibit labor productivity and job creation. The report uses the terms workforce and labor force interchangeably. More specifically, the study is intended to help inform a national strategy for skills development and related policies and institutions in support of competitiveness, productivity, and job creation.

The study presents empirical analyses of skills development as it relates to the labor market to promote labor competitiveness and job creation. A sector-specific approach to skills development has been adopted while paying attention to employment-intensive sectors and addressing growth-intensive investments. The study reaches conclusions and offers policy recommendations based on its efforts to answer six questions:

- What has been the trajectory of Cameroon's economic growth? Which sectors have contributed to growth?
- Where are jobs being created?
- What types of skills are used in the sectors where the highest percentages of the population are employed? Are the employed productive?
- What are the demand and supply barriers to skills?
- Which policies and institutions are at play? Are they sufficient for Cameroon to reach full-fledged middle-income country status?
- What needs to or could be reformed to enhance skills development and productivity for competitiveness and growth?

The sectors analyzed by the study are infrastructure, forestry/wood and wood processing, agriculture, and agribusiness (with a focus on cotton textiles, palm oil, tourism, and extractives); another sector, technology and innovation, has also been included. The priority sectors were chosen based on the following:

- Their estimated potential for job creation.
- Their estimated potential for increasing productivity. The skills development perspective of job creation is seen as being relatively narrow, because the constraints to job creation in a particular sector in Cameroon often lie outside traditional labor policies, including skills development.
- Labor concentration.
- Whether jobs in the sectors cut across the formal and informal sectors where most of the poor and vulnerable are engaged.
- Prospects for creating economic opportunity through job creation and workforce value added in most of the selected sectors.
- Their potential to remain labor-intensive, while also being the most amenable to structural transformation.

Given the large informal sector in Cameroon, the diagnostic and policy work includes analyses of and recommendations for opportunities in the formal sector and increasing productivity in the informal and formal sectors. A particular challenge in studying skills for the informal sector has been to identify appropriate tools.

Recognizing the need for a mix of tools to address the challenge of skills development, the conceptual framework for this study integrates three themes and subthemes. First, the study uses the Aggregation-Accumulation Framework to model growth and skills development using proxies and, together with the Skills Toward Employment and Productivity (STEP) framework, shows the potential for shifting the production possibility frontier. Second, the study includes an assessment of the stock and flow of workforce skills, since policy conclusions and recommendations differ for the two. Third, the study applies the Systems Approach for Better Education Results (SABER) Workforce Development (WfD) framework to analyze policies and institutions that have been conducive to or retarded skills development.

The Aggregation-Accumulation Model helps measure the change in gross domestic product over time (the independent variable) due to changes in skills accumulation as measured by educational attainment (the dependent variable), with all other factors of production (land, capital) held constant. It is acknowledged that educational attainment is a weak proxy for assessing the distribution of skills and is largely insufficient to inform policy. But in the absence of better measures to assess skills, educational attainment is the best quantitative measure. Learning assessments would also serve as a good measure for skills. However, learning has not been measured consistently in Cameroon. The country participates in the regional Program for the Analysis of Education Systems (PASEC) assessment, and has maintained its position as one of the top three placements in PASEC. But PASEC tests have changed over time, casting doubt on the comparability of country results.

The study takes stock of economic growth until 2012, the aspects that have contributed to or detracted from skills accumulation, the structure of the labor market and its shift over time from the primary agricultural sector to the tertiary services sector, and the education and skills of the workforce. Demand-side analysis has been conducted by reviewing the value chain analyses financed by the Private Sector Development and Competitiveness Project of the World Bank's Finance and Private Sector Development Department, to assess the types of skills most sought by the primary, secondary, and tertiary sectors. Supply-side analysis has been undertaken by assessing the extent to which skills development is being fostered by the education and training sector.

The strategy and indicators for measuring the supply and demand of skills were developed by:

- Reviewing the evolution of growth and sector contributions to growth, employment, and associated education levels of the workforce
- Drawing on labor market analyses by the National Institute of Statistics and the International Labour Organization
- Mapping the demand for skills using the 2011 employers' survey
- Linking sector-oriented employment and skills needs for value added in the value chain analyses by the World Bank's Africa Region Trade and Competitiveness Department
- Conducting empirical analysis using the SABER-WfD tool for the diagnostics of the existing skills development policy and institutional framework for workforce development
- Drawing on an extensive literature review.

Several key conclusions emerged. First, there is significant deadweight loss with respect to the available skills in the system and the use of those skills. That is, the most highly educated people—those who have completed university education—have the highest unemployment rates. That is partly because they tend to opt out of lower-skill jobs and partly because of the shortage of jobs requiring highly skilled workers. Moreover, most university graduates have generalized skills as opposed to specialized skills. And university graduates often avoid taking jobs in rural and remote areas. Finally, the education and training system is highly inefficient, making education and training costly for households. These costs outweigh the private and social benefits of education and training. Combined, these factors create a mismatch between the quantity and quality of skills. Supply is not commensurate with the demand for workforce skills.

Second, about 90 percent of the workers in Cameroon are underemployed and in informal jobs. Only 5 or 6 percent work in the formal sector, and the business environment is not conducive to self-employment. Entrepreneurs cite high taxes, a difficult tax regime, extensive corruption, problems with access to credit, excessive bureaucracy, unfair competition, problems with energy and water, transportation challenges, and a cumbersome judicial system as the main disincentives to starting a company and doing business. Workforce training and skills are also ranked among the list of barriers. These are major problems for the medium-to-long term, even though most enterprises are small or medium in size. Over time, the skills of the workforce would become incommensurate with the increased potential that the market could actually bear. Another challenge is that most workers in the informal sector lack entrepreneurial and technical skills—a major contributor to reduced productivity. This report also discusses constraints on skills development that all sectors are facing.

Third, Cameroon lags behind most countries in competitiveness: the country is ranked 168 of 189 economies. It is ranked at 132 for starting a business, mainly because of cumbersome and time-consuming procedures, long wait times for obtaining licenses to operate, high costs, and the absence of minimum capital to start small and medium-size enterprises. Cameroon lags behind Malaysia, Thailand, and Vietnam in the size of the manufacturing sector, despite having similar relative size and equal growth of the services industry. Cameroon has latent potential to improve its manufacturing base through the promotion of light manufacturing in agribusiness, wood processing, and ancillary sectors to the extractives industry. The main impediments are the business environment (tax regime, excessive bureaucracy, unfair competition, cumbersome judicial system, etc.) and the low skills base, leading to low productivity.

Well-performing economies on the *Doing Business* indicators (World Bank 2013) tend to be more inclusive along two dimensions. They have smaller informal sectors, so more people have access to formal markets and can benefit from regulations such as social protection and workplace safety regulations. They are also more likely to have gender equality under the law. Women make up nearly half the population in Cameroon, and boosting their productivity would benefit the country.

Finally, country-level, time-based benchmarking shows that Cameroon's system is between "latent" and "emerging" for all the functional dimensions of policies and institutions in the SABER-WfD analytical framework—strategic, system oversight, and service delivery. The findings represent an average. A deeper examination of the underlying scores across the nine policy areas reveals some confounding aspects, requiring a more nuanced approach to understanding the system. Specifically, there is a strategic framework (policy areas of strategic direction and coordination, but not demand-led) that is a latent system. This is largely due to centralized preparation of vision and strategy documents and action plans. System oversight and service delivery dimensions are also latent. That is, there is limited collective engagement across education and training ministries, and other ministries that provide specialized skills. This is due to a highly fragmented approach to workforce skills development oversight and service delivery. On other policy dimensions, Cameroon has latent potential.

Taking into account all these elements, the prospects for Cameroon to move from lower-income to middle-income status are promising. There are implications for creating more dynamic and responsive workforce skills and a competencies development system to address potential new jobs and requirements. A new strategy is required to foster the accumulation of skills and competencies for value added in labor-intensive sectors, economic diversification, and structural transformation. Cameroon requires a unified, action-oriented framework for skills development to promote collective action for improving system oversight and ensuring service delivery for results.

This report culminates with a proposed framework for action constructed on 10 principles: optimization, concentration and assimilation, adequacy, specialization versus generalization, facilitation, concatenation, relevance, maximization, portability, and structural transformation. For each of these areas, some directions are proposed, including suggestions for global good practices that Cameroon could draw upon. Recommendations are also provided for revised and renewed governance and institutional arrangements. These include developing a management information system for jobs and promoting public-private partnerships. Some alternative financing options for skills programs are also discussed. Finally, monitoring and evaluation systems are proposed.

The expected outcomes are reducing systemic inefficiencies, promoting options, and boosting the contribution of the informal sector to support Cameroon's competitiveness and growth. The main risk is that the government might not endorse the recommendations. But that might not be a substantial risk, since mitigation measures have included extensive country-level consultations through crowd-sourcing and close engagement with the government's multi-sector team.

Note

1. The DSCE was approved by an Inter-Ministerial Committee on August 26, 2009 and covers the period 2009–19.

Abbreviations and Acronyms

A2D	Douala Development Agency
AAACP-ACP	Agricultural Commodities Program
AAF	Accumulation-Aggregation Framework
AAM	Aggregation-Accumulation Model
ACE	Africa Centers of Excellence
ACP	Agricultural Commodities Program
ADC	Airports of Cameroon
AES-SONEL	National Electric Company *Société Nationale d'Electricité*
AFD	French Development Agency *Agence Française de Développement*
AfDB	African Development Bank
AFOP	Support program for the renovation and development of vocational training in agriculture, livestock, and fishing
AFVAC	Association of Families of Victims of Traffic Accidents
AJEHOV	Association of Young Humanitarian Volunteer Students
AJVC	Cameroon Green Youth Association
A/L	Advanced Level
ALMP	Active labor market programs
ALVF	Association for the Fight against Violence against Women
ANOR	Standards and quality agency
ARIZ	Monitoring Financial Risks
ASET	Applied science, engineering and technology
ASPPA	Project to support strategies of farmers and the professionalization of agriculture
ATPO	Association of Palm Oil By-Products Transformers *Association des Transformateurs des Produits Oléagineux*
AVD	Vital Actions for Sustainable Development
AYICC	African Youth Initiative on Climate Change
BAC	Baccalaureate

BEPC	First-cycle secondary education Certificate
	Brevet d'Études du Premier Cycle
BHA	Hydraulically assembled wood
BTS	Advanced Technician Certificate
C2D	Contract for Debt Relief and Development
	Brevet de Technicien Supérieur
CAD	Computer-aided design
CAM	Computer-aided management
CAP	Certificate of Professional Competence
	Certificate d'Aptitude Professionnelle
CAS	World Bank Country Assistance Strategy
CBF	Cameroon Business Forum
CCI	International Trade Center
	Centre du commerce international
CCIMA	Chamber of Commerce, Industry, Mines, and Crafts
CDC	Cameroon Development Corporation
CEFOPRAF	Center for Professional Training Brotherly Love
CEM	Cameroon Economic Memorandum
CEMAC	Central African Economic and Monetary Community
CEO	Chief executive officer
CEP	Primary Study Certificate
	Certificat d'Étude Primaire
CEPROMINES	Vocational Training Center for the Mining Professions
	Centre de Formation professionnelle aux Métiers Miniers
CFAF	CFA franc
CFC	Common Fund for Commodities
	Fond commun pour les produits de base
CFM	Vocational Training Center
	Centre de Formation Professionnelle aux Métiers
CFMIN	Vocational Training Center for Industry Trades of Nyom
	Centre de Formation Professionnelle aux Métiers de l'Industrie de Nyom
CFPC	Continuous Professional Training Center of the Room
	Centre de Formation Professionnelle Continue de la Salle
CFPE	Vocational Training Centers of Excellence
	Centres de Formation Professionnelle d'Excellence
CFPM	Mining Vocational Training Center
	Centre de Formation Professionnelle des Mines
CFPR	Public intensive vocational training centers

CFPS	Vocational Sectoral Training Centers
CFR	Rural training centers
CIEP	International Center of Education Studies of Paris
CIMSGWD	Cameroun Inter-Ministerial Steering Group for Workforce Development
CMPJ	Multifunctional Center for Youth Development
	Centre Multifonctionelles de Promotion de la Jeunesse
CNUCED	United Nations Conference on Trade and Development
	Conférence des Nations unies sur le Commerce et le Développement
CONFEJES	Conference of Ministers of Youth and Sports of the Francophonie
CTSE	Technical Committee of Monitoring and Evaluation
CQP	Vocational Qualification Certificate
	Certificat de Qualification Professionnelle
CRA	Regional centers for agriculture
CRESA	Regional Center for Specialized Education in Agriculture, Forestry and Wood
CVET	Continuing vocational education and training
DAE	Economic Affairs Directorate
DDLC	Development Department and Local Community
DEFACC	Agricultural Education Cooperative and Community Division
	Division de l'Enseignement Agricole Coopérative et Communautaire
DEPC	Directorate of Studies, Programs, and Cooperation
DEPCO	Studies Division of Planning and Cooperation
DFOP	Department of Vocational Training and Guidance
	Direction de la Formation et de l'Orientation Professionelle
DHS/EDS	Demographic and Heath Survey
DMJ	Dynamic World Youth
DPPC	Department of Project Planning and Cooperation
DRMO	Guidance for the Regulation of Labor
	Direction de la régulation de la main d'œuvre
DSCE	Strategy Document for Growth and Employment
DUT	University technical education diploma
ECAM	Household survey
ECCD	Early childhood care and development
ECD	Early childhood development
EDB	Economic Development Board
EESI	Employment and Informal Sector Survey

EFSEAR	School for Training Rural Development Specialists
EGEM	School of Geology and Mining
EIDA	Engineering Industry Development Authority
ENATH	National School of Tourism and Hospitality
ENEF	National School of Forestry and Water Resources
ENSAI	National School of Agro-Industrial Sciences
EPA	Economic partnership agreement
ESW	Economic and sector work
ETA	Technical Schools of Agriculture
EU	European Union
FAAS-FASA	Faculty of Agronomy and Agricultural Sciences
FAO	Food and Agriculture Organization
FCJ	Young Council Foundation
FDI	Foreign direct investment
FEFWE-FMBEE	Faculty of Employment in Wood, Water and Environment
	Faculté des Métiers Bois, Eaux et Environnement
FIDA	International Fund for Agricultural Development
	Fond international pour le développement de l'agriculture
FIJ	Youth Integration Fund
FNE	National Employment Fund
FNE-PADER	Support Program for Rural Jobs
FNE-PAJERU	Rural and Urban Youth Support Program
FNE-PREJ	Retirement and Youth Employment Program
FSLC	First School-Leaving Certificate
G4S	Group 4 Securicor
GAR	Results-based management
GCE A/L	General Certificate Examination Advanced/Level
GCE O/L	General Certificate Examination Ordinary/Level
GDP	Gross domestic product
GER	Gross enrollment ratio
GIC	Common Initiative Group
GEI	Group for Education and Investment
GICAM	Association of Private Sector Employers
	Groupement Inter-patronal du Cameroun
GIPA	Interprofessional Group for Craftsmen
	Groupement Interprofessionnel des Artisans
GPECT	Provisional Management of Jobs and Skills
GTHE-ENSET	General Technical Higher Education
HE	Household enterprise

HRDF	Malaysia's Human Resource Development Fund
HRFM	Human Rights and Freedom Movement
ICES	International Computers and Electronics Systems
ICT	Information and communication technology
IDA	International Development Association
IFAD	International Fund for Agriculture Development
IFC	International Finance Corporation
IGF	National Forum on Internet Governance
ILO	International Labour Organization
IMF	International Monetary Fund
INS	National Institute of Statistics
IRAD	Agricultural Research Institute for Development
IT	Information technology
ITES	Information technology enabled-services
IVET	Initial vocational education and training
JICA	Japanese International Cooperation Agency
JVE	Young Volunteers for the Environment
LMIS	Labor market information systems
MDG	Millennium Development Goal
MIC	Middle-income country
MICROPAR	Referral Program for Micro-Enterprises
MIDENO	North West Development Authority
MINADER	Ministry of Agriculture and Rural Development
MINAGRI	Ministry of Agriculture
MINAS	Ministry of Social Affairs
MINDCAF	Ministry of State Property Survey and Land Tenure
MINDUH	Ministry of Urban Development and Housing
MINEDUB	Ministry of Primary Education
MINEFOP	Ministry of Employment, Vocational Education, and Training
MINEPAT	Ministry of Economy, Planning, and Regional Integration
MINEPDED	Ministry of Environment and Protection of Nature
MINEPIA	Ministry of Livestock, Fisheries, and Animal Industry
MINESEC	Ministry of Secondary Education
MINESUP	Ministry of Higher Education
MINFI	Ministry of Finance
MINFOF	Ministry of Forests and Wildlife
MINFOPRA	Ministry of Public Service and Administration Reform
MINJEC	Ministry of Youth and Civic Education

MINJEUN	Ministry of Youth
MINJUSTICE	Ministry of Justice
MINMIDT	Ministry of Industry, Mines, and Technological Development
MINPMEESA	Ministry of Small and Medium Size Enterprises, Social Economy, and Handicrafts
MINPROFF	Ministry of Women's Empowerment and Family
MINRESI	Ministry of Scientific Research and Innovation
MINTOUR	Ministry of Tourism
MINTSS	Ministry of Labor and Social Security
MTEF	Medium-term expenditure framework
NAF	National Accreditation Framework
NASSCOM	National Association of Software and Services Companies
NEET	Not in employment, education, or training
NER	Net enrollment rate
NGO	Nongovernmental organization
NQF	National Qualifications Framework
NSWF-ENEF	National School of Water and Forests
OHADA	Organization for the Harmonization of African Business Law
O/L	Ordinary level
ONCPB	National Office for the Commercialization of Basic Agricultural Products
	Office national de commercialisation des produits de base
OTIC	Intermediary technical assistance institutions
PADER	Support Program for Rural Jobs
PAIJA	Support Program for Youths Inclusion in Agriculture
PAPESAC	Support Cluster for Professionalization of Higher Education in Central Africa
PASEC	Program for the Analysis of Education Systems
PCFC	Project Competitiveness of Sectors of Growth
PCR	Primary completion rate
PED	Graduate Employment Program
PETU	Technological Excellence Cluster
PIAASI	Integrated Support Program for Informal Sector Actors
PIM	Brazil's Better Early Childhood Development Program
PhD	Doctor of Philosophy
PMJE	World Youth Parliament for Water
PNVRA	National Program to Promote Public Access to Agricultural Research

PPF	Production possibility frontier
PRECASEM	Capacity Development in Mining Project
PRIMATURE	Prime Minister's Office
PRSP	Poverty Reduction Strategy Paper
PSVC	Private sector value-chain
PTA	Parent-teacher associations
PTEC	Professional Excellency Training Center
PTR	Pupil-teacher ratio
RCSEAFW	Regional Center for Specialized Education in Agriculture, Forestry, and Wood
REJEFAC	Youth Network for Central African Forests
RGE	General Census of Enterprises
ROJAC	Network of Youth Organizations for Citizen Action
SABER	Systems Approach for Better Education Results
SAP	Skills for Africa Program
SAR	Rural Crafts Section
SAR/SM	Rural and household artisans
SCADA	Supervisory control and data acquisition
SCNPD	National Civic Service for Participation in Development
SDF	Singapore's Skills Development Fund
SF	Science of Forestry
SITE	Strengthening Informal Training and Enterprise
SM	Household Department
SME	Small and medium enterprises
SMIG	Guaranteed minimum professional wage
SNPHPC	National Union of Palm Oil Producers of Cameroon
SOCAPALM	Cameroonian Society of Palm Growers
SODECOTON	Cotton Development Corporation
SOWEDA	South West Development Authority
SSA	Sub-Saharan Africa
SSF	Solidarity Without Borders
STEM	Science, technology, engineering, and mathematics
STEP	Skills Toward Employability and Productivity
SYNACSU	National Synergy School Health Clubs and University
TGCR	Techniciens Génie Civil Réunis formation
TINAGRI	Technicians and Engineers in Food
TVA	Value-added tax
TVET	Technical industrial vocational and entrepreneurship training

UICN	International Union for Conservation of Nature and Natural Resources
UITTW/UIT	University Institute of Technical Training in Wood
	Institut Universitaire de Technologique Bois
UNDP	United Nations Development Programme
UNESCO	United Nations Organization for Education, Science, and Culture
UNEXPALM	Palm Oil Operations Union
UNWTO-OMT	United Nations World Tourism Organization
UPI-IUP	Informal production unit
USAID	United States Agency for International Development
UTA	Annual work unit
UTI	University technical training institutes
VCA	Value chain analysis
WDI	World Development Indicators
WfD	Workforce development
WSCD	Workforce skills and competencies development
WWF	World Wildlife Fund
YDF	Youth Development Foundation
ZEP	Education priority area

CHAPTER 1

Introduction and Background

Objective and Scope

The overarching goal of this study is to facilitate Cameroon's strategic objective of ensuring that the country has a well-educated human resources base to support its quest to emerge as a strong middle-income economy by 2035. This strategic objective is communicated in various national documents, especially the vision documents *Cameroun emergent à l'horizon 2035* and the 2009. Strategy Document for Growth and Employment (*Document de Stratégie pour la Croissance et l'Emploi 2009*, or DSCE), which emphasize a shift away from focusing on poverty reduction and toward fostering growth as the source of prosperity and employment, premised on income redistribution and poverty reduction.

The DSCE identifies agriculture, agribusiness (cotton textiles, palm oil, cocoa, and coffee), forestry (wood and wood processing), mining, and tourism as the key engines of economic growth and employment. Light manufacturing in these sectors is emerging as a viable option. Building on these themes and the country's vision, the World Bank sees the focus on adding value through labor-intensive production, promoting competitiveness, and supporting structural, spatial, and social transformation as critical drivers of economic growth.[1]

This study is intended to support Cameroon in preparing a national strategy for skills development, related policies and institutions to boost competitiveness and productivity, and job creation. The study also notes that many factors other than skills can limit productivity and job creation, including weak governance, bureaucracy, infrastructure, and taxation policies that directly affect the business environment.

The study focuses on skills development for the informal and formal labor markets. For this purpose, the authors have undertaken empirical analyses on growth accumulation effects, skills development through the education and training system (skills accumulation effects), and value chain analysis that shows the constraints for the demand and supply of skilled and unskilled labor in Cameroon. Labor markets are dynamic. There will always be skills gaps and mismatches. Hence, the study reviews the education and training system and its potential to build a skilled workforce through the accumulation approach.

This report also presents a comprehensive diagnostic of skills development policies and institutions in Cameroon. It analyzes the various mechanisms for skills development and their alignment with emerging sector demand. The underlying idea is that the development of a critical mass of skilled labor with strong foundational and higher-order skills could contribute to improving competitiveness, meeting the labor needs of the transforming economy, and promoting growth. The business and investment climate faces several challenges that require attention—weak governance, excessive bureaucracy, inadequate infrastructure, and cumbersome taxation policies. These challenges retard firm productivity and competitiveness and in turn reduce labor demand. However, their effects are not analyzed in depth because these factors are considered exogenous to skills development.

The study bridges the knowledge gap about the skills mismatch in Cameroon, and addresses the question of how education and training can make valuable contributions to developing skills, spurring growth, increasing competitiveness, and helping Cameroon evolve into higher-value products and services. A significant challenge is to unify the currently fragmented approach to increasing the supply of skills, which is delivered by several ministries and private organizations. The fragmentation of skills supply—combined with a large rural population, extensive informality, and high underemployment—poses considerable challenges.

The study is a natural next step to the analytical and operational work on competitiveness and growth that has been undertaken over the past five years. Specifically, the study complements the value chain studies in agriculture, agribusiness (cotton textiles and palm oil), forestry (wood and wood processing), and tourism that have already been prepared. The study also complements the detailed analysis by the National Institute of Statistics on employment, the role of the informal sector, and labor characteristics, including skills levels, based on the second Enterprise Surveys data set. The extent to which firms can attract and absorb workers is discussed.

This introductory chapter defines the context, rationale, and scope of the study; sets out the conceptual framework; describes the questions addressed by the study; explains the methodology; and identifies the data sources.

Context and Rationale

Cameroon's Socioeconomic Context for Skills and Competencies

Cameroon is a lower-middle-income country aspiring to reach full middle-income status by 2035. During the first two decades after independence (1960), growth in Cameroon was resource intensive, with productivity and efficiency playing only minor roles. Between 1996 and 2003, despite less favorable external conditions, structural reform–led growth was possible because of the country's long-term foundations for enhanced productivity. Over the past decade, growth has slowed as the foundations and policy resolve have weakened in agriculture and nonmining industries (World Bank 2013a, 2014c). While populations in most of the world are aging, Cameroon (like other African countries) has one of the world's youngest populations. Cameroon cannot afford to miss the demographic dividend to achieve its vision.[2]

The DSCE has identified economic diversification through five sectors and two subsectors for the purposes of generating employment and orienting growth. The sectors are infrastructure, forestry (wood and wood processing), agriculture and agribusiness (with a focus on cotton textiles and palm oil), tourism, and extractives. This study analyzes the demand, supply, and development of skills in these sectors. A sixth sector, technology and innovation, has also been included. This is an area that requires urgent attention in Cameroon, to help raise the country's competitiveness to international levels.

The first two criteria for selecting the priority sectors are their estimated job creation potential and estimated productivity gains. The skills development perspective of job creation is seen as being relatively narrow, because in many cases the constraints to job creation in a sector lie outside the country's traditional labor policies, including skills development. For example, the main constraints to improving job creation and raising productivity in the cotton sector involve the large number of small family plantations, lack of knowledge about new technologies, transportation barriers, and lack of information on market pricing signals. Although these types of constraints lie outside the skills area, they could do more for jobs than other types of investments. Therefore, a larger perspective has been taken to recognize the broader context.

The criteria for selecting the priority sectors are also that the selected sectors have high labor concentration; jobs cut across the formal and informal sectors, where most of the poor and vulnerable are engaged; there are prospects for creating economic opportunity through job creation and workforce value added; and the sectors could potentially continue to remain labor intensive while also being most amenable to structural transformation. Sectors that contribute to growth are not necessarily or automatically labor intensive.

By focusing investments on skills development and complementary business development areas in these sectors, the Government of Cameroon could create significant value added through jobs and workforce contributions to growth and productivity. Together the sectors could expand the national market through synergistic interdependence. They could create sustained jobs and steer the country away from seasonal employment. And they could put Cameroon on the path to becoming self-sufficient and promote export-oriented growth. The aggregate output and accumulation of workforce skills over time would enable the country to sustain growth and attain its vision of becoming a full-fledged middle-income country by 2035. To achieve this, Cameroon's competitiveness and access to national, regional, and international markets needs to be improved.

This study attempts to understand the skills in demand by employers, the constraints on the development of those skills, and the skills that make a difference in raising productivity. Formal wage work accounts for only 4–6 percent of employment in Cameroon. Therefore, the study looks broadly at the informal sector—which accounts for about 90 percent of employment—and formal sector firms. From the perspective of skills development, the study seeks to identify the types of skills that could raise productivity for workers in the informal sector. Drawing on the literature, the roles of the formal education sector and informal learning opportunities (such as apprenticeships and on-the-job training) are studied to determine policy recommendations.

Conceptual Framework for the Study

Skills development drives productivity and can boost employment and earnings. But employment depends on job creation. Skills development is essential to improve productivity and attract foreign direct investment (Ansu and Tan 2012). Cameroon has long protected local industries from foreign competition and direct investment. Local investment levels are also low. Weak skills have led to suboptimal jobs and earnings; thus, informality prevails and the majority of informal sector workers are underemployed.

Cameroon's approach to general education and training requires review. Higher levels of specialized—not generalized—higher education are required for Cameroon to achieve structural transformation. Moreover, structural transformation takes time. Thus, this study's conceptual framework integrates three themes and subthemes:

- The analysis uses the Aggregation-Accumulation Framework to model aggregate growth, with gross domestic product (GDP) serving as the proxy, and skills accumulation, with years of educational attainment serving as the proxy. The framework shows that, all else held equal, changes in educational attainment can increase GDP over time.
- To estimate the supply of skills, the analysis takes into consideration the stock and flow of the workforce. Therefore, the study addresses
  a. The *stock of workers* in the selected sectors and their characteristics—especially skill levels (opportunities and constraints). The analysis uses a framework to assess their job-relevant skills, workers' constraints and barriers to finding employment, the demand for their skills, and the socioeconomic constraints to the supply of skills as filters for the different sectors.
  b. The *flow of future workers*, by analyzing the current education and training sector using the Skills Toward Employability and Productivity (STEP) framework and its potential contribution to economic growth. Skills are assessed by disaggregating the concept into developing foundational skills (getting off to the right start through early childhood development); ensuring that all children learn literacy and numeracy; building job-relevant skills; encouraging entrepreneurship, innovation, and management skills; and fostering skills for labor mobility to permit ease of movement from the formal to the informal sector and vice versa, since the workforce is often dynamic—especially in an environment such as Cameroon, where job stability is not ensured.

- The analysis uses the Systems Approach for Better Education Results–Workforce Development (SABER-WfD) framework to analyze the policies and institutions that have been conducive to or have retarded skills development.

Main Questions Addressed by the Study

The report is structured to respond to six main questions. First, what has been the trajectory of Cameroon's economic growth and which sectors have contributed to growth? Second, where are the jobs? Third, what types of skills are being used in the sectors where the largest percentages of the population are employed, and are the employed productive? Fourth, what are the demand and supply barriers to skills? Fifth, which policies and institutions are creating jobs and raising productivity, and are they sufficient for Cameroon to reach full-fledged middle-income country status? Sixth, what needs to be or could be reformed to enhance skills development and productivity in Cameroon for competitiveness and growth?

Methodology and Data Sources

The study conducts a dynamic analysis, taking into account intertemporal and data constraints. Analytical inputs to the formation of the study's skills development strategy include the following:

- The private sector value chain framework and analysis that have been undertaken in the key growth and competitiveness sectors. The sectors are identified in the government's vision (embodied in the DSCE) for Cameroon to ensure structural transformation from a lower-middle-income country to a full-fledged middle-income country by 2035. The value chain analysis serves as the basis for understanding the demand for workers by analyzing the geographic locations of sector activity as well as the stock of workers and their composition, education levels, and value added to the sector; assessing existing skills and competencies; and understanding skills needs, skills gaps, and potential skills upgrading strategies for workforce development over the next 15 years. The key skills considered pertinent here are entrepreneurial, managerial, and behavioral skills.
- Analyses of the latest available household survey data[3] and government analytical reports on the Survey of Employment and the Informal Sector in Cameroon (Government of Cameroon 2012a, b and c),[4] which provide key information on the current state of public wage and nonwage sector employment and the current education levels of employees. The key skills considered pertinent here are cognitive, noncognitive, and job-relevant skills.
- The original quantitative simulation model created for the purpose of preparing the Country Status Report titled *"Le système d'éducation et de formation du Cameroun dans la perspective de l'émergence"* (World Bank 2013b). The model brings together the flow of students in the education and training sector and

spans five ministries of education and training in Cameroon. The simulation model assesses the impact of the growing school age and youth population on educational attainment and its potential effects on the working-age population and labor market outcomes. The quantitative simulation helps to explain how gaps in the skills required by firms could be bridged. Here foundational skills, higher-order job-relevant skills, and skills for labor mobility are considered important.

- The SABER-WfD framework and diagnostic tool:[5]
  a. For systematic documentation of policies and institutions that influence the performance of Cameroon's education and training system. The tool encompasses initial, continuing, and targeted vocational education and training that are offered through multiple channels, focusing on programs at the secondary and post-secondary levels.
  b. To benchmark against evidence-based global standards.
  c. To foster dialogue and action on reforms.

The analyses were undertaken through consultations with a government multisector team and youth groups. The analyses serve as the basis for prioritizing interventions. The SABER-WfD framework and diagnostic tool is useful for identifying the strengths and weaknesses of the system, especially in developing a system that is responsive to the labor market. SABER-WfD has nine policy drivers grouped under three dimensions: strategic direction, system oversight, and service delivery. The instrument does not guide the prioritization and sequencing of reforms, so it is used in conjunction with the value chain demand-side analyses to determine areas for prioritization and sequencing.

Notes

1. World Bank (2014c) and other finance and private sector development value chain reports including World Bank (2013b), have demonstrated the need for economic diversification.

2. The demographic dividend is the growth in a country's economy resulting from changes in the age structure and dependency ratios of its population due to the demographic transition. The first dividend occurs with the decline of birth rates and increase in labor supply. The second occurs when a significant number of workers are motivated to invest for their financial security in retirement. Governments have a window of 30 to 50 years to capitalize on the larger share of working age population, if it is productively employed for economic development and growth (World Bank 2013a).

3. *Enquête Camerounaise auprès des ménages* (Household Surveys, ECAM) 2007/08.

4. *Deuxième enquête sur l'emploi et le secteur informel* (Employment and Informal Sector Surveys 2012, EESI II) (INS 2012).

5. The Systems Approach for Better Education Results (SABER) Workforce Development (WfD) framework was introduced by the World Bank's Human Development Network Education Team in 2012.

CHAPTER 2

Macro Aggregation-Accumulation Model

Introduction

This chapter addresses several questions: What has been the trajectory of Cameroon's economic growth? What is the current employment structure in the economy, and in which sectors? What is the projected trajectory of growth? And what new types of jobs are likely to emerge?

The chapter brings together the concepts of aggregation and accumulation as an approach to understanding the twin effects of movement along the production possibility frontier for Cameroon. The discussion explores trends in economic growth over time, sector contributions and shifts over time, associated movements in jobs, shifts in labor force participation and productivity over time, the stock and flow of skills mixes and mismatches, and the government's approach to tackling jobs and skills challenges. The Skills Toward Employability and Productivity (STEP) framework is superimposed to show the path of skills accumulation and its potential effects for value added and prospects for improving competitiveness and growth.

Labor-Intensive Competitiveness and Growth: Aggregation-Accumulation Model

The Aggregation-Accumulation Model (AAM) helps measure changes in gross domestic product (GDP) over time (the independent variable) caused by changes in skills accumulation (the dependent variable), holding all other factors of production (land, capital) equal (figure 2.1). Cameroon's trajectory over time is captured with actual data on GDP and educational attainment.[1] The drivers of the change are discussed, and the potential positive impact over time is explained.

Along the x-axis in figure 2.1, the STEP framework demonstrates skills accumulation over time. Together the AAM and STEP framework show how the production possibility frontier can shift. The underlying assumption is that even if Cameroon moves from labor-intensive to capital-intensive competitiveness and growth, workers' skills would still need to be addressed, because Cameroon's labor market does not ensure job stability. The argument is that by enhancing the quality and quantity of the skills base in conjunction with changes in the business environment, Cameroon can elevate its regional and global competitiveness and create an enabling environment for stable jobs.

The AAM is based on estimating GDP as a measure of growth and output over time, as well as a proxy for measuring productivity (output per worker-hour). The trend over time shows output aggregation. Age in years serves as a proxy for measuring educational attainment and skills accumulation. The values for 2010 are actual data. The estimated GDP trend line shows the projections for Cameroon from 2010 through 2025. The intersection of the age and GDP trend lines shows the levels of aggregation and accumulation points. In 2010, there was significant visible and invisible underemployment and high child labor in Cameroon. Over time, there was also investment in education and some investment in training. In 2010, there was considerable deadweight loss (measured as the distance between the GDP trend line and the educational attainment curve for ages 13 years and older) of skills usage in the system. Investments in skills development for youth ages 14 years and older could result in greater value added through a better skilled workforce. This could help strengthen the light manufacturing base that is already prevalent in the sectors analyzed by this study.

The STEP framework provides a means of integrating skills development across the potential workforce over the lifecycle (figure 2.2). Moving up the steps correlates with the y-axis dimension of skills accumulation in figure 2.1, where educational attainment measured in years is used as the proxy. Tracing the path and assessing the progress at each step, it would be appropriate to conclude the following about Cameroon:

- The country has been relatively successful in moving forward with steps 1 and 2, although step 1 requires some concerted attention. The requirements in step 2 of fostering inquiry, providing basic vocational training, imparting and acquiring behavioral skills, fostering cognitive skills, and promoting the socialization of school-age students are already receiving some attention. But sustained efforts are needed and trade-offs should be carefully assessed in guiding transitions to the next levels.
- The country is having difficulty in making the transition to step 3—building job-relevant skills. Key challenges include making skills development programs more accessible to purchasers or beneficiaries, and encouraging providers or suppliers to design and offer more responsive and adaptable programs suited to the needs of the market. Demand-side financing options need to be actively considered. There are other options. But the cost-effectiveness of comparable programs to determine scalability requires more attention. Fostering responsive supply-side programs means providing the right incentives linked to performance and results, and an enabling environment conducive for entrepreneurs

Figure 2.1 Aggregation-Accumulation Effect in Cameroon, 2010, 2020, and 2025

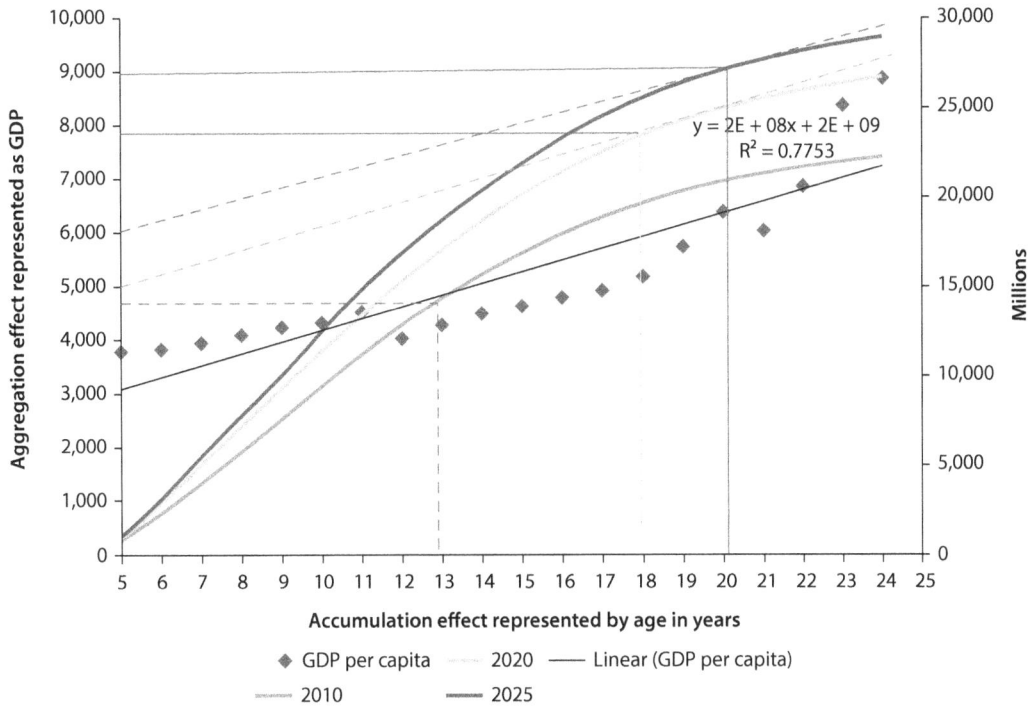

$$y = 2E + 08x + 2E + 09$$
$$R^2 = 0.7753$$

- GDP per capita — 2020 —— Linear (GDP per capita)
- 2010 —— 2025

Source: World Bank staff calculations on the basis of World Development Indicators data 2014.
Note: Age in years serves as a proxy for measuring educational attainment and skills accumulation.

Figure 2.2 The STEP Framework as an Integrated Set of Programs across the Lifecycle of Workers

	Step	Pre-school age	School age	Youth	Working age
5	Facilitating labor mobility and job matching			Apprenticeships, skills certification, counseling	Intermediation services, labor regulation, social security portability
4	Encouraging entrepreneurship and innovation		Fostering inquiry	Universities, innovation clusters, basic entrepreneurship training, risk management systems	
3	Building job-relevant skills		Basic vocational training, behavioral skills	Vocational training, higher education, apprenticeships, targeted programs	Firm-provided training, re-certification, re-skilling
2	Ensuring that all students learn		Cognitive skills, socialization, behavioral skills	Second chance education, behavioral skills	
1	Getting children off to the right start	Nutrition, psychological and cognitive stimulation, basic cognitive and social skills			

Source: World Bank 2010.
Note: The figure should be read from bottom up.

Fostering Skills in Cameroon • http://dx.doi.org/10.1596/978-1-4648-0762-6

to promote skills development. The certification and recertification of providers and skills require urgent attention.
- The country is having great difficulty with step 4—encouraging entrepreneurship and innovation.
- The country is lagging behind on step 5—facilitating labor mobility and job matching.

For Cameroon to emerge as a middle-income country, structural transformation through economic opportunity will be critical. Inclusive workforce skills development in concert with a better business environment could elevate value added by labor and enterprises, boost competitiveness, and help to sustain growth. These efforts would advance Cameroon's development frontier. The rest of this chapter disaggregates the model and explains the aggregation and accumulation effects. Specific aspects of skills development are discussed in subsequent chapters.

Aggregation Effect, 1960–2012

Economic growth in Cameroon was modest during 2003–13 (figure 2.3) and was undermined by the global economic crisis, which weakened demand for Cameroon's nonoil exports, such as wood, timber, and rubber. Nonoil exports are the drivers of the country's economic growth, although activity in the oil industry picked up in 2012. In recent years, the economy has rebounded, with real GDP growth approaching 4.7 percent in 2012. However, only about 14 percent of the labor force has secure employment.

Figure 2.3 GDP per Capita, 1960–2012

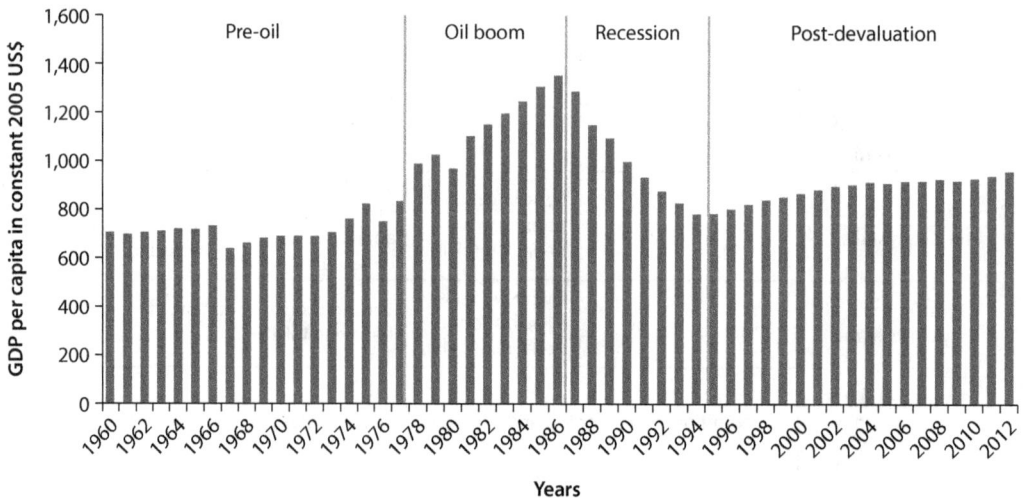

Source: World Bank 2014d.

Per capita GDP rose 52 percent between 1978 and 1986. The oil sector contributed significantly to the government budget, growing from 1.4 percent of GDP (9 percent of total revenue) in 1980 to about 9 percent of GDP (41 percent of total revenue) in 1985. The government adopted a development strategy dominated by expanding the capital budget, which increased from an average of 2 percent of GDP during 1965–77 to an average of 9 percent during 1978–86, and reducing average current outlays from 16 to 12 percent. This strategy resulted in a relatively large public sector. National physical infrastructure improvements included more roads and irrigated land. However, the share of private investment in GDP remained largely unchanged (Ghura 1997; Charlier and N'cho-Oguie 2009).

GDP per capita was $1,165 in 2012. Although Cameroon has attained lower-middle-income country status, poverty rates are still relatively high. Although the annual population growth rate is high (more than 2 percent), real growth in GDP per capita averaged only 1 percent per year over the past decade (2003–13). Poverty rates fell by 13 percentage points between 1996 and 2001, but have since stagnated at around 40 percent.[2] Further, average national poverty figures mask major regional disparities. While 56 percent of the population lived in urban areas in 2007, 87 percent of the poor were in rural areas. Further, there is a growing income gap between regions, urban and rural areas, and rich and poor people. Between 2001 and 2007, poverty rates increased in four regions (Adamaoua, Far North, North, and East; figure 2.4), with the two northern

Figure 2.4 Poverty Headcount and Number of Poor, 2001, 2007, and 2011

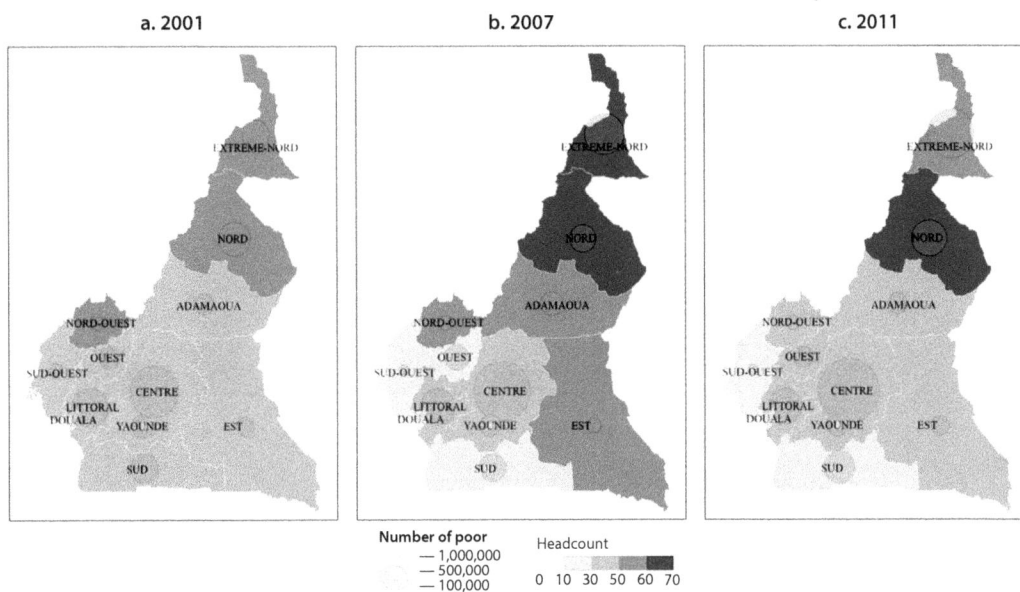

a. 2001 b. 2007 c. 2011

Number of poor
— 1,000,000
— 500,000
— 100,000

Headcount
0 10 30 50 60 70

Sources: Tegoum 2013; Himelein 2014; World Bank staff estimates using the Cameroon Household Surveys from 1996, 2001, and 2007, and the Demographic and Health Survey from 2011.

regions seeing the largest increases and human development indicators—including access to schooling, primary completion rates, literacy, access to water and sanitation, and life expectancy—registering slower growth in these regions than in other parts of the country. Spatial and geographic disparities between rural and urban areas and poverty-based gender disparities have also become more pronounced.

The evolution of poverty is consistent with the pattern of economic growth (World Bank 2014d). Average real nonoil economic growth per capita of 1.2 percent per year over time is meaningful but not high. A limited reduction in rural poverty is therefore realistic. Moreover, although the primary sector (agriculture, forestry, fisheries, and stock breeding) was the most dynamic over 2007–11, the relatively small share of the primary sector in nonoil GDP (around 25 percent) is also consistent with limited progress on poverty reduction in rural areas.

During 1986–2011, the sector contributions to GDP growth also shifted, reflecting changing workforce needs. In 1990 and 2005, the tertiary sector (services) was the largest contributor to GDP growth, followed by the secondary sector (mining, manufacturing, utilities, and construction, but excluding oil) and the primary sector (agriculture, forestry, fisheries, and stock breeding). By 2011, the growing tertiary and primary sectors overshadowed the contribution of the secondary sector (figures 2.5 and 2.6). This could be attributed to the post-oil boom recession era (1986–94), and the post-devaluation period (1994–2012).

The World Bank's 2010 Country Assistance Strategy identified Cameroon's main challenges as stimulating a healthy growth rate and ensuring that growth is shared equitably. Debt relief in 2006 increased fiscal space for government spending linked to poverty reduction. Cameroon is one of the

Figure 2.5 Sector Contributions to GDP, 2006–11

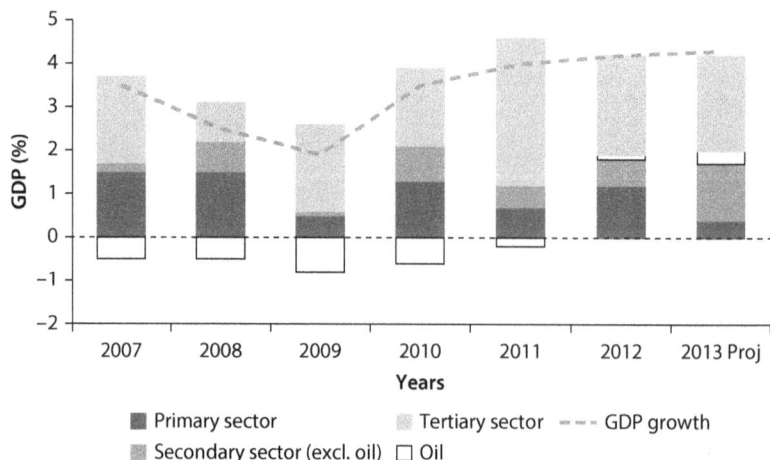

Sources: National Institute of Statistics, various years; World Bank staff calculations.

Figure 2.6 Sector Contributions to GDP, 1990, 2005, and 2011

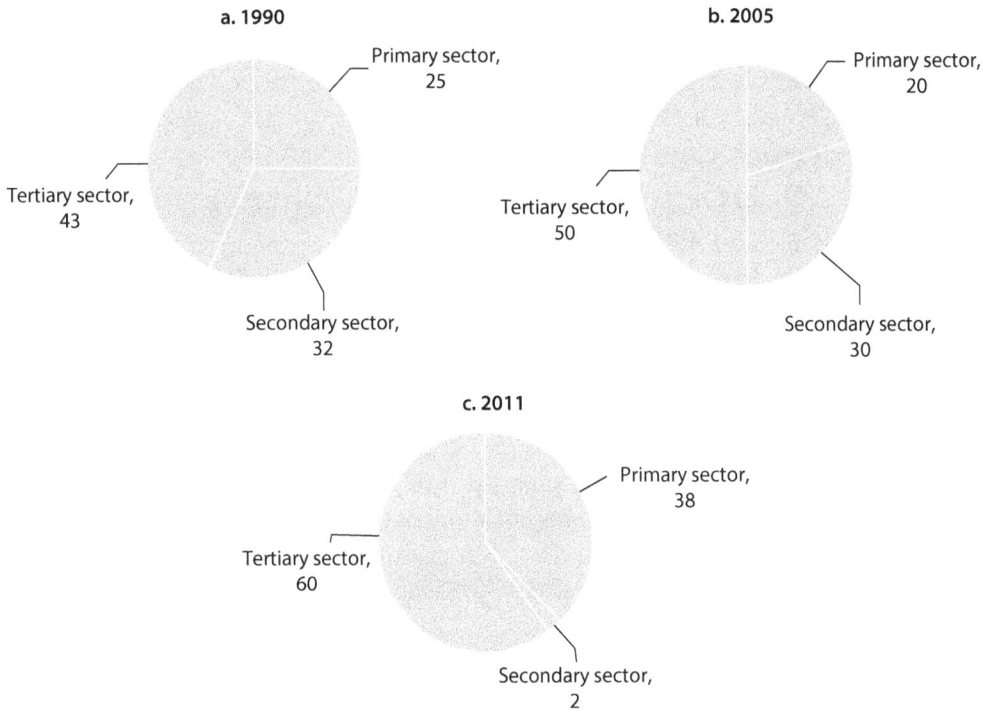

a. 1990

Primary sector,
25

Tertiary sector,
43

Secondary sector,
32

b. 2005

Primary sector,
20

Tertiary sector,
50

Secondary sector,
30

c. 2011

Primary sector,
38

Tertiary sector,
60

Secondary sector,
2

Sources: Data for 1990 and 2005 are from Charlier and N'Cho-Oguie 2009; data for 2011 are from World Bank 2012a.

least aid-dependent countries in Sub-Saharan Africa and works with relatively few development partners.

The World Bank's 2003 Poverty Reduction Strategy Paper for Cameroon stressed human resource development as a core component of the government's broad-based development strategy and efforts to meet the targets set by the Millennium Development Goals (MDGs). Strengthening the human resource base was also identified as an important aspect of poverty reduction. The volume and quality of human capital were seen as fundamental to long-term economic growth, including their effects on the quality of growth that could translate to employment creation and income generation (Ghura 1997; Charlier and N'cho-Oguie 2009). Government policies and efforts have helped to advance this goal. In 2009–10, the government revised its strategy to move from reducing poverty to boosting growth and employment.

In 2012, despite concerted efforts, Cameroon was largely off track for achieving the MDGs. Recent data indicate that the MDG for universal primary schooling, which was once considered possible to achieve, is not feasible. The gender parity index fell from 0.88 in 2004 to 0.85 in 2010.[3] Further, lack of progress on the MDGs related to water and sanitation, teaching and learning materials, and school reentry support structures for girls might be affecting education enrollment and attainment for out-of-school children (particularly girls and vulnerable groups, including ethnic minorities) and life expectancy in general. Still, government efforts over time have raised Cameroon to lower-middle-income status (table 2.1).

Demographics and Employment

The results of the third population census in 2005 showed that Cameroon had 18.1 million inhabitants. By 2010, the population had jumped to 20.6 million. Cameroon has a large, relatively healthy, young population (figure 2.7). The share of young people is expected to increase over the next two decades. The young people could help increase the country's economic competitiveness in the subregion and region. Over the next decade, a significant number of young people are expected to enter the job market. As in other countries in Sub-Saharan Africa, youth make up about 40 percent of the population in Cameroon and could generate a demographic dividend, with human resource benefits—or costs, if not appropriately addressed. Cameroon's young population offers a huge opportunity to build an educated, trained, skilled, and employable workforce to drive economic diversification and economic transformation.

Table 2.1 Macroeconomic, Employment, and Education Indicators, 2010

Macroeconomic	
GDP growth (annual %)	4.6
Exports of goods and services (% of GDP)	29.2
Imports of goods and services (% of GDP)	31.9
Tax revenue, 1999 (% of GDP)	11.2
Poverty headcount ratio at national poverty line, 2007 (% of population)	39.9
Employment	
Population (millions)	20.6
Unemployment, total (% of total labor force) (national estimate)	3.8
Urban population	11.4
Employment in agriculture, 2010 (% of total employment)	53.3
Employment in industry, 2010 (% of total employment)	12.6
Employment in services, 2010 (% of total employment)	34.1
Education	
Ratio of girls to boys in primary and secondary education (%)	86.9
School enrollment, primary (% net)	91.5
School enrollment, primary (% gross)	110.6
School enrollment, secondary (% gross)	50.4
School enrollment, secondary, 1981 (% net)	14.7
Literacy rate, adult total, 2010 (% of people ages 15 years and older)	71.3
Literacy rate, adult total, 2011 (% of people ages 15 years and older)	65.1

Sources: World Bank 2013b, 2014d.
Note: GDP = gross domestic product.

Figure 2.7 Demographic Profile

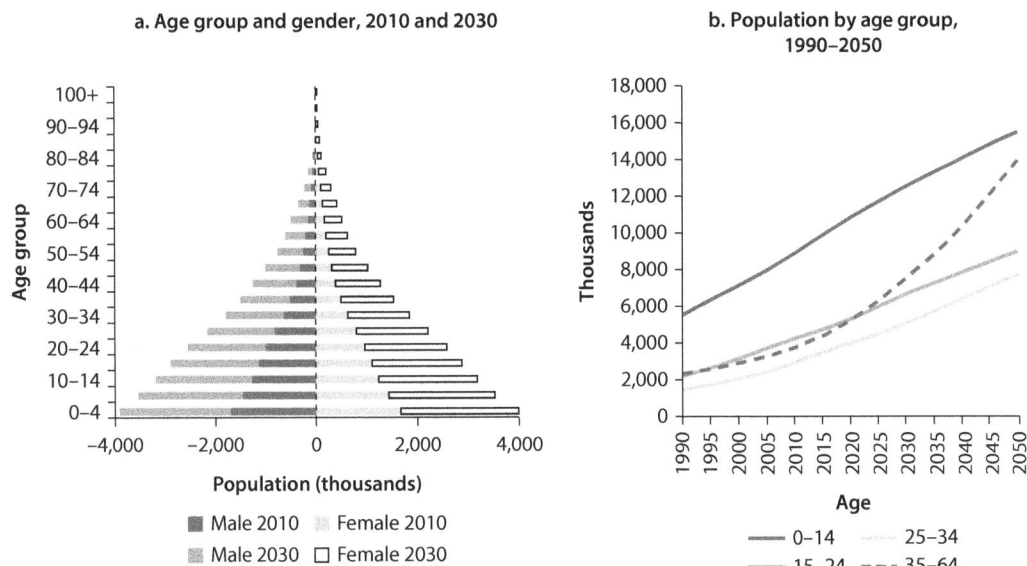

a. Age group and gender, 2010 and 2030

b. Population by age group, 1990–2050

Male 2010   Female 2010
Male 2030   □ Female 2030

— 0–14   25–34
— 15–24   --- 35–64

Source: Population Division of the Department of Economic and Social Affairs of the United Nations Secretariat, various years.

A recent report on youth labor markets in Sub-Saharan Africa and around the world finds that the lack of prospects for secure employment, along with increased education, access to modern technology, and exposure to the perceived advantages of developed economies, risks creating frustration among young people (Elder and Koné 2014). That frustration, in turn, could result in political unrest and emigration. According to a 2010 report by the McKinsey Global Institute (2012), only about 23 percent of young people in Cameroon had stable employment, 73 percent were in vulnerable employment, and 4 percent were unemployed. Therefore, the political economy aspects warrant equal attention. The Strategy Document for Growth and Employment (Government of Cameroon 2009) sets a national target for youth employment of 50 percent by 2020—an ambitious goal. A key to reaching the target will be to maintain access to education and training while improving their quality.

Since 2000, the emphasis has almost exclusively been on improving access to education. But improved access to education is not enhancing economic growth. The main reasons for this are the relatively low quality of education and mismatches in skills and competencies. Further, formal private sector jobs have been very slow to grow, resulting in a growing number of jobs in the informal sector. Although informal could be considered normal, the potential contribution of the informal sector to the economy, especially for enhanced tax payments, is not being taken into account. And low tax revenue is undermining Cameroon's growth and competitiveness.

Changes in employment and workforce participation have been relatively slow over the past decade and will not increase significantly without concerted policies and enforcement. Table 2.2 shows the trends over time. Between 2001 and 2010, the population grew by about 2.3 percent per year. The active workforce increased by 2.8 percent per year. But the workforce participation rate declined, as did the unemployment rate, leading to the conclusion that informality increased over the period. The rate for the active workforce ages 15–59 years was around 19.6 percent in 2001, representing only 7.1 percent of the active workforce in the age group—a decrease of 60 percent. Youth ages 25–34 years experienced a less dramatic change, with the rate decreasing from 18.7 percent in 2001 to 8.2 percent in 2010—a decrease of 53 percent.

The breakdown by sector shows that most employment is in the informal sector, increasing from 82.2 percent in 2001 to about 90 percent in 2010 among workers ages 15–59 years. In the informal sector, there was a significant reduction in the share of workers in agriculture, from 68.1 percent in 2001 to 56.6 percent in 2010, while the number of agricultural jobs rose from about 3.0 million to 3.5 million. The number employed in the informal nonagricultural sector increased during the period. Economic activity among those ages 25–34 years fell only slightly, from 94.8 percent in 2001 to 93 percent in 2010. Employment in the formal sector also decreased for this age group, from 21.2 percent in 2001 to 19.1 percent in 2010, with an increase in the number of unskilled workers.

In 2012, Cameroon had an estimated population of 21 million. Therefore, over the next decade the government can anticipate a growing workforce. Taking into account the change in unemployment over time, it is important to assess the potential direction of future employment and the spread between skilled and unskilled employees.

Most young adults are unemployed, holding out for public sector jobs, underemployed in the public sector, or working unpaid or poorly paid in household enterprises. Three aspects deserve examination: workforce participation and its evolution over the past two decades and distribution across economic sectors, to understand the stock of workers; the consequences of the evolution of employment creation; and estimated labor productivity from an intertemporal perspective and its effects on inter-sector mobility.

Table 2.2 Changes in Workforce Participation and Unemployment Rate by Population Age Group
(%)

Age	Workforce participation rate			Unemployment rate		
(years)	2001	2005	2010	2001	2005	2010
15–59	66.1	64.1	60.0	35.0	12.0	11.3
25–34	93.0	90.3	88.0	18.7	9.1	8.2
35–49	94.5	93.8	93.0	7.9	3.4	3.3
50–59	91.6	90.5	88.7	5.7	3.0	2.3

Sources: World Bank 2013b; calculations using data from the National Institute of Statistics.

Workforce participation rose from 3.5 million in 1985 to 5.8 million in 2005—an annual growth rate of 2.5 percent (World Bank 2013b). During the same period, there was a shift in the population distribution across economic sectors. By 2010, the workforce showed increasing signs of being skewed toward the informal nonwage sector (figure 2.8).

Figure 2.8 Employment Structure and Distribution of Employment by Sector and Location, 2010

a. Employment structure

Public, 6

Formal private, 4

Informal agriculture, 53

Informal non-agriculture, 37

b. Distribution of employment

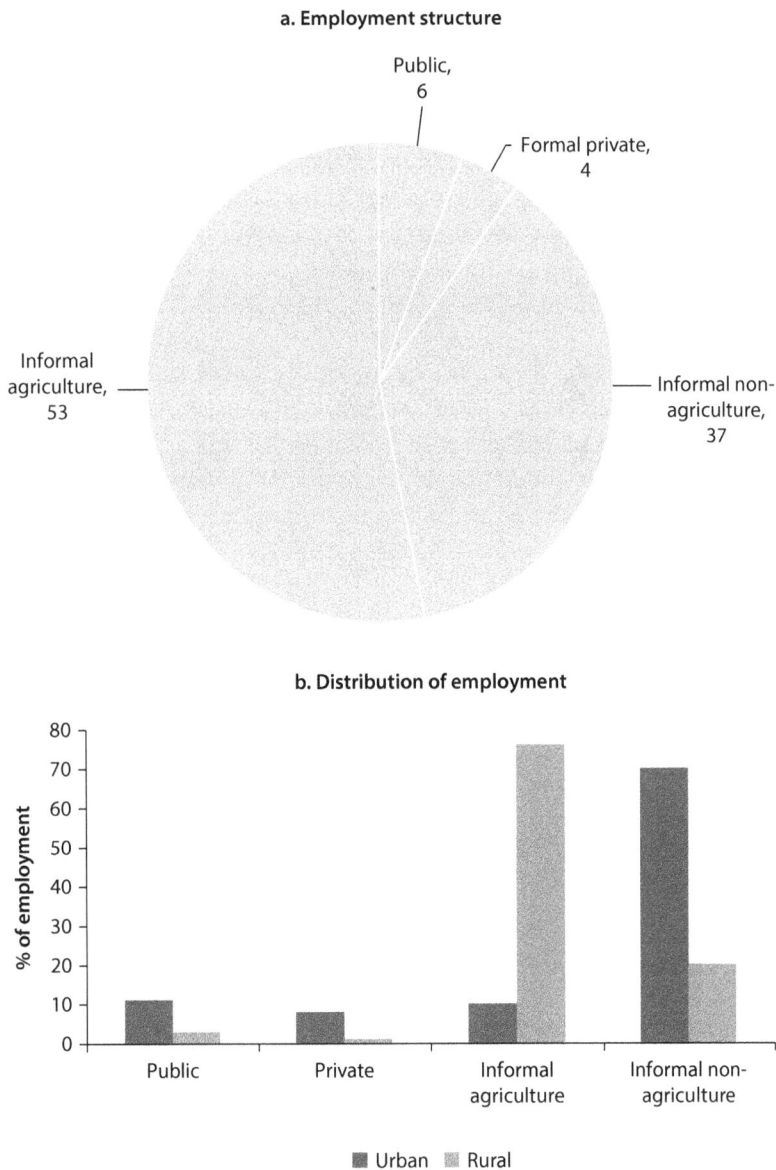

Urban   Rural

Source: National Institute of Statistics, Employment and Informal Sector Surveys II 2010.

Data on employment by sector from 1986 to 2010 reveal declining trends for agriculture and industry and a growing trend for services (figure 2.9). During 1978–86, there was an increased emphasis on capital spending that was reflected in substantial improvements in infrastructure. The increase in the primary sector's contribution to GDP while there was a decline in employment in agriculture might have been caused by improved technology and productivity. In 1986, the estimated active workforce in the primary sector (agriculture, forestry, and fisheries) was 2.04 million. By 2005, that number had fallen to 1.9 million. The share of the workforce employed in agriculture witnessed a considerable decline, from 57.6 percent in 1985 to 32.3 percent in 2005, a drop of nearly 1.3 percentage points per year. Between 1985 and 2005, only about 150,000 workers were employed in the secondary sector (industry). During the same period, the number employed in the tertiary sector (services) increased from 1.35 million to 3.81 million, or from 38.1 percent of the labor force to 65.2 percent. Thus, employment opportunities in the tertiary sector increased dramatically.

The preference for employment in the tertiary sector is creating significant competition and entry barriers. Within the tertiary sector, it is important to distinguish between the formal sector (where firms are registered and are not required to pay import duties, and employees earn reasonable salaries and social security benefits) and the informal sector (which comprises some small enterprises and retail services, often involves intermittent employment, and is fraught with unemployment). During 1985–2005, it seems that the number employed in the modern services subsector nearly doubled. But this was a relatively small increase relative to the working-age group (ages 15–64 years). A large portion of this age group entered the informal services subsector. That is, employment in this subsector increased from 858,000 individuals in 1985, or 24 percent of the

Figure 2.9 Employment by Sector, 1986–2010

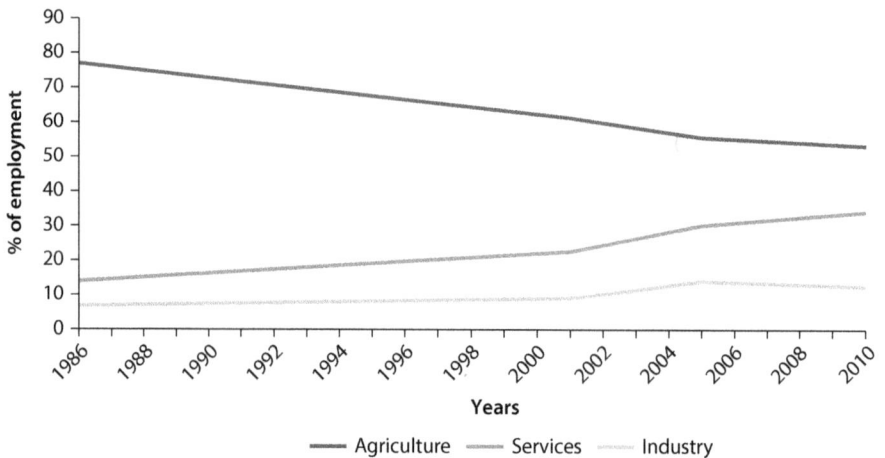

Sources: For 1986–2006, World Development Indicators and staff calculations; for 2007–10, Cameroonian authorities and World Bank staff calculations.

labor force, to 2.8 million in 2005, or 48 percent. It is unclear to what extent the sector has served as a key input into the production function for economic growth. The increase could reflect unemployment redistribution that masks the overall constraints to access the overall formal and tertiary formal sectors.

Workforce Participation and Productivity

During 1977–2011, improved productivity, defined as output per worker-hour, contributed about 14 percent to real GDP growth, whereas labor and capital each contributed about 40 percent (figure 2.10).

The apparent average productivity of the aggregate workforce in Cameroon—in the formal and informal sectors—and the value added over time declined between 1985 and 2000.[4] This could be attributed to the effects of climate on agriculture, the increase in the salaries of public officials in 2008, and the revaluation of the guaranteed minimum wage in 2008. Workforce productivity showed signs of picking up after 2000 (figure 2.11).

Figure 2.10 Total Factor Productivity, 1977–2011

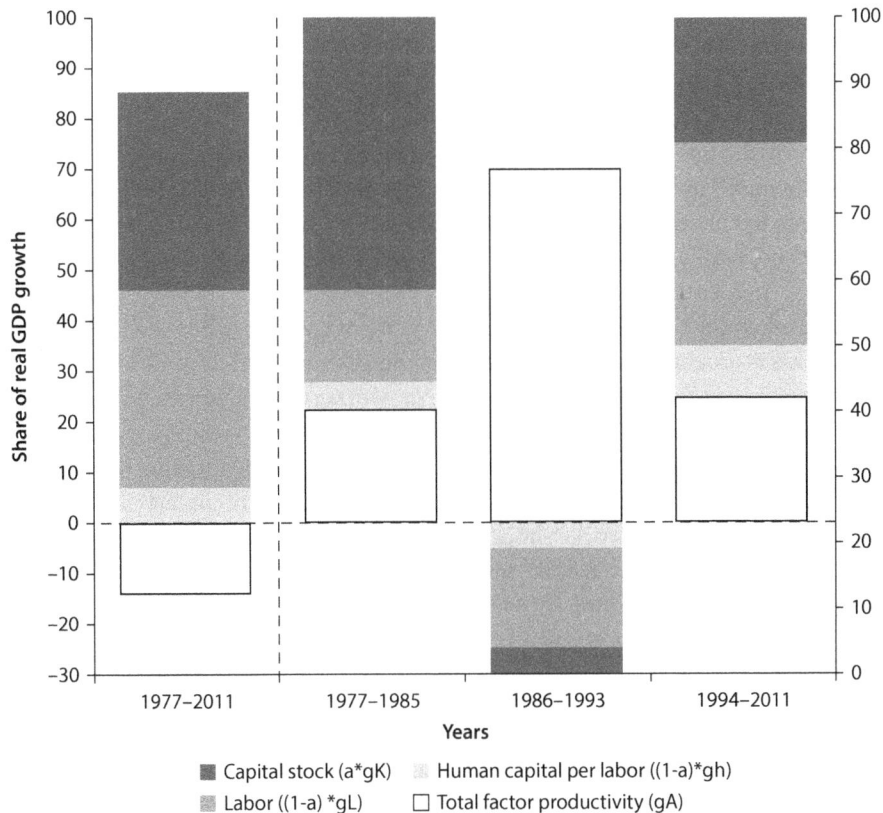

Legend:
- Capital stock (a*gK)
- Labor ((1-a)*gL)
- Human capital per labor ((1-a)*gh)
- Total factor productivity (gA)

Sources: Data from the National Institute of Statistics, various years; World Bank staff calculations.

Figure 2.11　Apparent Productivity of the Workforce, by Economic Sector, 1985–2007

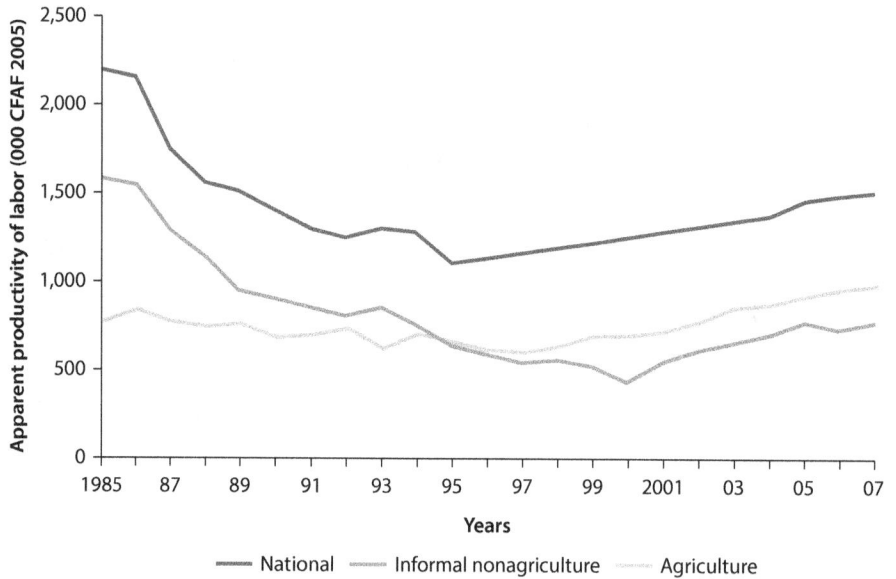

Source: World Bank 2013b.

The trajectory appears to be in concert with the period of devaluation follow-ing the recession between 1986 and 1994. Labor productivity decreased dramati-cally in the informal nonagricultural subsector from 1985 to 2000, possibly because of the increase in the overall workforce, a manifestation of disguised unemployment, or both. Underemployment is apparent mostly among the active workforce in the informal agricultural subsector, although in rural areas, among females and family, apprentice, and nonclassified personnel. Overall, the major-ity (82.2 percent) of the workforce is underemployed. However, invisible underemployment declined by about 5.2 percentage points between 2005 and 2010. This is an encouraging evolution for the government.

Productivity (also known as output per worker-hour) among the growing working-age population in the informal sector seems to be declining (figure 2.12) (Government of Cameroon 2012c). Analysis by the National Institute of Statistics (INS 2012) finds that optimal productivity (measured in monetary terms to be $2 worth of output per worker-hour) is attained by a typical firm in the informal sector when the firm has at least three workers in addition to the entrepreneur. Not surprisingly, an increase in average salary has a positive effect on worker productivity. This is contrary to the effect in the formal sector. For firms in the informal sector, seniority and the entrepreneur's years of education do not have a significant influence on productivity.

Of the 3,635 informal sector firms analyzed, most were managed by female entrepreneurs. Their productivity seems to have been less than that of their male counterparts. Overall, in a typical informal sector firm, 47 percent of productivity gains were made by the workforce and only 22 percent was

Figure 2.12 Evolution of Workforce Productivity, by Average Age of Workers

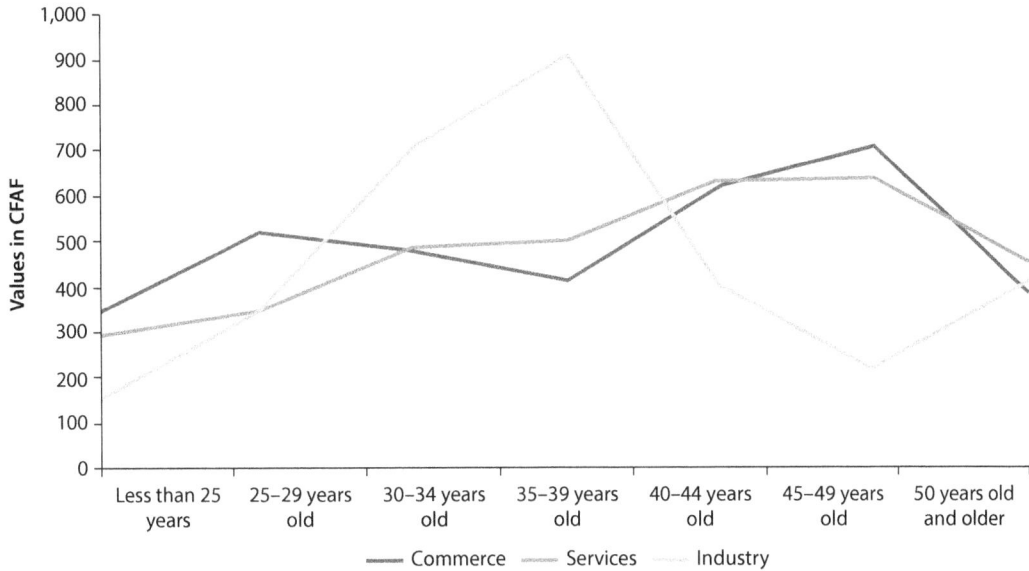

Source: INS 2012.

from capital. This seems to be the case almost systematically across the different economic sectors. In global terms, productivity in the informal sector was 10.5 times greater for firms that utilized technological innovations than those that did not. The analysis by sector showed that the production levels jumped by about 20 times in the commercial and services sectors.

Promoting growth alone does not improve living conditions for all. Thus, the World Bank promotes the notion of pro-poor growth (World Bank 2005). Among the active working population, 90 percent are in the informal sector, of which approximately 52 percent are in the informal agricultural or farm sector (INS 2005) and about 35 percent in the informal nonfarm sector are battling low productivity and underemployment. Further, over 20 percent of the active working population in rural areas is in the informal nonfarm subsector. The concentration of workers in this subsector is not because work in the subsector is attractive, but because the formal sector is closed to those workers. Their working conditions are precarious; they earn low revenues, use outmoded production mechanisms, and are by and large poorly managed; and the informal sector is the only means of avoiding unemployment (Bem and others 2013).

The informal small- and medium-size firms are not registered with the Chamber of Commerce, and they do not adhere to formal accounting procedures as per the Organization for the Harmonization of African Business Law[5] requirements (INS 2006). These firms are by and large inefficient. Proprietors and employees in the informal sector are poorly prepared, with low-quality basic education and post-basic education, especially vocational and technical training. Inclusive workforce development is fundamental to addressing pro-poor growth.

Notes

1. It is acknowledged that educational attainment is a weak proxy for assessing the distribution of skills and is largely insufficient to inform policy. However, in the absence of better measures to assess skills, educational attainment serves as the best quantitative measure. Learning assessments would also serve as a good measure for skills. However, learning has not been measured consistently in the country. Cameroon participates in the regional Program for the Analysis of Education Systems (PASEC) assessment. So far Cameroon has maintained its position as one of the top three placements in the PASEC. But the PASEC tests themselves have undergone change over time, casting doubt on the comparability of the results.

2. The most recent poverty data are from 2007.

3. United Nations Development Programme database for Cameroon (2012 update).

4. This represents the labor force participation in various sectors of the economy and the respective "productivity" (output per worker-hour) that is attributable to each sector. The calculation helps to determine the apparent productivity of the workforce and assess change over time. But the aggregate figures need to be complemented by separating the modern services subsector and the informal services subsector. For the purposes of this report, value added in the informal services subsector is estimated to be the difference between (i) the value added in the public and services sector and (ii) the value added in the modern informal sector by estimating the average salary or remuneration (from the household survey).

5. The Organization for the Harmonization of African Business Law (OHADA) was created in Port-Louis, Mauritius, on October 19, 1993. It became effective on September 18, 1995. OHADA is intended to create for African member countries an economic zone with juridical security to attract foreign direct investments and to consolidate national investments. But OHADA law is heavily inspired by the French business laws. OHADA law does not take into account sufficiently the socioeconomic context of Africa. The member countries of OHADA have predominantly a large informal sector. In Cameroon, a little over 90 percent of all employment is in the informal sector. OHADA law is not adapted to the informal sector. A study has been undertaken to outline the extent to which OHADA law could be adapted to the national-level specificities (informal sector) of Cameroon (Kwemo 2012). The details of the study are not discussed in detail in the World Bank report since the topic is beyond the scope of the study.

CHAPTER 3

Enterprises and Workforce

Introduction

What is the current status of skills among Cameroon's workforce? Do workers have the education and training required to increase productivity? And what are the key constraints to skills development?

Like many other countries in Sub-Saharan Africa, Cameroon's labor market has few formal jobs and a large informal labor force. Unemployment is low because most Cameroonians cannot afford not to work. But most jobs have low productivity and generate little income. Domestic help personnel are required to work up to 54 hours per week, and security guards and chauffeurs are required to work 56 hours. But the average work week is only 39 hours, reflecting involuntary underemployment in workers' main occupations, which is caused by employment conditions or an inefficient economy. Thus, the challenge is to improve the productivity and earnings of those already working—whether in the formal or informal sector—while also creating more jobs in the formal sector. These goals could be achieved through a thriving private sector, a skilled workforce, and a streamlined public sector that creates an enabling environment for changing policies and institutions.

The Strategy Document for Growth and Employment (DSCE) sets ambitious targets for Cameroon (Government of Cameroon 2009). A responsive labor market is a prerequisite for Cameroon to move up from lower-middle-income to full-fledged middle-income status. This chapter discusses the emerging landscape of the labor market, the distribution of employment by economic sector, the education levels and skills of the current labor force, and the training programs in place. The chapter captures the private sector/demand-side assessment of the stock of workers and their skills, skills mismatches, and other labor supply constraints. Investment climate constraints affecting enterprise productivity are also assessed.

The most recent survey data were used to identify the workforce characteristics of enterprises in Cameroon. The data analyses are based on three data sets: Demographic and Health Surveys, Household Surveys, and Enterprise Surveys (Appendix A). Enterprise Surveys are conducted by the World Bank and

International Finance Corporation and their partners across all geographic regions. Enterprise Surveys cover small, medium-size, and large firms,[1] and focus on the many factors that shape the business environment. These factors can be accommodating or constraining for firms and play an important role in whether a country will prosper. An accommodating business environment encourages firms to operate efficiently by providing incentives for firms to innovate and raise productivity—key factors for sustainable development. A more productive private sector, in turn, expands employment and pays the taxes needed for public investments in education, health, and other services. In contrast, a poor business environment increases the obstacles to conducting business activities and decreases a country's prospects for reaching its potential in employment, production, and welfare (World Bank and IFC 2014).

Landscape of Enterprises and Employment[2]

Enterprise and Workforce Characteristics

Enterprises by Region, Size, and Number of Workers

Yaoundé is the political capital of Cameroon; Douala is the economic capital. The country has 10 geographic regions. Micro, small, medium-size, and large enterprises are concentrated in Douala (35.1 percent) and Yaoundé (23.9 percent), followed by the West, South-West, and North-West regions (table 3.1). Regions in the Anglophone part of the country appear to be more entrepreneurial and inclined toward private sector employment, while the Francophone part of the

Table 3.1 Regional Distribution of Small, Medium-Size, and Large Enterprises, 2009

Region	Primary sector (%)	Secondary sector (%)	Tertiary sector (%)	Undeclared (%)	Number of enterprises	Share of total (%)
Douala	0.2	11.8	86.1	2.0	33,004	35.1
Yaoundé	0.1	14.5	84.1	1.3	22,436	23.9
West	0.6	16.1	81.3	2.0	8,327	8.9
South-West	0.6	15.1	83.7	0.5	6,866	7.3
North-West	0.3	16.7	82.3	0.7	6,487	6.9
Adamaoua	0.6	8.2	90.7	0.5	2,740	2.9
Center (excluding Yaoundé)	1.1	7.4	90.4	1.2	2,695	2.9
East	0.6	6.0	93.1	0.3	1,736	1.8
Far North	0.5	7.5	90.8	1.2	2,585	2.8
Littoral (excluding Douala)	1.5	10.7	84.8	3.0	1,704	1.8
North	1.3	14.9	82.8	0.9	2,942	3.1
South	0.4	9.0	90.2	0.4	2,447	2.6
Total	**345**	**12,154**	**80,109**	**1,361**	**93,969**	**100**
(%)	(0.4)	(12.9)	(85.3)	(1.4)		

Sources: INS 2009b; World Bank 2009b.

country—with the exception of Yaoundé—is more oriented toward the Francophone system of public sector employment. Most enterprises are in the tertiary sector (85.3 percent), followed by the secondary sector (12.9 percent) and primary sector (0.4 percent). Some enterprises did not declare their sector of economic activity.

Micro-enterprises (those with fewer than five employees) account for three-quarters of the total (table 3.2), and men manage two-thirds of these enterprises.[3] Only 25 firms have 1,000 or more employees.

The number of permanent and temporary employees in micro and small enterprises is only a few thousand less than the number in medium-size and large firms (table 3.3). There are far more male than female employees in nearly all categories, with especially large disparities in large enterprises. Female employees account for 27 percent of permanent employees and 24 percent of temporary employees. Large firms employ the most permanent workers, followed by micro-enterprises.

Workforce by Economic Sector

In the three economic sectors—primary, secondary, and tertiary—men make up 70–80 percent of the temporary and permanent workforce and about 75 percent of the total workforce (table 3.4). Women are more likely to work in the tertiary sector under "other services" besides commerce and banking and insurance, and some work in transport, where they account for 44 percent of permanent employees and 53 percent of temporary employees.

Table 3.2 Definitions of Enterprises by Size, 2009

Enterprise size	Definition		Share of enterprises (%)
	Number of employees	Annual earnings (CFAF)	
Micro	5 or fewer	Less than 15 million	75
Small	6–20	15 million to 100 million	19
Medium	21–100	100 million to 1 billion	5
Large	More than 100	More than 1 billion	1

Sources: INS 2009b; World Bank 2009b.

Table 3.3 Permanent and Temporary Employees, by Gender and Size of Enterprise, 2009

Enterprise size	Permanent employees			Temporary employees		
	Men	Women	Total	Men	Women	Total
Micro	88,351	32,202	120,553	9,012	5,899	14,911
Small	44,153	23,400	67,553	5,993	2,392	8,385
Medium	35,890	14,087	49,977	5,603	1,233	6,836
Large	112,597	35,583	148,180	12,470	893	13,363
Total	280,991	105,272	386,263	33,078	10,417	43,495

Sources: INS 2009b; World Bank 2009b.

Table 3.4 Distribution of Employees, by Gender and Sector, 2009

Sector	Subsector	Permanent employees			Temporary employees		
		Men	Women	Total	Men	Women	Total
Primary	Agriculture	20,361	6,169	26,530	772	122	894
	Livestock management	405	144	549	42	36	78
	Silviculture	6,533	254	6,787	289	29	318
	Fisheries	30	9	39	9	3	12
	Subtotal	**27,329**	**6,576**	**33,905**	**1,112**	**190**	**1,302**
Secondary	Mining	953	209	1,162	25	3	28
	Food industry	15,208	4,239	19,447	6,604	123	6,727
	Other manufacturing industries	39,843	10,150	49,993	4,608	1,727	6,335
	Electricity, water, and gas	6,378	2,152	8,530	1,055	32	1,087
	Construction	7,389	1,368	8,757	2,383	238	2,621
	Subtotal	**69,771**	**18,118**	**87,889**	**14,675**	**2,123**	**16,798**
Tertiary	Commerce	84,907	20,551	105,458	3,756	1,382	5,138
	Transport	12,346	2,695	15,041	634	110	744
	Banking and insurance	7,072	5,512	12,584	257	290	547
	Other services	77,382	51,462	128,844	12,554	6,304	18,858
	Subtotal	**181,707**	**80,220**	**261,927**	**17,201**	**8,086**	**25,287**
Undeclared		2,184	358	2,542	90	18	108
Total		**280,991**	**105,272**	**386,263**	**33,078**	**10,417**	**43,495**

Sources: INS 2009b; World Bank 2009b.

An overwhelming number of permanent employees are either self-employed or work in small, medium-size, or large enterprises in the tertiary sector, especially in the "other services" and commerce subsectors (figure 3.1).

Workforce by Gender, Region, Education Level, and Sector

The DSCE projected that there will be 800,000 salaried employees in the formal sector by 2020. But there were only 386,263 permanent employees in the private sector in 2010, of which about 281,000 (73 percent) were male and 105,000 (27 percent) were female. These numbers reflect the low absorptive capacity of enterprises. Public enterprises have about 196,000 permanent employees. Most are concentrated around Douala (47 percent) and Yaoundé (21 percent). Only about 73 percent of the active labor force—the majority of them men—are permanently employed or working as apprentices and drawing a regular salary. These data reflect the fragile state of Cameroon's formal sector.

Most workers who have no education, are out of school, or have not completed primary education work in agriculture, followed by industry (figure 3.2). These tend to be nonwage jobs. By contrast, workers with post-secondary education and not in technical, industrial, vocational, and entrepreneurship training (TVET) earn wages.

Figure 3.1 Distribution of Permanent Employees by Sector

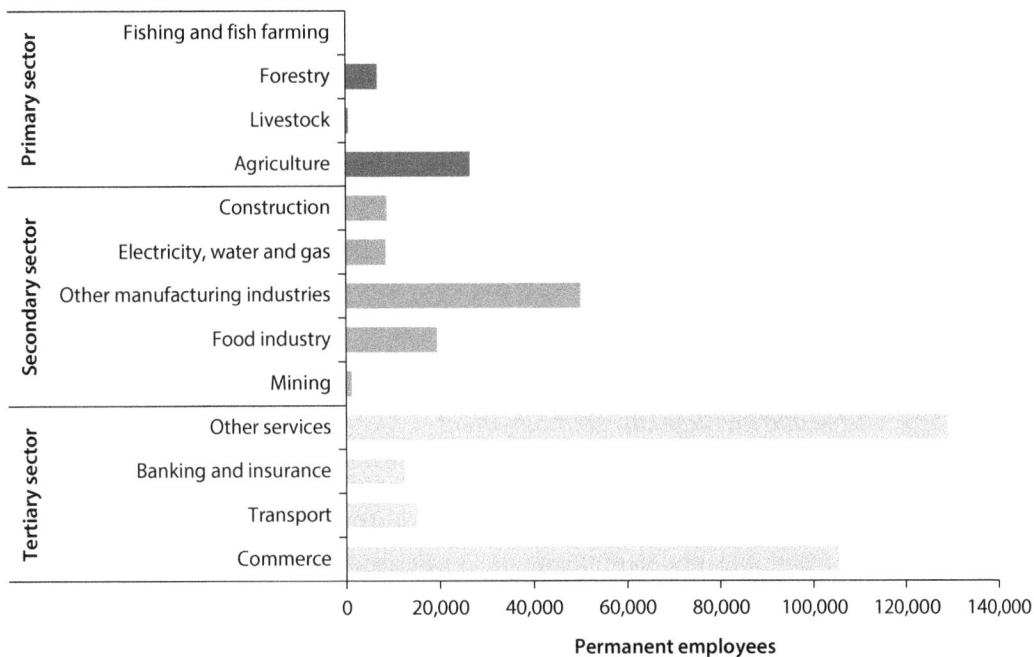

Sources: INS 2009b; World Bank 2009b.

Figure 3.2 Education Levels and Employment by Economic Sector, 2009

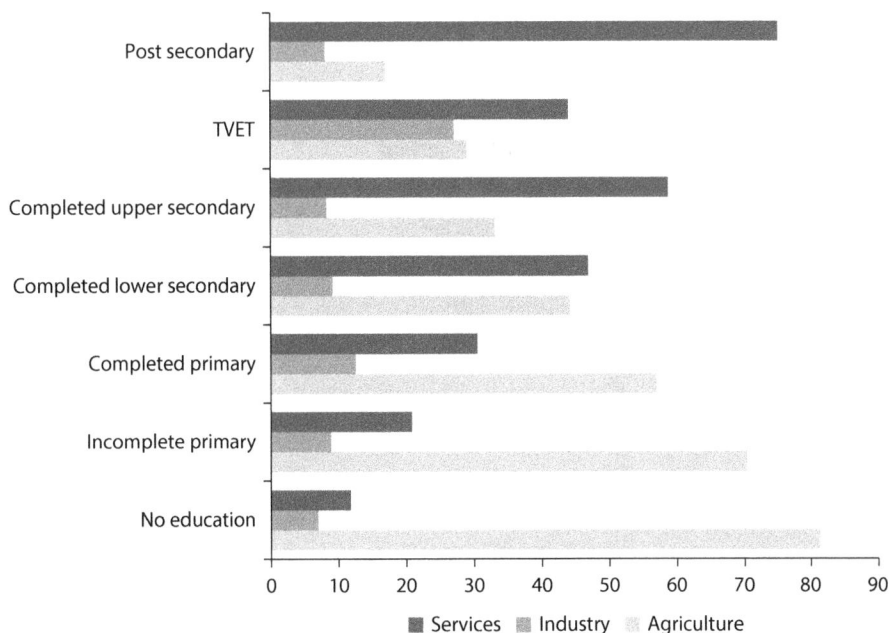

Sources: Cameroon Demographic and Health Survey 2009; World Bank staff estimates.

Few employees with incomplete primary education work in the public sector (figure 3.3). Those who have completed lower secondary, upper secondary, and post-secondary education are more likely to be in government service, where there is job security and assured pay. Many others are also in TVET, which provides them with a purpose to continue education—although they are not assured of jobs once they complete training.

A large share of the less educated workforce finds refuge in the informal sector (figure 3.4). Again, most are underemployed. More women are in the informal sector, working multiple jobs or transient low-paying jobs. Thus, their employment situation is more precarious than for men. Nearly 87 percent of women entrepreneurs in the informal sector operate without a professional address. Frictional unemployment is high.

Visible and Invisible Underemployment

Visible underemployment is considerably higher for women than men—as is invisible underemployment (figure 3.5). Invisible underemployment characterizes those employed whose hourly wage is less than the minimum hourly wage. Invisible underemployment is calculated by taking the ratio of the number of employed earning less than the minimum hourly wage to the employed population (Government of Cameroon 2012, 38). In 2010, visible underemployment was highest among those with a university education,

Figure 3.3 Education Levels and Public and Nonpublic Employment, 2009

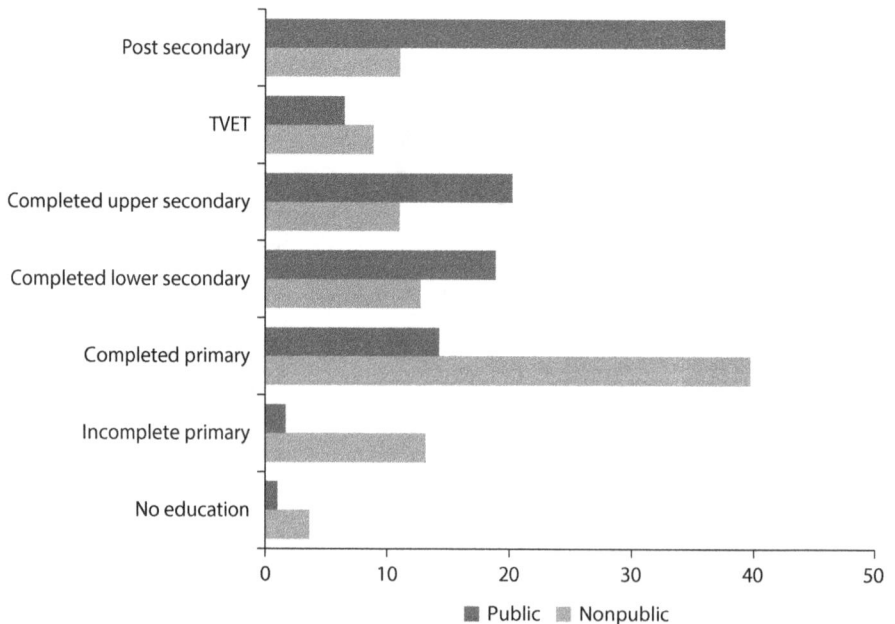

Sources: Cameroon Demographic and Health Survey 2009; World Bank staff estimates.

Figure 3.4 Education Levels and Wage, Nonwage, and Agricultural Employment, 2009

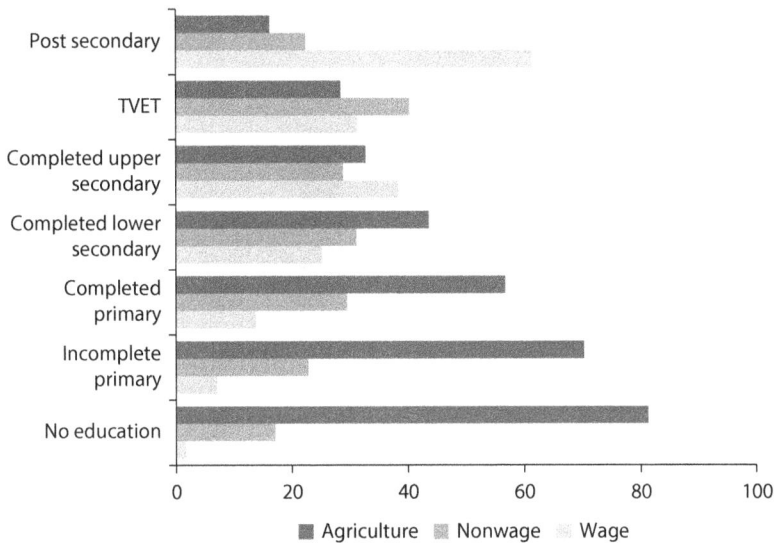

Sources: INS 2009a; World Bank staff estimates.
Note: The wage category includes those employed in the public sector receiving wages plus those working in the private, nonagriculture sector receiving wages. The nonwage category includes those working in the nonfarm sector (small enterprises/informal sector). The agriculture category includes those employed in the private agriculture sector receiving wages plus those working in the farm sector (small/family farms).

while invisible underemployment was highest among those with no education. Visible underemployment fell in most regions, with the Adamaoua and West regions showing the greatest declines, but it increased significantly in the South-West region. Invisible underemployment fell slightly in most regions. Visible underemployment was higher in urban areas, while invisible underemployment was much higher in rural areas. Visible underemployment mainly increased in the tertiary sector, while invisible underemployment was higher in the primary sector. Visible underemployment increased significantly in the public sector, while invisible underemployment increased in the informal agricultural sector.

One of the main goals of the DSCE is to reduce national underemployment from 76 percent of the workforce in 2005 to 50 percent by 2020. Underemployment dropped by 5 percentage points between 2005 and 2010. Still, in 2010 there was high invisible underemployment, at 82 percent and visible underemployment of 8.5 percent. The encouraging trend between 2005 and 2010 needs to be sustained through higher levels of employment creation in the formal sector—a goal that can be achieved through structural transformation projects. During 2005–10, education and training programs underwent qualitative and quantitative changes.

Figure 3.5 Visible and Invisible Underemployment by Gender, Education Level, Region, Residence, Economic Sector, and Institutional Type, 2005 and 2010

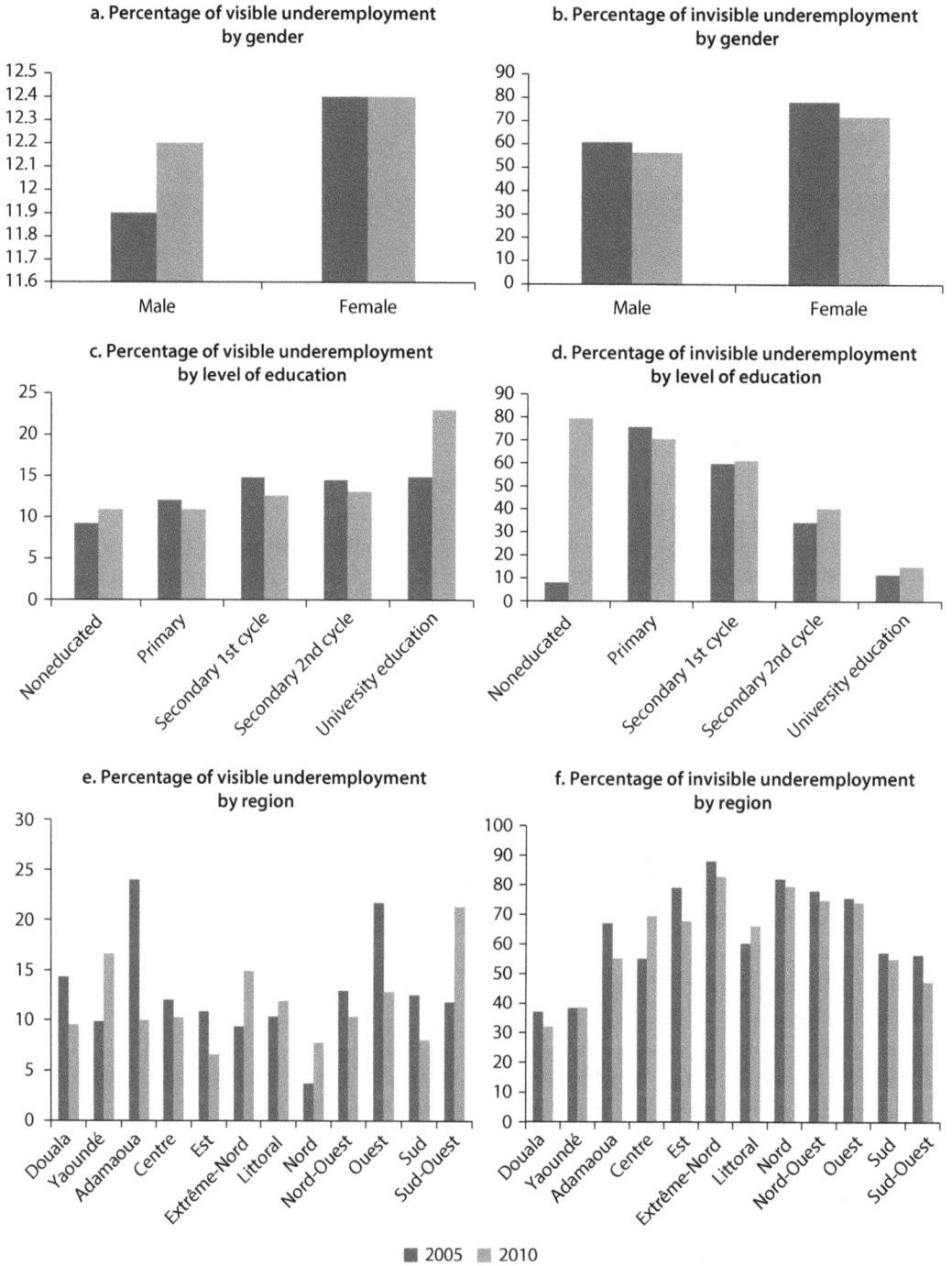

a. Percentage of visible underemployment by gender

b. Percentage of invisible underemployment by gender

c. Percentage of visible underemployment by level of education

d. Percentage of invisible underemployment by level of education

e. Percentage of visible underemployment by region

f. Percentage of invisible underemployment by region

■ 2005   ■ 2010

figure continues next page

Figure 3.5 Visible and Invisible Underemployment by Gender, Education Level, Region, Residence, Economic Sector, and Institutional Type, 2005 and 2010 *(continued)*

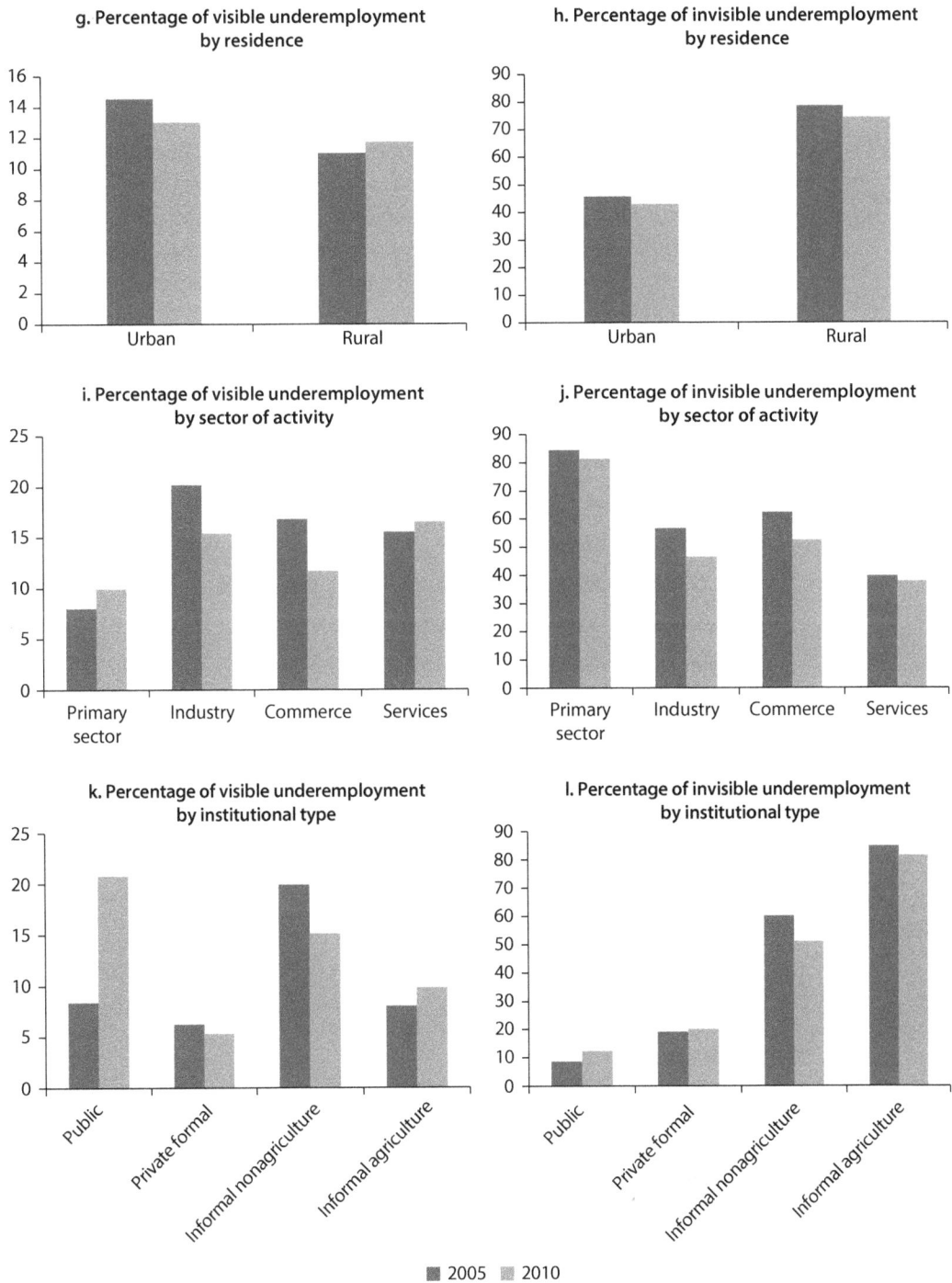

g. Percentage of visible underemployment by residence

h. Percentage of invisible underemployment by residence

i. Percentage of visible underemployment by sector of activity

j. Percentage of invisible underemployment by sector of activity

k. Percentage of visible underemployment by institutional type

l. Percentage of invisible underemployment by institutional type

■ 2005 ▨ 2010

Sources: INS, EESI 1 2005 and EESI 2 2010.

Enterprise-Level Constraints

The majority of enterprises and workers in Cameroon are in the informal sector. Entrepreneurs say that most of the barriers they face relate to the business environment: practices in the informal sector (a key finding of the World Bank Enterprise Survey; World Bank 2009b), high taxes and a difficult tax regime, widespread corruption, problems accessing credit, excessive bureaucracy, unfair competition, poor infrastructure, high financing costs, little or no informal dialogue to promote collective action, weak energy and water systems, transportation challenges, a cumbersome judicial system, problems with training and skills, and inadequate labor legislation (figure 3.6). As a result, Cameroon is not competitive in global markets. If the human dimension—training and skills—is not addressed, increasing the supply of machinery, capital investments, and finance will not raise productivity.

Figure 3.6 Main Barriers to Entrepreneurship
(% cited by entrepreneurs)

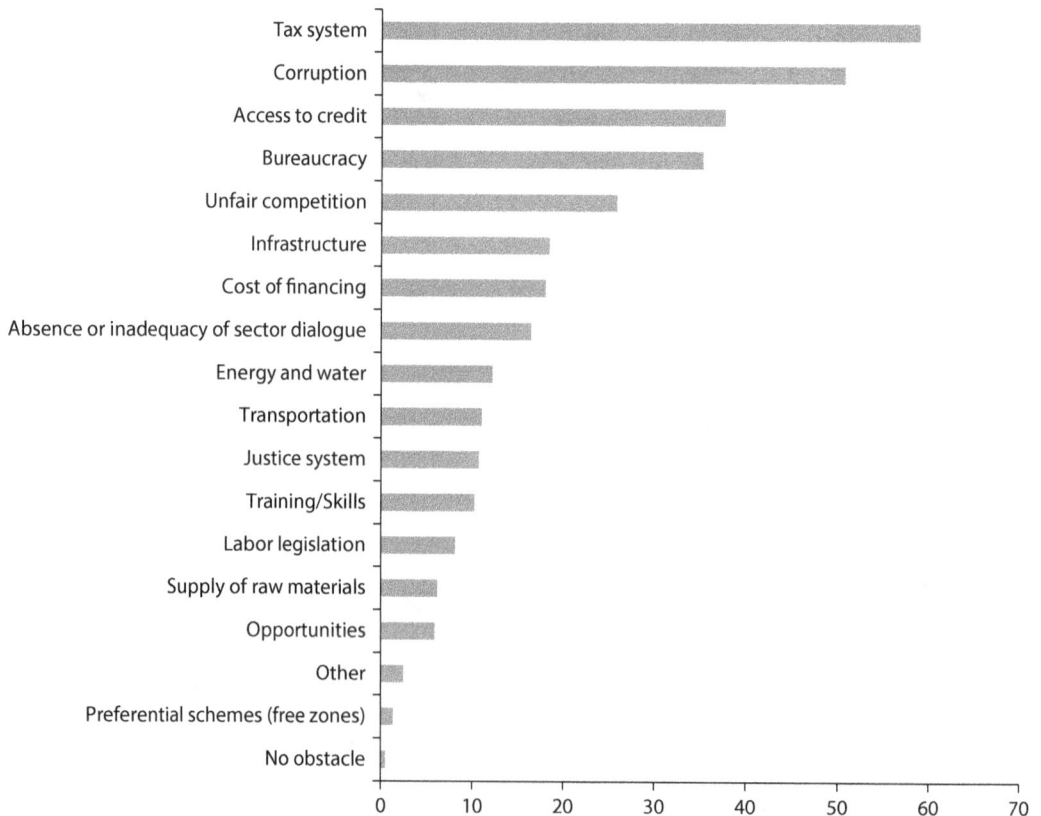

Source: Government of Cameroon 2010, 66; World Bank 2009b.

Benchmarking Skills and Workforce Productivity

The 2009 Enterprise Survey found that 15.5 percent of managers of enterprises in Cameroon did not have a formal education. Those managers employed 6.8 percent of the workforce. About 28.7 percent had completed primary education, and they employed 13.3 percent of employees. Another 28.2 percent of managers had a secondary education and employed 24.4 percent of employees. And 27.1 percent had completed university education, but they managed only 12.8 percent of employees. Thus, the less educated managers oversee a larger share of employees. This is one of the main weaknesses of the country's private sector—and, coupled with poor infrastructure, financial constraints, and a weak business environment, it has caused enterprise productivity to suffer. Labor productivity benchmarking for a sample of countries is shown in figure 3.7.

There are a few binding constraints to raising productivity for small and medium-size enterprises in Cameroon (table 3.5). Respondents cited weak entrepreneurial skills as well as technical skills among workers, but not behavioral skills.

Benchmarking Innovation and Workforce Indicators

Cameroon lags behind most countries in competitiveness, with a ranking of 168 among 189 economies. The country ranks at 132 for starting a business, mainly because of cumbersome and time-consuming procedures, long wait times for

Figure 3.7 Labor Productivity Benchmarking in Various Countries

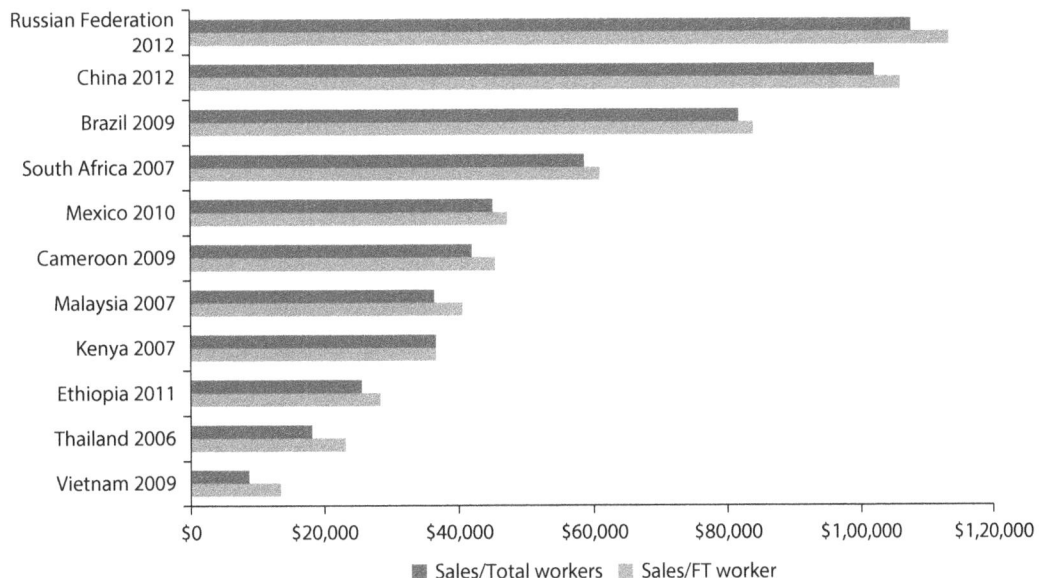

Source: World Bank 2009b.
Note: Weighted averages, no controls. Sales are in 2009 US$.

Fostering Skills in Cameroon • http://dx.doi.org/10.1596/978-1-4648-0762-6

Table 3.5 Binding Constraints to Raising Productivity

Constraint	Skill type	Explanation
Weak entrepreneurial skills	Managerial skills of the firm's owner	Needed for efficient and reliable production processes; business is well known
	Technical skills of the firm's owner	Know-how and ability to innovate products in response to shifts in market demand
Weak worker skills	Technical skills	Efficient production and high-quality output

Source: World Bank 2009b.

obtaining licenses to operate, high operating costs, and the absence of minimum capital to start small and medium-size enterprises. As of June 2013, no reforms had been reported in any of these areas since the previous year. Economies that improve in the areas measured by the World Bank's *Doing Business* report are more likely to implement reforms in other areas, such as governance, health, education, and gender equality. Economies that perform well on the *Doing Business* indicators do not necessarily have smaller governments. A key area of regulation measured by *Doing Business* that consistently affects firms relates to employing workers. But Cameroon lags behind many countries in this area. It has no business registry, and the absence of a minimum capital requirement hinders business development and growth.

In the formal sector, Cameroon scores well on seven Enterprise Survey indicators for innovation and workforce relative to the average for Sub-Saharan Africa, and on some indicators compared with lower-middle-income countries elsewhere. In 2009, 68.3 percent of the firms surveyed had annual financial statements that were reviewed by external auditors. The high-risk governance environment could explain this requirement of all firms. But a plausible explanation is also that Cameroon has very few trained and certified accountants, so firms have to seek external auditors to audit their financial statements. A second explanation is that firms receiving foreign direct investment are required to have their financial statements externally reviewed. On the use of innovation and technology for business, Cameroon ranks on par with other lower-middle-income countries for use of e-mail to communicate with clients and suppliers, but lags behind in having firm-specific websites. Finally, Cameroon lags behind other lower-middle-income countries in hiring temporary and permanent full-time workers (table 3.6).

Investment Climate Constraints to Enterprise Productivity

Economies that perform well on the *Doing Business* indicators tend to be more inclusive along at least two dimensions. They tend to have smaller informal sectors, meaning that more people have access to the formal market—whether in the tertiary sector or in the primary and secondary sectors—and can benefit from regulations such as social protections and workplace safety regulations. They are also more likely to have gender equality under the law as measured by the World Bank Group's *Women, Business, and the Law* indicators. This means not hampering the productivity of formal businesses through overly burdensome rules.

Table 3.6 Innovation and Workforce Indicators

Indicator	Small firms (1-19 employees)	Medium-size firms (20-29 employees)	Large firms (100+ employees)	Cameroon	Sub-Saharan Africa	Lower-middle-income average
% of firms with internationally recognized quality certification	9.1	31.6	58.0	20.4	13.0	16.0
% of firms with annual financial statements reviewed by external auditors	61.6	78.1	79.3	68.3	42.3	48.2
% of firms with their own website	14.8	38.6	68.1	27.5	16.3	32.0
% of firms using e-mail to communicate with clients/suppliers	49.4	70.1	85.6	59.3	44.0	58.3
Average number of temporary workers	1.6	5.9	24.9	5.3	5.2	11.5
Average number of permanent, full-time workers	8.6	32.0	201.4	35.3	25.7	60.9
% of full-time female workers	30.4	23.8	21.4	27.6	22.9	31.1

Sources: World Bank 2009b; World Bank and IFC 2014.

And it means not needlessly depriving the economy of the skills and contributions of women. Other important factors are a well-educated workforce, well-developed infrastructure, and stable macroeconomic policies.

A thriving private sector with new firms entering the market—creating jobs and developing innovative products—could contribute to a more prosperous Cameroon. The government could play a crucial role in supporting a dynamic ecosystem for firms that establishes an enabling environment, by developing rules, strengthening property rights, establishing a system for resolving disputes at manageable cost, increasing the predictability of economic transactions, creating financial regulations that permit access to seed funding/capital for entrepreneurs to test innovations, and setting boundaries for enforcement. Entrepreneurs would have greater access to capital to start small and medium-size firms, create jobs, and serve as engines of growth. There are opportunities for business development in the leading growth sectors—agriculture and agribusiness, forestry/wood processing, infrastructure (including energy, mining, and petroleum), and tourism—identified in the DSCE.

Skills Utilization and Labor Laws

Knowing Cameroon's labor laws is crucial to understanding the working conditions for employees and their motivation to use their skills. This relates directly to creating an enabling environment for skilled and unskilled workers to take jobs, whether full-time or part-time. It also relates to the salary levels of the workforce. Cameroon's labor laws are based on the *Code du travail, 1974* and the

Code du travail du Cameroun, 1992. There is also a National Labor Council. The key elements of the Labor Code are the following:

- Industrial and commercial enterprises: 40-hour work week
- Public sector: 48-hour work week
- Agricultural sector: 48-hour work week
- Domestic help: 54-hour work week
- Security guards and chauffeurs: 56-hour work week.

But in practice the average work week in Cameroon is only about 39 hours. There is visible underemployment among the active workforce when workers work less than 35 hours per week in a principal job either due to the employer or because there is no economic justification for working more. Invisible underemployment is also prevalent because much of the active workforce earns less than the guaranteed minimum hourly wage.

Figure 3.8 Benchmarking the Composition of Economic Sectors across Countries

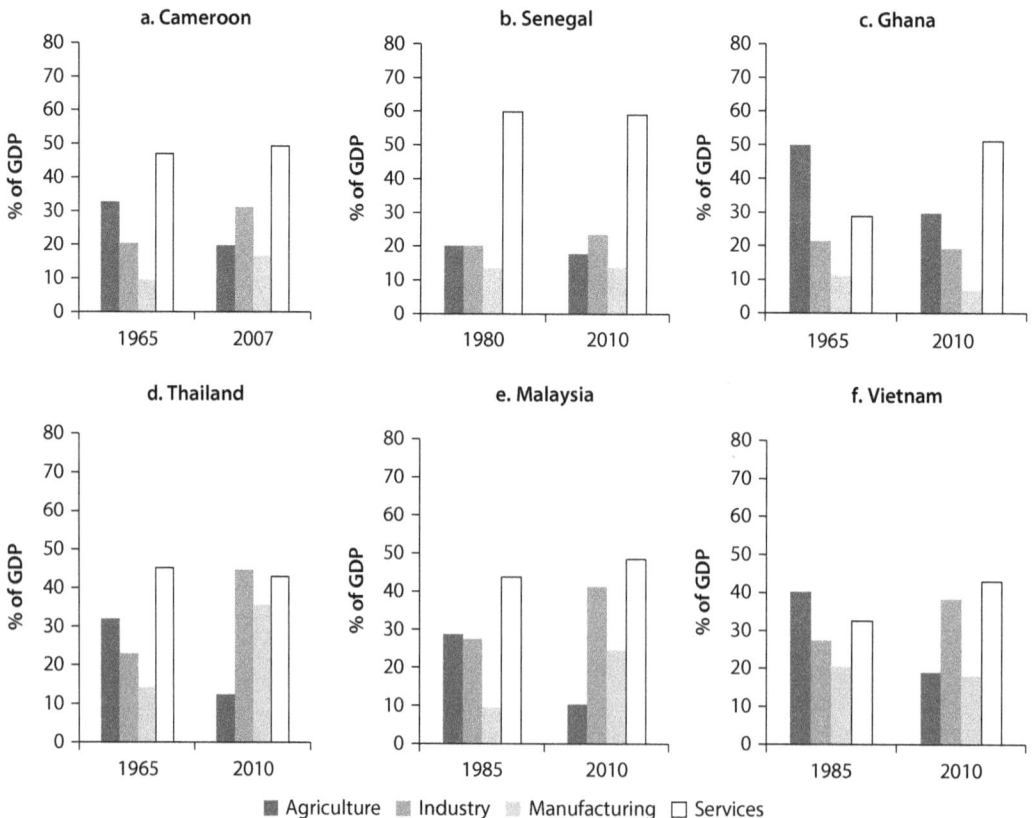

Sources: World Development Indicators, various years; World Bank staff estimates.

Fostering Skills in Cameroon • http://dx.doi.org/10.1596/978-1-4648-0762-6

National underemployment includes both forms of underemployment—visible and invisible. According to official data, in 2005 nearly 75 percent of the active workforce was underemployed. The situation had not improved by 2010. If anything, it deepened: nearly 90 percent of the active workforce was in the informal nonwage sector. Unemployment insurance does not exist in Cameroon. About 60 percent of the unemployed who were surveyed preferred a salaried job, about 22 percent preferred to work independently, and less than 20 percent were indifferent about the type of employment. By contrast, about 70 percent preferred to be employed full-time with a 44-hour work week (Government of Cameroon 2005; Njobo 2013).

For Cameroon to accelerate economic growth, it needs to build a thriving and competitive private sector and a simpler public sector to create an enabling environment for policy and institutional development. In 2009–10, Cameroon elaborated value chains in the sectors that were identified as contributing the most to growth. The value chains set out the minimum thresholds for entering markets, creating jobs, and developing innovative products. The thresholds include the skills and competencies that would best serve future needs for developing the sectors. The next chapter discusses value added in the anticipated growth sectors and the opportunities and constraints.

Benchmarking Cameroon and two other countries in Sub-Saharan Africa against three Southeast Asian countries shows that the sector composition is consistent (figure 3.8): agricultural contributions have declined over time and industry has increased. Manufacturing does not show such a dramatic upward change in Cameroon, whereas it does in Thailand and Malaysia. And services has always been larger than any other sector. If Cameroon aspires to have an export-oriented economy like some Southeast Asian countries, fostering light manufacturing could bring large payoffs. It is worth noting that the shares of industry in the three Southeast Asian economies are almost on par with services, and that there has been a significant increase over time.

Notes

1. Enterprise Surveys are administered to a representative sample of firms in the nonagricultural formal private economy. The sample is consistently defined in all countries and includes the manufacturing sector, services sector, and transportation and construction sectors. The public utilities, government services, health care, and financial services sectors are not included. The surveys collect a wide range of qualitative and quantitative data through in-person interviews with firm managers and owners about the business environment in their countries and the productivity of their firms. Topics covered include infrastructure, trade, finance, regulations, taxes and business licensing, corruption, crime, informality, finance, innovation, labor, and perceptions about obstacles to doing business. The data collected through the surveys link a country's business environment characteristics with firm productivity and performance. The surveys are useful to policy makers and researchers, and are repeated over time to track changes and benchmark the effects of reforms on firms' performance.

2. This section draws on INS (2009b) and World Bank (2009b).

3. In 2009, enterprises were not categorized by type due to the lack of acceptable definitions. Through the process of preparing the Enterprise Surveys, the National Institute of Statistics proposed acceptable criteria for classification. Appropriate amendments were made and legislation was passed (No.001/2020 of April 13, 2010). This put in place the definitions for small and medium enterprises. The three criteria are: (i) number of employees working full time for one year, part time or temporary; salaried, village-level owners, or associated entities with continuous activity in the enterprise as financial beneficiaries; and the nature of the business; (ii) legal entity/status resulting from trading in goods or services, excluding taxes; and (iii) formal or informal (unregistered, that is, with no registration number; with no formal accounting as per the prevailing financial management system in Cameroon.

CHAPTER 4

Key Economic Sectors for Jobs, Value Added, Competitiveness, and Growth

Introduction

What skills are valued in the sectors studied by this report? And what are the payoffs to those skills?

The Strategy Document for Growth and Employment (DSCE) identifies unemployment and weak productivity as key challenges for Cameroon's development (Government of Cameroon 2009). Thus, the document recommends the following:

- To develop more robust formal and informal employment opportunities by strengthening human development
- To increase productivity in agriculture, mining, and key value chains (such as timber, tourism, and information and communications technology)
- To stimulate growth through investments in critical infrastructure (particularly energy, roads, port infrastructure, and water supply) and improvements in the business climate and regional integration.

The DSCE sets an ambitious target of reducing underemployment from 76 percent of the workforce in 2005 to 50 percent by 2020, by creating tens of thousands of formal jobs. But the results achieved during the first two years of its implementation suggest that the DSCE is far from achieving that goal.

Key Sectors

The government has identified infrastructure, forestry (wood and wood processing), agriculture (agribusiness with a focus on cotton textiles and palm oil), tourism, extractives, and information and communications technology as sectors that would generate the most value added and so accelerate economic growth. The sectors are labor intensive, and could support Cameroon's structural transformation.

Infrastructure

Infrastructure has great potential for workforce value added and economic growth. Developing workers' skills in infrastructure involves fostering a range of generalists and specialists. For the purposes of this study, infrastructure is defined as construction of public and private buildings and public works. Infrastructure requires a host of light manufacturing enterprises, and there are specific workforce and skills requirements in the infrastructure value chain. For example, light manufacturing entrepreneurs engage in the fabrication of construction materials such as ceramics, tiles, bricks, cement-based items (such as balustrades for stairs), and metal gates and doors. Public works require social and environmental assessments conducted by qualified engineers, sociologists, anthropologists, communication specialists to sensitize communities and the public, and sector experts for the construction of health, education, and water and sanitation facilities. Between 1993 and 2005, employment opportunities in public works increased by nearly half in Cameroon. Decentralized management is the approach used for all construction and public works.

Projections of workforce requirements over 2009–12 showed a significant increase in the need for construction, rehabilitation, and maintenance of public and private buildings and for public works. The International Labour Organization (ILO) estimated that global workforce requirements for infrastructure would increase 53 percent during that time, although the workforce for roads was projected to increase by only 1.2 percent (ILO 2010). But the demand for construction of schools and other education facilities and health centers represents a significant market for the workforce. Based on government projections for investment in infrastructure, for each of the four fiscal years from 2009 to 2012, the ILO estimated that direct jobs would increase by 36,000 in Cameroon, with 47 percent in construction and 45 percent in roads. That rhythm is set to continue during 2013–20.

In 2005, 51.3 percent of public works enterprises in Cameroon were in Douala, followed by 26.6 percent in Yaoundé.[1] Together they comprised a major source of jobs. Maroua in the Far North region accounted for 6.5 percent and Garoua in the Northern region for 3.4 percent, followed by Bemenda, Limbé, and Bertoua. All other townships in the survey combined had just 5.3 percent of public works enterprises. The remaining 7 percent are from other parts of the country.

About 70 percent of the workforce is employed in 72 percent of the public works enterprises and each year contributes less than CFAF 20 million toward government revenue (about US$40,000). About 25 percent of employees in the remaining 22 percent of the public works enterprises contributes between CFAF 50 million and CFAF 100 million (US$100,000 to US$200,000) per year, and the remaining 5 percent employed in just 6 percent of public works enterprises contributes more than CFAF 100 million (US$200,000 per year). Between 2003 and 2006, workforce productivity declined, because of the drop in the national demand for construction and public works. Personnel costs rose 7.3 percent during that time, and the value added of the workforce fell from 1.86 percent in 2003 to 1.40 percent in 2006.

The structure of all infrastructure employment changed considerably between 2005 and 2006 (table 4.1). The demand for skilled workers increased, while that for unskilled workers decreased. Construction and civil works engineering accounts for about 86 percent of all infrastructure employment.

In 2005, 35.2 percent of infrastructure workers were ages 10–24 years, 36.3 percent were 25–39, and 21.7 percent were 40–54 (table 4.2). Thus, a huge number were youth, including those of school age (10–16 years). About 89.6 percent of technical personnel at the concept stage had completed higher education, and 22.4 percent of unskilled workers (those without specific qualifications) had completed lower secondary education; 17.8 percent had completed the first cycle of technical secondary education; and 39.6 percent had completed primary education.

Major constraints for infrastructure development in Cameroon include a shortage of qualified workers in areas such as accounting, governance, and production of construction materials. There is also a dearth of qualified environmental experts to conduct environmental assessments. Most workers have only primary education (table 4.3).

Table 4.1 Structure of Employment for All Infrastructure, 2005 and 2006
(%)

Category	2005	2006
Specialists	5.1	5.3
Skilled technicians	6.7	8.0
Technicians	17.1	22.7
Unskilled workers	68.7	64.0
Total	**100.0**	**100.0**

Sources: ILO 2010; National Institute of Statistics and International Labour Organization staff calculations.

Table 4.2 Characteristics of the Infrastructure Workforce, by Age Group and Type of Work, 2005
(%)

Age group	Technical personnel/ concept stage	Technical personnel/ rehabilitation	Specialized workforce	Workforce without specific qualifications	Share of total
10–24	0.0	8.6	36.5	35.8	35.2
25–39	44.6	48.1	37.5	33.8	36.3
40–54	40.7	38.9	17.1	27.0	21.7
55–69	10.5	4.5	8.9	2.5	6.3
>70	4.3	0.0	0.0	0.9	0.4
Total	**100.0**	**100.0**	**100.0**	**100.0**	**100.0**

Sources: ILO 2010; National Institute of Statistics and International Labour Organization staff calculations.

Table 4.3 Education Levels of Infrastructure Workers, 2005

(%)

Level of education	Technical personnel/ concept stage	Technical personnel/ rehabilitation	Specialized workforce	Workforce without specific qualifications	Share of total
None			5.6	3.9	4.7
Primary		5.4	46.2	39.6	42.2
1st cycle general secondary		7.8	13.9	22.4	16.9
2nd cycle general secondary	10.5	3.3	7.0	6.3	6.7
1st cycle secondary technical		16.0	14.6	17.8	15.6
2nd cycle secondary technical		42.8	8.1	8.6	8.7
Higher education	89.6	24.7	4.6	1.4	5.1
Total	**100.0**	**100.0**	**100.0**	**100.0**	**100.0**

Sources: ILO 2010; National Institute of Statistics and International Labour Organization staff calculations.

Entrepreneurs in Cameroon consider that the skills imparted by the country's prominent, large, and specialized institutes of technical training are adequate. But skills for potential entrepreneurs require attention. Skills development in commerce and business management—including the basics of economics, taxation, project management, accounting, and specialized software for accounting, auditing, and recordkeeping—are critical for increasing workforce value added. Management training is also required, particularly for civil works inspectors on industry standards, project managers, human resources managers, accountants, and auditors. Finally, there is a tendency to abandon projects or to have significant delays. Employment suffers and workers have little incentive to complete projects.

For potential employees, prior technical training in a host of specializations is needed, including in areas such as carpentry, masonry, electricity, plumbing, painting, and roofing. Some workforce development solutions include capacity development by integrating training on a large scale of the required quality within agreed timeframes, to facilitate job opportunities and on-the-job training. Government plans for skills development have not been synchronized with market needs. Further, multinational corporations have not been willing to build the required capacity and transfer knowledge on new techniques and technologies. The government needs to foster the conditions for such initiatives and devote efforts to new forms of technical training and technology transfer.

Infrastructure has been shifting from labor-intensive to capital-intensive processes, and is increasingly computerized. More higher-end skills are needed, including supervisory engineers and long-term skills development. But medium- and short-term skills development is also crucial. Yet, the unskilled account for most infrastructure workers. And infrastructure is heavily oriented toward seasonal employment.

Structural transformation will require skilled workers with engineering, science, and technology backgrounds. Training needs to be tested and certified.

Priority areas include specialized higher education in engineering (civil, mechanical, sanitation, water, plumbing, and electrical), technology (computer-aided design), and computer-aided management. But the paradox for infrastructure in Cameroon is that the sector's most highly educated and its illiterate workers find employment last. Nearly half the workers ages 25–34 with at least an undergraduate degree were unemployed (ILO 2010; ILO staff estimates based on the Household Survey III). Thus, a high-quality technical education could better serve people in that age bracket seeking work in infrastructure. And workers with a strong engineering and technology background could attract foreign direct investment and help the country to achieve structural transformation.

Forestry (Wood and Wood Processing)

Cameroon has the second largest natural forest area in Sub-Saharan Africa, strict laws on forest management, and the region's most developed forestry industry. Limits on exports of wood logs have helped create jobs, particularly among small enterprises involved in wood processing. The largest enterprises are owned by firms from Belgium, China, France, Greece, Italy, Lebanon, Malaysia, and the Netherlands. Most of them operate in Douala, Yaoundé, and Limbé.

In 2005, Cameroon's wood industry contributed about 6 percent to gross domestic product (GDP). That same year, the wood and wood processing industry accounted for 170,000 jobs—150,000 in the informal sector and 20,000 in the formal sector. Because startup costs are relatively low, many illegal and unregistered small enterprises are in operation. They mostly employ unskilled workers such as artisans and carpenters. The laws of 1999 paved the way for second-stage transformation in the country's value chain.

The wood industry had generated a value of CFAF 228 billion (US$456 million) in 2005. The government sought to diversify products, attract new importers, and develop local wood producers. Those efforts were expected to create 21,000 full-time jobs and 15,000 part-time jobs, with the value added estimated at CFAF 126 billion (US$252 million). The estimated cost was CFAF 1.36 billion (US$2.72 million), for a benefit-cost ratio of CFAF 0.92 in gross revenue for every franc invested. The government provides subsidies for large enterprises. Small enterprises receive none, so they tend to be informal.

The value chain in the wood industry is based on government classification of enterprises (table 4.4). Most wood enterprises (134) are involved in stage 1 transformation, 36 in the first two stages, 21 in the first three stages, and eight in all four stages (MINFOF 2012).

Wood enterprises and jobs are concentrated around the Center, East, Littoral, and South regions (table 4.5). Their location is linked to forest cover and infrastructure, making transportation of raw materials and final products relatively efficient. The most recent data from the Ministry of Economy, Planning, and Regional Integration (MINEPAT) and the Ministry of Forests and Wildlife indicate that 77.6 percent of the wood industry workforce is composed of specialized workers. This is in keeping with the national legislation of collective enterprises for the wood industry (access, transformation,

Table 4.4 Value Chain in the Wood Industry

	Stage 1 transformation	Stage 2 transformation	Stage 3 transformation	Stage 4 transformation
Definition	Primary processing of wood logs; sawmill trades	Transformation of stage 1 products into semi-finished or finished outputs through supplementary processing		Making products available for final consumption
	Heavy manufacturing Capital-intensive	Light manufacturing amenable/labor-intensive		Light manufacturing amenable/ labor-intensive
Examples	• Sawing timber of all sizes • Creating squared washers and studs • Slicing and peeling veneer	• Hydraulically assembled wood • Reconstituted solid wood • Paneling, parquet floors, wrinkles, decks • Drying sawn products	• Fabricating wood briquettes/bricks • Laminating and gluing • Fabricating particle board • Backing wood to prevent deterioration • Other wooden gadgets	• Furniture • Doors and door frames • Windows • All ready-to-use wood products

Sources: Government of Cameroon Decision 2637/D/MINFOF of December 6, 2012; MINEPAT 2014.

Table 4.5 Regional Distribution of Employment in the Wood Industry

Enterprise typology	Region	Full-time employees (%)
Wood transformation enterprises	Center	39.0
	East	30.6
	Littoral	20.5
	South	9.8
Artisanal enterprises	Center	40.7
	East	22.0
	Littoral	20.1
	South	17.2

Sources: Government of Cameroon Decision 2637/D/MINFOF of December 6, 2012; MINEPAT 2014.

and forest by-products). Professional workers comprise about 18.1 percent, and only 3.5 percent are high-level graduates (with a master's degree or professional engineers). Moreover, only 2 percent of this last category is employed.

All stages of the forestry and wood industry are labor-intensive and offer employment opportunities. Jobs in rural areas include sawers, assistant sawers, porters, chauffeurs, and assistant chauffeurs; in urban areas, employment opportunities include vendors, transporters, door-to-door salespeople, and food vendors who use processed wood materials (such as bowls, plates, and trays). In addition, there are potential spillover benefits in linking the outputs of the wood industry to value added in tourism.

Cameroon could increase the economic contribution of its forestry and wood industry. There are not enough qualified workers for stages 2 and 3 in the transformation of raw materials to produce export-quality products (carpentry, panels, woodworking, wood construction, cooperage, drying, packaging, and pallets). The country also suffers from the absence of a well-organized structure for vocational and technical training for the wood industry; lack of opportunities for apprenticeships; and lack of forestry experts (mid- to high-level expertise) with knowledge about conservation, reforestation, and forestry management.

An analysis of vocational and technical education and training in Cameroon's public and private wood industry found many weaknesses, including the following:

- Several training centers affiliated with universities offer training in wood processing—but they are not producing enough graduates and offer few courses.
- The centers have poorly qualified but highly paid trainers, making courses expensive.
- Most training centers do not have conducive learning environments: not just staff, but also learning materials and equipment (MINEPAT 2014; Pro-Invest 2014).

However, the training centers are the only providers of formal training for wood processing. There are also many informal training centers and programs offering low-quality training. Cameroon needs to invest in training in the commercial production of saplings, scaling up the use of sustainable technology, and upgrading the skills of trainers.

Agriculture and Agribusiness

The Government of Cameroon has identified six areas in agriculture as *key profitable areas*: cotton, palm oil, maize, manioc, banana-plantain, and aviculture. The main stages in the value chain for agriculture are the supply of inputs, production on farms, collection, processing, and final delivery (World Bank 2008). Cameroon could become a major source in Sub-Saharan Africa for manioc, maize, and banana-plantain—creating a lot of jobs and revenue, as well as developing skills.

This study analyzed only cotton and palm oil. Cotton is a major source of revenue for populations in the relatively poor parts of Cameroon—especially the North region. Cotton can also benefit other sectors (such as tourism) at the national level, and could earn major revenue through regional and international exports. Palm oil offers promise for agribusiness and has high potential for exports. There is also a significant national market for it. Most cotton is cultivated in the North region, while palm oil, cocoa, and coffee grow well in the West, South, and Central regions.

Cameroon has a good foundation for agro-industry. The country's one million small farms specialize in traditional agriculture, improved rainfed agriculture, intensive irrigated cultivation, pastoralism, and agro-pastoralism, producing many cereals and other foods. Medium-size and large farms are more specialized and typically have professional managers, salaried employees, and more mechanization. There are about 20 large public and private agro-industries, and their outputs are often exported. They have salaried employees and depend on inputs from small and medium-size farms.

Agricultural production is organized in a hierarchy of inputs, with improvements and changes in scale at each level (table 4.6).

Table 4.6 Hierarchy of Agro-Industry and Worker Needs

Small scale	Medium scale / taking to scale		Large scale
Farm-level; inputs use relatively small	Farm-level; improved management of inputs	Commercial level production	Agro-industrial large enterprises; extensive use of inputs
Manual (Intensive; 1 ha in total)	Manual (Intensive; 3 ha in total)	Manual (Intensive tending toward extensive; 5 ha in total)	Tractors or manual (extensive)
Small-scale inputs	Medium-scale inputs	Medium-larger scale inputs	Large-scale inputs
Markets close to farms	Markets in the proximity of farms	Markets far off; products have to be transported	In-house production; raw material transported to site of production
Limited use of equipment	Greater use of equipment	Use of technologically adapted equipment	Modern equipment
Family workers	Combination of family workers plus some salaried workers/contractors	Mostly salaried workforce	Only salaried workers
Entrepreneurship skills; unskilled workforce; apprenticeship	Entrepreneurship skills; some managerial skills; unskilled and skilled workforce	Entrepreneurship skills; management skills; skilled workforce	Management skills; skilled workforce

Source: World Bank 2008.

Agriculture suffers from a limited number of workers trained in good farming practices, management skills, and access to inexpensive inputs. As in other sectors, many agricultural jobs are informal. Investors could offer opportunities for investment—but investors would need to see a potential for returns. Young people do not consider agriculture an exciting career path. Reestablishing agriculture as agribusiness, with the potential for technology-based innovations, would make it more attractive.

Institutions and Agriculture

Reforms in the 1990s promoted liberalization and privatization of economic activities in Cameroon. As in the other sectors, there are various programs in the agriculture sector (table 4.7). Each program has distinct capacity-building elements.

Several programs for institutional capacity development support the current workforce and could help transfer technological know-how. But government officials have said that the programs bring financing but little knowledge transfer.

In the short term, food prices need to be lowered to help poor people. Over time, small farmers need to become more productive. Increasing access to better inputs and production technologies could improve output, which would require technical training for farmers in areas such as information sharing—such as through text messages. Lower transportation costs would also help.

All cost reduction strategies will require improving production technologies and the knowledge of farmers. Approaches to fertilizer use, direct imports of fertilizers, rationalized distribution channels by using collective management techniques, and information on value-added tax could improve production, lower costs, and make Cameroon's products more competitive.

Table 4.7 Programs and Institutions in the Agriculture Sector

Program	Institutions involved	Focus
National program to promote public access to agricultural research	World Bank/IDA Government (MINAGRI, MINEPIA, MIDENO, SOWEDA, SODECOTON) African Development Bank	National policy for improving and sustaining agricultural productivity; technical capacity (operational and financial) development; improving information on services; accelerating technology transfer.
Program for reform of the fertilizer subsector	USAID National Office for the Commercialization of Basic Agricultural Products	Support to private sector producers; commercialization of fertilizers; institutional capacity development
Project to support Strategies of farmers and the professionalization of agriculture	Churches Nongovernmental organizations International donors/development partners (French Development Cooperation program such as C2D—*Contrat des désendettements et de développement*)	Institutional capacity development; professionalization of small farmers
All ACP Agricultural Commodities Program	European Union (cocoa, coffee, milk) World Bank, FAO, Centre du commerce international, UNCTAD, and CFC (cotton) International Fund for Agricultural Development	Preparing sustainable strategies for agricultural production to improve revenues and access to resources for producers

Source: World Bank 2008.
Note: ACP = Agricultural Commodities Program; CFC = Common Fund for Commodities; FAO = Food and Agriculture Organization; IDA = International Development Association; MIDENO = North West Development Authority; MINAGRI = Ministry of Agriculture; MINEPIA = Ministry of Livestock, Fisheries, and Animal Industry; SODECOTON = National Cotton Development Company; SOWEDA = South West Development Authority; UNCTAD = United Nations Conference on Trade and Development; USAID = U.S. Agency for International Development.

Cameroon's agricultural products enjoy regional markets in the Central African Republic, Chad, Equatorial Guinea, Gabon, and the Republic of Congo. The Economic Partnership Agreement negotiated between the Central African Economic and Monetary Community (CEMAC) countries and the European Union could lower Cameroonian tariffs and open the country's market to foreign competition. Investments in technology, inputs, and credit will be key drivers. Using options such as savings and insurance to raise agricultural productivity (as in Rwanda) and combining financing and skills development approaches would help maximize returns.

Cotton Textiles

Cameroon has a regional comparative advantage in converting cotton textiles into mass clothing, and in distribution. These are the third and fourth stages in the value chain. (The first two are the transformation of raw cotton into fiber, and fiber into cloth, thread, and the like.) Cameroon is the only country in Central Africa that has the manufacturing capacity for making final products that satisfy the national market.

Cameroon needs to foster regional exports. Workers can produce innovative cotton cloth and textiles. They have long produced *stretch material*, know their clients' needs, and are nearby. Cotton textiles could also boost tourism.

Some constraints make it difficult for cotton to move to foreign markets. Most output is produced by informal workers who have limited knowledge, expertise, and training. Apprenticeships are the main way to transfer know-how. Another problem is that regulations on intellectual property are weak. Shortcomings arise from infrastructure weaknesses, the low level of pre-service training, and the few options for re-tooling or learning new methods of production.

Some workforce skills development solutions include capacity development by integrating training in basic homogenous techniques of production, mastering export-oriented procedures for external markets, promoting capacity for large deliveries, and improving job opportunities and training.

Palm Oil

Palm oil production could reduce poverty in Cameroon. Because such activities are not mechanized, they require that jobs be created in forests. Revenue from palm oil is fairly stable. The industry is relatively small and caters to national and regional consumption. It is not a full-fledged secondary level transformation industry. About 135,000 hectares are farmed and about 30,000 hectares have been reserved for agro-industry, with a transformation capacity of about 250,000 metric tons of palm oil, which could grow by nearly 10,000 hectares per year. Table 4.8 shows the evolution of raw palm oil production in Cameroon over time. Palm oil cultivation area increased by nearly a third between 2003 and 2008 (table 4.8).

It has been estimated that palm oil production generates approximately 65,000 direct and indirect jobs. Plantations (agro-industries) use many unskilled hourly workers, making it a village-level industry. Elevating the agro-industry to a larger scale would create more jobs.

The five main agro-industries in Cameroon produced about 145,000 metric tons of palm oil in 2008 (table 4.9). The enterprises employ around 30,000

Table 4.8 Raw Palm Oil Production, 2003–08
(tons)

Production level	2003	2004	2005	2006	2007	2008
Agro-industrialists	116,520	119,390	127,435	128,854	131,485	131,485
Village level plantations	52,680	58,680	64,880	70,680	76,680	82,680
Total	169,200	178,070	192,115	199,534	208,165	214,165

Sources: World Bank 2009b; Ministry of Employment, Vocational Education, and Training; International Labour Organization 2009a.

Table 4.9 Agro-Industry Locations and Palm Oil Production, 2008

Company	Location	Production (tons)
SOCAPALM	Mbongo, Nkapa, Kienke, Eseka	83,000
CDC	Limbe, Idenau	18,000
SPFS	Apouh (Edea)	15,000
SAFACAM	Dizangue (Edea)	12,000
PAMOL	Lobe	16,000

Sources: World Bank 2009b; Ministry of Employment, Vocational Education, and Training and International Labour Organization 2009; international consultants.

direct employees, for a global investment of CFAF 110 billion (US$220 million). Privatization has led to significant returns. In agro-industry, the objective is to remove entry barriers for new operators with available capital and knowledge about the production of palm oil for commercial purposes. SOCAPALM was privatized successfully. This resulted in more forest areas being cultivated for harvesting palm oil.

Most village plantations are artisanal. In 2009, the trade union that represents small farmers—the Palm Oil Operations Union (UNEXPALM)—brought together nearly one million planters among 10,000 small farmers who cultivate about 35,000 hectares. They produced about 30,000 tons of raw palm oil. Improvements in harvesting could increase those yields.

More extension workers are needed to improve cultivation. A major challenge has been to attract a qualified workforce from the Anglophone regions of the country to work in the more remote Southern and Eastern regions. More densely populated and urbanized areas are home to the most qualified workers, but more data on palm oil workers are needed.

The palm oil value chain is amenable to labor-intensive production (table 4.10).

Cameroon's ability to produce palm oil is relatively weak. Maximum production yields 18–19 tons per hectare, compared with 25 tons per hectare in Indonesia—which, along with Malaysia, is among the world's top producers. For the more extensive production system, Cameroon can produce nine tons per hectare, while Asian countries can produce 11.

Wages are among the top costs of palm oil production. Farmers say that they pay workers about CFAF 20,000 (about US$40 on average) per ton produced. But workers say that they receive only CFAF 12,000 (about US$24). According to the guaranteed minimum wage, a worker is supposed to receive CFAF 28,000 (US$56) per month. For small farmers, transportation is a close second cost.

The palm oil industry is a precarious option for young workers. They do not have access to the factors of production: land, human, and financial capital. In urban areas, youths tend to attend school and university. In rural areas, they are less likely to do so.

Tourism

Tourism could create decent jobs and foster Cameroon's economic growth. With modest investment in infrastructure, tourism has the potential to create more than 5,100 short-term and permanent direct, indirect, and induced jobs (MINEFOP and ILO 2009b). Building three-star hotels with conference facilities could create jobs and generate investments.

The government has not invested effectively in tourism. Weak infrastructure (communications, roads, and sanitation) and the lack of a service culture are major obstacles. Further, the Ministry of Tourism (MINTOUR) does not have regional departments, and there are no synergies between the ministry and national security to promote tourism in the country. The World Tourism Organization (UNWTO-OMT) envisioned the arrival of 500,000 visitors in 2007,

Table 4.10 Workforce in the Palm Oil Value Chain

Category	Characteristics	Potential and needs
Producers • Gatherers/pickers • Village plantations	• Represented by UNEXPALM • Supply 10% to 20% to artisans • Cultivation of primary product typically in old abandoned industrial plantations • Focus on rapid returns to capital investment • Generally poor and vulnerable • Often take the route of risk mitigation over profit maximization • Data/statistics on numbers of producers unavailable	• Most important category for skills development • Data/statistics on numbers of producers
Agro-industrialists	• Producers are protected by two trade unions: the National Union of Palm Oil Producers of Cameroon (SNPHPC) • The Association of Palm Oil by-Products Transformers (ATPO) [30,000 jobs with 6,000 jobs for transformation] • Five large and most established (old) ones: Ferme Suisse, Pamol, Safacam, CDC, and SOCAPALM • Procuring primary products • Organizing collection (in bulk/wholesale)	• Mid- and high-level management skills • Village plantations mostly inaccessible to agro-industrialists
Local transformers	• Informal sector • Artisanal transformers • Setup in makeshift or rented premises • Mostly manual transformation, not automation • Low level of outputs (15% to 18% at most from the best performers compared with industry equivalent of 22%) • The by-products are used as fuel for cooking walnuts • Amenable to light manufacturing	• Product diversification, management, and marketing skills • A major handicap since the almonds of palms are highly sought by the soap-making industry • Information about markets for primary and by-products • Data/statistics
Commercial agents	• Importers who supply to transformers • Wholesalers who target mostly agro-industrialists • Middlemen linked to wholesalers • Located in the informal rural setting or urban setting	• Marketing skills, negotiating skills • Information • Data/statistics
Transporters	• All types and modes (walking, pushcarts, bicycle, cars, vans, and trucks) at different stages of transformation	• Management and organization skills • Defensive driving skills
Fats and soap-making industry	• Stage II transformation • Use modern factories to transform palm oil—light manufacturing • Export quality production • High distribution costs—not competitive	• Knowledge about the industry • Management skills

Source: World Bank 2009b.

Note: CDC = Cameroon Development Corporation; SOCAPALM = Palm Growers Society of Cameroon; UNEXPALM = Palm Oil Operations Union.

but only 196,000 arrived. The global fiscal crisis and its impact on Cameroon's economy further depressed tourism the following year (2008).

MINTOUR's budget rose 234 percent for recurrent and 333 percent for investment spending between fiscal years 1996/97 and 2009. Yet the budget for tourism accounts for just 1 percent of the national budget. Moreover, the tourism industry is poorly organized, caters to few tourists, and has not contributed much to GDP.

Tourism is most prominent in the Littoral, South and Central regions. For example, it has generated 5,633 jobs in Limbé (Littoral) and 3,979 in Kribi (South).

Tourist agencies are also concentrated around the two regions. Most tourist hotels are unclassified (no stars). Domestic travel is difficult because there is limited infrastructure—only major highways, with inadequate railroads and unreliable flights.

About 20 public entities are engaged in tourism activities (table 4.11). Coordinating them is a challenge, and the industry remains in the nascent stage. However, Cameroon's plants and animals could generate significant tourism revenue.

Tourism training is offered by 38 public and private institutions:

- Among the public institutions, five technical training institutes offer hotel management. The most prominent are in Kribi and Limbé. The University of Yaoundé I has two faculties for hotel management and tourism, but they only provide licenses for tourist guides. The School for Hotels and Tourism of

Table 4.11 Public Entities Involved in Tourism

Entity	Responsibility
Ministry of Environment and Protection of Nature	Management of protected areas
Ministry of Forestry and Fauna	Management of forests, fauna, conserved areas, hunting, and exports of trophies
Ministry of Culture	Inventory of principal cultural activities and promotion of national culture
Ministry of Higher Education	High-level training and mastery in tourism studies
Ministry of Secondary Education	Mid-level training in tourism studies
Ministry of Technical and Vocational Education and Training	Technical and vocational training in tourism studies
Ministry of Finance	Tourism finance, accounting for tourism satellites, immigration, and exchange
Ministry of Economy, Planning, and Regional Integration	Programming investments, territorial management (tourist zones)
Ministry of Agriculture and Rural Development	Export of foodstuffs
Ministry of Defense	Security of people and tourists
Ministry of the Interior and Decentralization	Oversight of local offices/agencies of tourism
National Security Delegation	Assuring security of persons, goods, border control, visa administration at national borders
Ministry of Small and Medium Enterprises, Social and Artisan Administration	Exports of artisanal products
Ministry of Commerce	Investment code
Ministry of National Health	National health and vaccinations
Ministry of Transport and National Airports Authority	Transport tariffs, Cameroon Airports Authority, Cameroon Airports Company administration
Ministry of Communication	Promotion of tourism through information for tourists and communication/media campaigns to sensitize the population
Ministry of External Relations	Visas and communication of information regarding Cameroon to tourists
Ministry of Scientific Research and Innovation	Research in codification of Cameroonian cuisine
Ministry of Public Works	Construction, maintenance, and rehabilitation of tourist sites, roads/highways in general, public water and sanitation, airports

Source: MINEFOP and ILO 2009b.

CEMAC, in N'gaoundéré, offers the most diverse training. The Ministry of Higher Education—in collaboration with the Ministry of Tourism and the French Cooperation—offers a license in tourism and hotel management in select universities, and the Training Institute in Garoua (North region) offers preparation for tourist guides.

- Among the private institutions, the most prominent are the Centers for Short-Term Rapid Training (accreditation programs, not diplomas) in Yaoundé and Douala and higher education institutions that provide an Advanced Technician Certificate in tourism and hotel management.
- Most ecotourism projects are initiated by nongovernmental organizations, such as the World Wildlife Fund, International Union of Nature and Natural Resources Conservation, and Birdlife International.

The quality of training varies, but in most cases it falls short of its potential (table 4.12).

Extractives

Among extractive industries, mining has the most potential to create a lot of jobs. But it requires significant infrastructure investments as well as a steady supply of commodities. Creating jobs in mining will depend on the extent of excavations and the choice of technology (labor-intensive or machine-intensive). Thus, it is difficult to project job creation in mining.

The government has identified diamond, cobalt-nickel, iron, and bauxite as some of the key minerals for excavation. The Capacity Development in Mining Project (PRECASEM) had estimated some levels of investment and employment for 2012–15 (table 4.13).

In keeping with the strategic development of the geology and mining sector in Cameroon, projections for the medium-term (2015–25) are as follows:

- Completion of iron ore excavation in Mbalam in 2016 and bauxite excavation in Minim-Martap in 2019, and the commencement of production

Table 4.12 Quality of Tourism Training

Aspect	Assessment
Training environment	Generally poor and not conducive to learning. Most training centers are in noisy neighborhoods, in rented buildings intended for residences. Short-term courses in hotels do not have the required facilities. Trainees pay all of their expenses.
Program options	Not well defined. No options for on-the-job training. Tourism has been reduced to hotels and restaurants. The conceptualization, organization, and distribution of tourism-related voyages/trips relating to tourism packages is entirely missing. This domain could offer significant job opportunities.
Relevance to market demand	Programs are poorly targeted, insufficiently elaborated, and not adapted to the tourism industry.
Pedagogical support	Highly theoretical and relatively disconnected from reality.
Training personnel	Not up to the standards required for training tourism professionals.

Source: MINEFOP and ILO 2009b.

Table 4.13 Minerals, Estimated Investment, and Employment, 2012–15

Project	Estimated investment	Estimated employment	Transformation (units)	Territorial management	Estimated exports
Diamond (Mobilong)	US$233 million	4,000 (direct jobs during the excavation phase of transformation)	Sediment sorting	Local infrastructure	6,000 carats
Cobalt-nickel	US$617 million	800 (direct jobs), 450 (indirect jobs)	Ore processing plant		4,000 to 5,500 tons of cobalt
Iron ore (Mbalam)	US$4.68 billion	3,000 (direct jobs)	Ore processing plant	Railway, port terminal, local infrastructure	No production
Bauxite (Minim-Martap)	US$5 billion	7,000 (direct jobs), 6,000 to 8,000 (indirect jobs)	Aluminum refinery, dam, hydroelectric power plant	Railway, port terminal, local infrastructure	No production

Source: Government of Cameroon 2013b.

Table 4.14 Estimated Impact of Mining Operations in the Medium Term, 2015–25

Project	Investment	Employment	Transformation factories	Territorial management	Estimated exports
Diamond (Mobilong)	US$223 million net	4,000 (direct jobs)	Sediment sorting	Local infrastructure constructed	6,000 carats
Cobalt-Nickel (Lomié)	US$617 million net	800 (direct jobs) 450 (indirect jobs)	Ore processing plant	Integration of roads and bridges	4,000–5,500 tons of cobalt
Iron Ore (Mbalam)	US$4.68 billion net; US$3.14 billion (Phase 2)	3,000 (direct jobs)	Ore processing plant Ore enrichment plant	Railway, port terminal, local infrastructure	30 metric tons of iron
Bauxite (Minim-Martap)	US$5 billion net	1,500-2,000 (direct jobs) 4,000 (indirect jobs)	Aluminum refinery, dam, hydroelectric power plant	Railway, port terminal, local infrastructure	3 metric tons of aluminum
Gold (Industrial South-East Region of Cameroon)	US$200 million (estimated)	500 (estimated jobs)	Processing plant	Local infrastructure	3,000 kgs of gold
Uranium (Poli-Kitongo Lolodorf Teubang)	US$1 billion (estimated)	500 (estimated jobs)	Ore processing plant and yellow cake manufacturing	Local infrastructure	800 tons per year of enriched mineral
Titanium (Akonoling)	US$300 million (estimated)	600 (direct jobs) 300 (indirect jobs)	Mineral processing	Local infrastructure	30,000 tons per year of rutile

Source: Government of Cameroon 2013b.

- Movement to the next stage of transformation following the excavation of diamond mines in Mobilong and cobalt in Lomié
- Construction of gold mines in the industrial South-East in 2018, uranium mines in Poli, Lolodorf, in 2019, and titanium mines in Akonolinga in 2019.

By 2020, the excavations would be complete and production would commence.

The jobs forecasts for the medium term (2015–25) are provided in table 4.14.

The long-term (2025–80) estimates translate to:

- Continued and progressive excavations and extraction of the mines already in place, except if new reserves are found in the neighboring areas (probable)
- Production of new resources currently known as Colombo tantalite, syénite néphélinique, granites (rose or black), or those discovered during the process of geological and mineral exploration.

With respect to jobs, taking into account the short-, medium-, and long-term needs, the occupations could be classified under the strategic categories listed in table 4.15.

An analysis of employment needs undertaken by the PRECASEM project reveals a considerable number of induced jobs by mineral and mining site. In the short term, they total about 24,300 jobs; in the medium term, approximately 13,400 jobs; and in the long term, about 10,400 jobs.

Table 4.16 shows the mapping of induced jobs by mineral, mining site, and time period.

Table 4.15 Strategic Occupations in Mining

Occupations	Needs	Where should the training be received?
Jobs in prospection		
• Geologist • Geometric topographer • Geochemist • Geophysicist • Driller	• In the short-term: stable • In the medium-term: depends considerably on the success of the first phase transformation phase	• Graduates and post-graduates from universities with specialized programs of study in geology
Jobs in construction		
• Civil engineering supervisors: head of civil engineering and construction • Masons • Plumbers • Logisticians (transport road and rail) • Electricians (industrial and buildings) • Mechanical engineers	• In the short-term: important • In the medium-term: depends on the extent and pace of excavations/exploration (commencement of mining operations)	• Graduates and post-graduates from universities with specialized programs of study in civil and mechanical engineering • Diploma holders from technical training institutes or vocational training centers
Jobs in excavation/exploration		
• Metallurgists/chemists • Head of mining subsector • Engine operators • Electro-mechanists • Maintenance technicians • Technicians in electronics/automotives • Welders/solders • Coordinator of health and security • Head of community relations	• Jobs depend on the pace of construction and excavation; they follow within a space of 2-5 years after sites have been constructed and excavated	• Degree holders from universities with specialized programs in engineering • Diploma holders from technical training institutes/vocational training institutes
Closing and renovation of sites		
• Social and environmental specialist	• Needed for the long term	• Degree holders/graduates from universities with specialized programs in environmental sciences

Source: Government of Cameroon 2013b.

Table 4.16 Estimated Induced Jobs in Mining

Mineral	Mining site	Induced Jobs		
		Short-term (2013–20)	Medium-term (2020–30)	Long-term (2030–80)
Diamonds	Mobilong	4,000	2,000	1,000
Cobalt-nickel	Lomié	800	800	800
Iron ore	Mbalam/Djoum	12,000	6,000	4,000
Bauxite	Mini-Martap	7,000	3,000	3,000
Gold	South-East	500	500	500
Uranium	Poli		500	500
Titanium	Akonolinga		600	600
	Total	**24,300**	**13,400**	**10,400**

Source: Government of Cameroon 2013b.

Table 4.17 Training Institutes and University Programs, by Location

Institute or program	Location
Centre de formation Professionnelle lassalien Van Haygen	Bertoua
Centre de Formation Professionnelle aux Métiers d'l'Industrie de Nyom (CFMIN)	Yaoundé
Centre de Formation professionnelle aux Métiers Miniers (CEPROMINES)	Yaoundé
Techniciens Génie Civil Réunis formation (TGCR)	Yaoundé
Professionnal Excellency Training Center (PTEC)	Edéa
Centre de Formation Professionnelle Continue de la Salle (CFPC)	Douala
Centre de Formation Professionnelle Amour Fraternité (CEFOPRAF)	Douala
Techniciens et Ingénieurs en Agro-Alimentaire (TINAGRI)	Ngaoundéré
Homelex Sarl	Douala
Matgénie	Yaoundé
Technical training colleges	
Lycée Technique	Edéa
Lycée Technique	Kousséri
Lycée Technique	Sanmélima
University-affiliated colleges/institutes	
École de Géologie et des Mines (EGEM)	Maiguenga
École Nationale Supérieure des Sciences Agro Industrielles (ENSAI)	N'Gaoundéré
Institut Universitaire de Technologie	N'Gaoundéré
Institut Universitaire du Sahel	Maroua
Les organismes d'intervention en Hygiène Sécurité Environnement Barakat SA	Douala

Source: Government of Cameroon 2013b.

Among the primary challenges for Cameroon is the dearth of a qualified workforce in all specialized areas. Although there are centers of professional training, technical training institutes, and some programs in universities (table 4.17), the quantity and quality of the trained workers are insufficient to meet the estimated demand. Further evaluation of the institutions is required to assess the programs being offered, the curriculum, their quality and relevance to the mining industry, whether graduates are finding jobs, and which programs are most popular and why.

Fostering Skills in Cameroon • http://dx.doi.org/10.1596/978-1-4648-0762-6

Information and Communications Technology

There is a large, untapped market for new entrants in Cameroon's markets, particularly in information technology (IT) and information technology–enabled services (ITES). Structural change could be fostered by developing basic skills, assessment, and certification programs in internationally benchmarked ITES. The potential of social media could also be harnessed.

IT skills can enhance competitiveness in a broad range of sectors, including e-government initiatives. Improving the country's competitiveness would require the following: (i) a sustained flow of employable skills, including IT skills: (ii) competitive labor costs; (iii) conducive business climate; (iv) infrastructure and quality relevant to the industry; and (v) sustained investments in IT-related secondary and post-basic education.

For Cameroon to achieve structural transformation, the country must identify skill gaps in technology and innovation. The assessment could form the basis for providing training and certifying skilled individuals. Cameroonian youth lack market-relevant skills in IT and ITES. Higher education enrollments in applied sciences, engineering, and technology are very low. Women's representation is especially low in science and technology courses, research professions, and leadership.

Foundations for Workforce Value Added

The value chain analyses conducted for this study focused on the lack of workers with needed skills (table 4.18). Slow job growth was cited as the second main problem, followed by lack of access to financial and social capital, problems with

Table 4.18 Sectors and Constraints in Workforce Availability

Constraints	Details	Infra-structure	Wood	Agriculture/ Agri-business	Cotton	Palm oil	Tourism	Tech-nology
Job-relevant skills constraints	Insufficient basic skills				X			X
	Technical skills mismatch	X	XXX	X	X	XXX		X
	Behavioral skills mismatch							
	Insufficient entrepreneurial skills	X						X
Lack of labor demand	Slow job-growth economy	X	X				X	X
	Employer discrimination					X		
Job search constraints	Job matching				X			X
	Signaling competencies							X
Firm start-up constraints	Lack of access to financial or social capital					XX	X	X
Social constraints on the supply side	Excluded-group constraints (ethnicity, gender)			X				X

Source: Authors' analysis about Cameroon based on constraints and details set out by Cunningham, Sanchez-Puerta, and Wuermli 2010.

job matching, insufficient entrepreneurial skills, insufficient basic skills, and employer discrimination. The value chain analyses were less useful at forecasting labor and skill needs.

Conclusion

Cameroon has latent potential for creating productive jobs in infrastructure, wood processing, cotton textiles, palm oil, and tourism. The strategic basis (enabling environment, laws, and regulations) exists to varying degrees for each of the sectors. The government needs to ensure a minimum threshold of capital-intensive investment for structural transformation of production processes. Labor-intensive structural transformation is also required. Workforce value added would be a key condition to enhance the skills development and accumulation effect. Together the aggregation and accumulation effects could result in sustained, inclusive growth.

An unduly heavy and centralized system—with a plethora of ministries, institutions, and oversight structures—is paralyzing action in Cameroon. Civil service reforms and streamlined workforce development could help. Structural reforms are needed to tackle the quantity and quality of workforce development. The government has already begun efforts in primary education, and is preparing to introduce basic education reform by 2016. Further, it has pledged to prepare forward-looking TVET and university education systems. These aspects are reviewed and the skills accumulation factors are analyzed in the next chapter.

Note

1. The most recent data available were for 2005 when the value chain analysis for infrastructure was prepared in 2010. The Employment and Informal Sector Surveys 2010 data set contains more recent data, but it was not available to the task team.

CHAPTER 5

Skills Accumulation and the Stock and Flow of the Workforce

Introduction

How is the government addressing workforce constraints? How are Cameroon's ongoing reforms in education and training likely to affect workforce development over the next decade? Will the flow of potential workers have the skills and competencies needed to increase economic productivity and contribute to growth? And what role should private employers play in developing workers' skills?

Investing in skills is costly. Few governments can afford to finance the extent and quality of worker skills required—creating a vicious cycle in which high costs constrain investment in skills, which impedes economic growth and so limits the resources available for investing in skills. Recognizing this, Ansu and Tan (2012) propose a two-pronged approach. First, skills development should be integrated with economic development plans. Purposeful and flexible arrangements would help meet employers' immediate demand for skills, particularly in prospective growth sectors. Second, longer-run efforts at system wide improvement could equip all citizens with strong literacy and numeracy skills, increase the education system's orientation toward science and technology, and strengthen links with the working world, particularly in tertiary education.

This chapter provides a critical review of skills accumulation in Cameroon. This is considered a gradual process that is best analyzed from the perspective of the education and training system. Age-based educational attainment is the proxy used to capture the skills accumulation process, from foundational skills at early grades through higher-order skills at the university level. Changes in levels of educational attainment over time were tested using an education and training simulation model. The quantitative and qualitative effects of ongoing basic education reforms, rates of return to education, and trends in the supply of labor are measured. The chapter also reviews how the policies, institutions, and programs of the technical, industrial, vocational, and entrepreneurship training (TVET) system contribute to skills formation at the vocational and professional technical levels. Employment trends offer the demand-side counterpart information.

Education System

Several ministries are in charge of Cameroon's education system, with one each for primary, secondary, vocational and professional technical, and higher education (box 5.1). Another ministry oversees youth affairs and policies. In addition, two education systems operate in parallel: one for Francophone areas and one for Anglophone (see appendixes B and C for greater detail on their structures). The government is trying to create a unified system.

Box 5.1 Cameroon's Education System

- **Pre-primary**: two years. Responsible entities— **Communities, Private Sector**.
- **Primary**: Responsible ministry— **Ministry of Primary Education**.
  - The Francophone system lasts six years and ends with the Primary Study Certificate.
  - The Anglophone system lasts seven years and ends with the First School Leaving Certificate.
  - Under both systems, the end of primary school marks preparation for vocational training or entrance to secondary.
- **Secondary**: six years (three lower secondary and three upper secondary)— **Ministry of Secondary Education**.
- **Post-primary**: two years (for rural artisans and domestic help.
- **Secondary and teacher training**: responsible ministry—Ministry of Higher Education **(MINESUP)**.
  - The Francophone system for **secondary general education** (based on a competitive entrance examination) lasts four years and ends with the *Brevet d'Études du Premier Cycle* (First-Cycle Secondary Education Certificate, BEPC). The Anglophone system lasts five years and ends with the General Certificate of Education Ordinary/Level.
  - For **secondary technical education**, there are two cycles. The first lasts four years and, in the Francophone system, ends with the *Certificate d'Aptitude Professionnelle* (Certificate of Professional Competence, CAP). The second cycle lasts three years. In the Francophone system, this cycle is open to BEPC and CAP graduates to receive a *Baccalauréat de Technicien* (Bachelor's Degree in Technical Education) or *Brevet de Technicien* (Technician Certificate). In the Anglophone system, the second cycle ends with the General Certificate of Education Advanced Level, which provides access to higher education or jobs. Both systems require the successful conclusion of the provisional level to graduate from the second cycle of secondary technical education.
- **Vocational and professional technical training**: responsible ministry—Ministry of Employment, Vocational Education, and Training **(MINEFOP)**.
  - Institutes offer short-term training and are affiliated with MINEFOP.

box continues next page

Box 5.1 Cameroon's Education System *(continued)*

- **Post-secondary or higher education**: responsible ministry—**MINESUP**.
  - Several public and private institutions offer post-secondary or higher education: Government universities: Yaoundé I, Yaoundé II, Douala, Buea, Dschang, N'gaoundéré, Maroua, and Bemenda.
  - University technical training institutes (UTIs), which last two to three years and are in Douala, Bandjoun, and N'gaoundéré. Entrance to UTIs is competitive for Cameroon nationals; an education portfolio comprising educational background and related experience is required for foreign nationals. Graduates receive a *Diplôme Universitaire de Technologie* (University Technical Education Diploma) or *Brevet de Technicien Supérieur* (two-year technical degree or Advanced Technician Certificate).
  - Private universities: Catholic University of Central Africa, Catholic University, University of Yaoundé-South Joseph Ndi Samba, and Institute Siantou Supérieur.
  - Major training institutes: most are affiliated with universities.

Source: Ministry of Education 2013.

Table 5.1 Gross Enrollments in Public and Private Education and Training, 2000–01 and 2010–11

(%)

Level	Public		Private	
	2000–01	*2010–11*	*2000–01*	*2010–11*
Pre-primary	13.3	27.2	58,0	61,9
Primary	102.8	112.9	27,0	22,2
1st cycle secondary general education	28.8	53.4	29,0	24,1
2nd cycle secondary general education	16.3	30.2	29,0	30,5
1st cycle secondary technical education	7.3	13.5	42,0	16,8
2nd cycle secondary technical education	3.8	8.1	39,5	26,4
Professional training	n/a	n/a	n/a	69,9
University education (Students/100,000 inhabitants)	454	1,103	7,6	14,6

Source: World Bank 2013a.
Note: n/a = not available.

Between 2007 and 2011, Cameroon increased access to and completion of primary education (table 5.1), although girls' completion rate grew less in the Education Priority Zones (ZEPs). There were notable increases in the net enrollment rate and primary completion rate (for both sexes) and a reduction in the repetition rate. Although there were improvements in the ZEPs— particularly in the Far North, North, Adamaoua, North-West, and East regions—in the disadvantaged pockets of urban and peri-urban areas, and the frontier parts of the country progress was much slower than in the rest of the country. For example, the overall primary completion rate rose from 51 percent in 2007 to 80 percent in 2011, but for girls it only went from

Figure 5.1 Transversal Profile and Probabilistic Profile of Student Flow, 2011

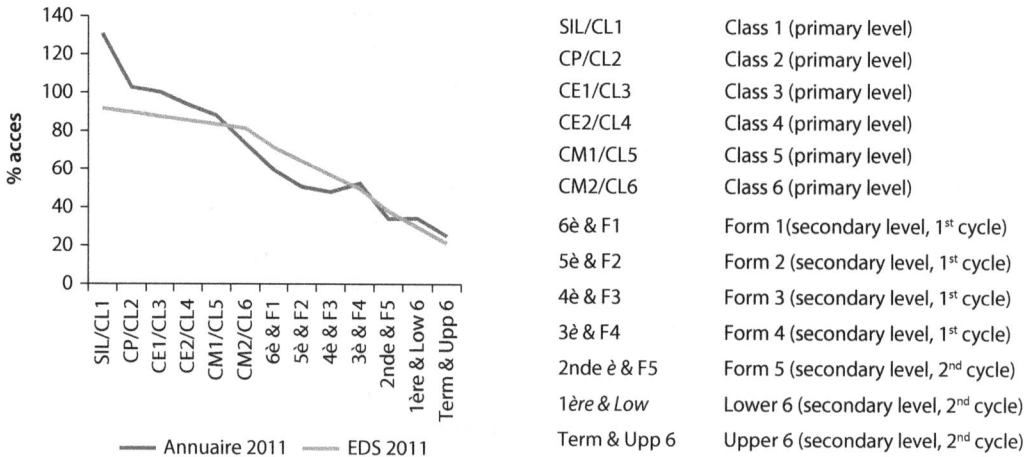

SIL/CL1	Class 1 (primary level)
CP/CL2	Class 2 (primary level)
CE1/CL3	Class 3 (primary level)
CE2/CL4	Class 4 (primary level)
CM1/CL5	Class 5 (primary level)
CM2/CL6	Class 6 (primary level)
6è & F1	Form 1(secondary level, 1st cycle)
5è & F2	Form 2 (secondary level, 1st cycle)
4è & F3	Form 3 (secondary level, 1st cycle)
3è & F4	Form 4 (secondary level, 1st cycle)
2nde è & F5	Form 5 (secondary level, 2nd cycle)
1ère & Low	Lower 6 (secondary level, 2nd cycle)
Term & Upp 6	Upper 6 (secondary level, 2nd cycle)

Source: World Bank 2013a.

Table 5.2 Education Levels and the Structure of Employment, 2010

Education level of graduates			Access to employment			
Education level	Number	% of total	Activity	Employment	Number	% of total
University complete	16,782	3.6		Senior management	13,444	2.9
University incomplete	50,723	11.0		Mid-level management	14,156	3.1
Upper secondary complete	29,425	6.4		Skilled employees	23,505	5.1
Upper secondary incomplete	78,467	17.0		Unskilled employees	36,496	7.9
Lower secondary complete	55,389	12.0		Informal nonagricultural	119,001	25.8
Lower secondary incomplete	96,930	21.0		Informal agricultural	115,047	24.9
Primary complete	46,157	10.0	Unemployed		6,445	1.4
No schooling and primary incomplete	87,699	19.0	Inactive		133,479	28.9
Total	461,573	100.0	Total		461,573	100.0

Source: World Bank 2013a.

38 percent in 2007 to 43 percent in 2011. The 2016 target for primary completion set in the government's education strategy for 2013–20 is ambitious, at 84 percent for the ZEPs.

Data for 2011 from two sources—the National Statistical Yearbook and the Demographic Health Survey—show student flow declining across the education system, factoring in dropouts and repetition rates (figure 5.1).

An analysis of student flow by level of education and sector of employment shows a changing pattern over time and important disconnects between jobs and the education levels of graduates (table 5.2).

Educational Attainment across Age Groups

Educational attainment has improved in Cameroon in recent decades. The primary completion rate rose from 53 percent in 2001 to about 80 percent in 2011 (figure 5.2). School life expectancy—the number of years of education children entering school can expect to receive in their lives—increased by four years over the same period, a sharp improvement relative to international comparators (figure 5.3). These improvements reflect the abolition of school fees for primary education in 2000, which increased enrollments, as did the

Figure 5.2 Primary Completion Rates, 1991–2011

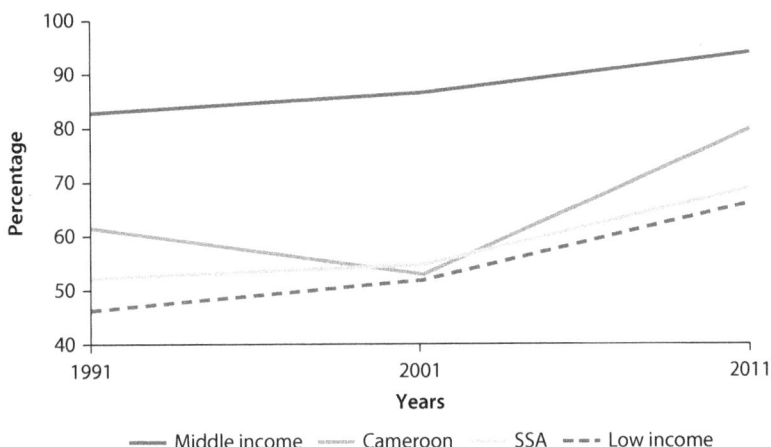

Source: World Bank 2003, 2013a; UNESCO Institute of Statistics.

Figure 5.3 School Life Expectancy, 2001–11

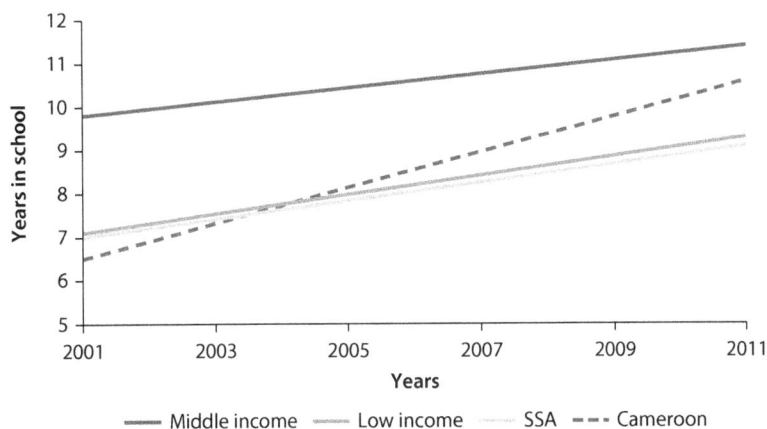

Source: World Bank 2003, 2013a; UNESCO Institute of Statistics.

improved service delivery that resulted from the contract teachers program in 2007–11. Secondary enrollments more than doubled over the past two decades, with nearly 1.3 million students in 2009. Overall, children spend 2.5 more years in school than they did two decades ago, totaling an average of 10 years—well into secondary school.

Average years of total schooling (primary and secondary) have also risen among Cameroon's working age population (figure 5.4). Countrywide, the share of this group (ages 15–64 years) with no schooling fell by more than half between 1990 and 2010, to just under 20 percent (figure 5.5). It is becoming increasingly common for workers to have completed secondary education. However, the increases have been lower than in full-fledged middle-income countries such as Malaysia and Thailand. And although access to education has increased, the quality of education has declined.

The evolution of the education system has been uneven (World Bank 2012b). Budget cuts in the 1990s caused a 10 percentage point drop (from 94 to 84 percent) in the primary education gross enrollment ratio. The budget cuts also affected teachers. Civil servants saw their salaries cut drastically in 1993, and teacher recruitment was restricted. Consequently, class sizes grew to more than 60 students, with significant variations between regions. Regions and communities used different strategies to address the growing need for teachers.

Figure 5.4 Schooling among the Working Age Population (Ages 15–64 Years), 1990–2010

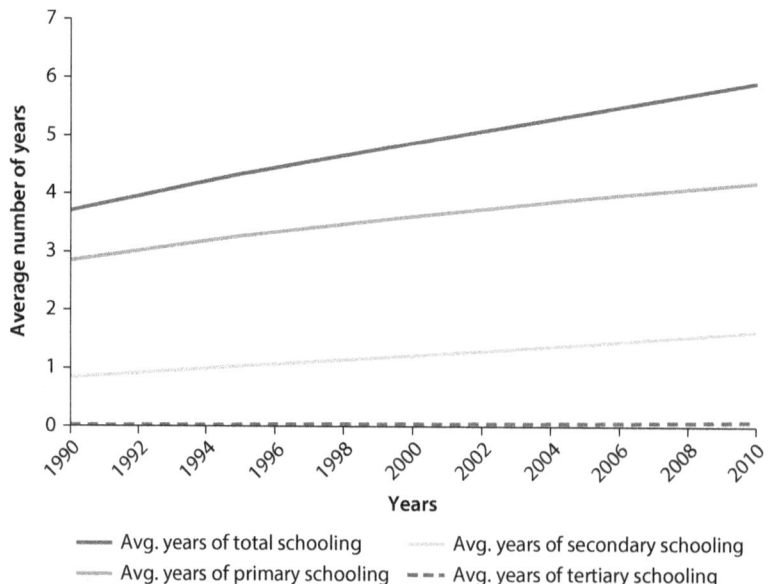

Figure 5.5 Highest Level of Education Attained among the Working Age Population (Ages 15–64 Years), 1990–2010

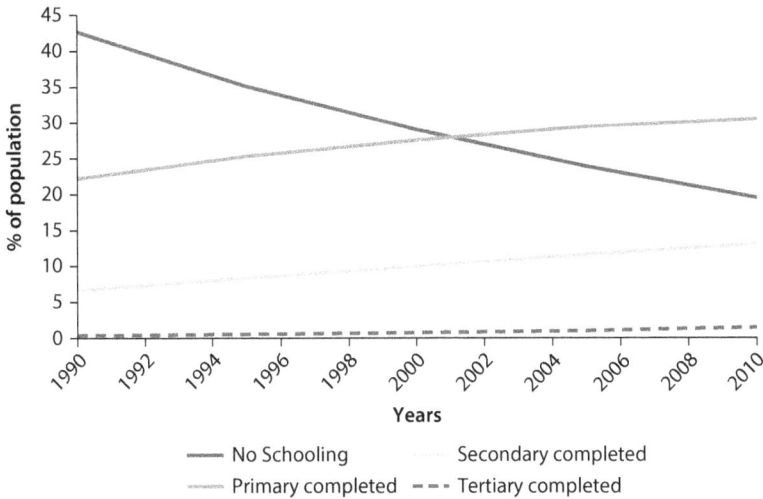

Source: Barro and Lee 2010.

Accumulation Effect (Ages 5–24 Years)

The stock of human capital in Cameroon nearly doubled between 1965–77 and 1978–86, from 1.3 years of education per working person to 2.5 years. Total and female primary and secondary school enrollment ratios increased, and overall literacy rose. During 1978–86, improvements in technology and productivity were attributable to the increased emphasis on human capital development. Relative to the average for Sub-Saharan Africa, Cameroon fared favorably on the educational attainment of its workforce. In 2005, the average Cameroonian worker had the equivalent of 3.18 years of primary education and 3.88 years of all levels of education, more than the average for Central and West Africa (3.10 years) and Sub-Saharan Africa (3.14) (Ghura 1997; Charlier and N'çho-Oguie 2009). Health indicators also improved markedly, reflecting an increase in the number of physicians and nurses relative to the population. Maternal and child mortality declined (World Bank 2013b).

Between 1986 and 2010, investments in human capital development—education, training, and jobs—peaked and then declined in real terms. The quality of primary education also improved and fell during this period. Public spending on education and training requires review and adjustment to increase efficiency.

The gains since the mid-1980s have not been uniform, especially among the poorer quintiles of the population, for whom enrollments are much lower at various education levels (figure 5.6). Table 5.3 provides data on enrollment and share in private education. By far, TVET has the highest percentage of enrollment in private institutions. However, TVET also had the lowest enrollment in 2010–11.

Figure 5.6 Enrollment in Education by Wealth Quintile, 2011
(%)

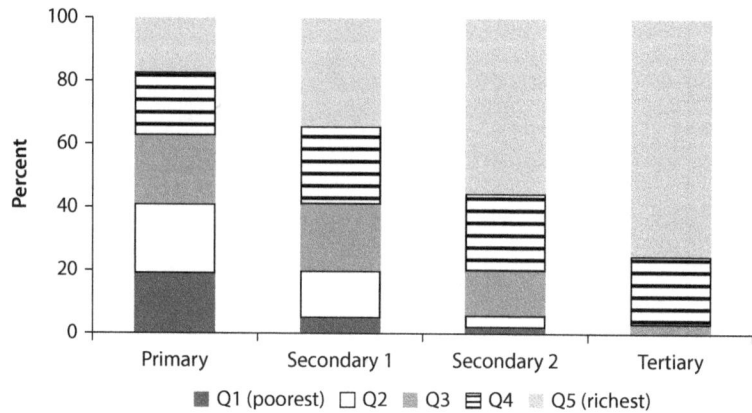

Source: World Bank 2013b.

Table 5.3 Education and Enrollment, 2010–11

Level of Education	Enrollment in 2010–11 (thousands)	Share in private education (%)
ECD	339.6	61.9
Primary	3,576.9	22.2
Secondary general	1,386.0	
1st cycle	*1,005.5*	24.1
2nd cycle	*380.5*	30.5
Secondary technical	356.1	
1st cycle	*254.0*	16.8
2nd cycle	*102.1*	26.4
TVET	39.5	69.9
University	189.8	14.6

Sources: Annual statistics from the Ministries of Primary Education, Secondary Education, and Higher Education; staff estimates for general secondary 1st cycle and secondary technical 1st cycle; World Bank 2013a.

The educational attainment of children and youth (ages 5–24 years) starts to decline when they reach around age 10 (figure 5.7).

There are also significant numbers in these age groups who have no education, are out of school, or have not completed primary education. Since 2010, the rising costs of schooling have started to be reflected in educational attainment levels among children and youth. Greater numbers of those ages 12 and older are not in school, training, or formal employment sector. Most have a secondary general education that does not prepare them for formal employment, few have secondary technical education, and even fewer have higher education. With growing numbers completing primary education and a portion of them completing lower

Figure 5.7 Educational Attainment of Children and Youth (Ages 5–24 Years), 2010

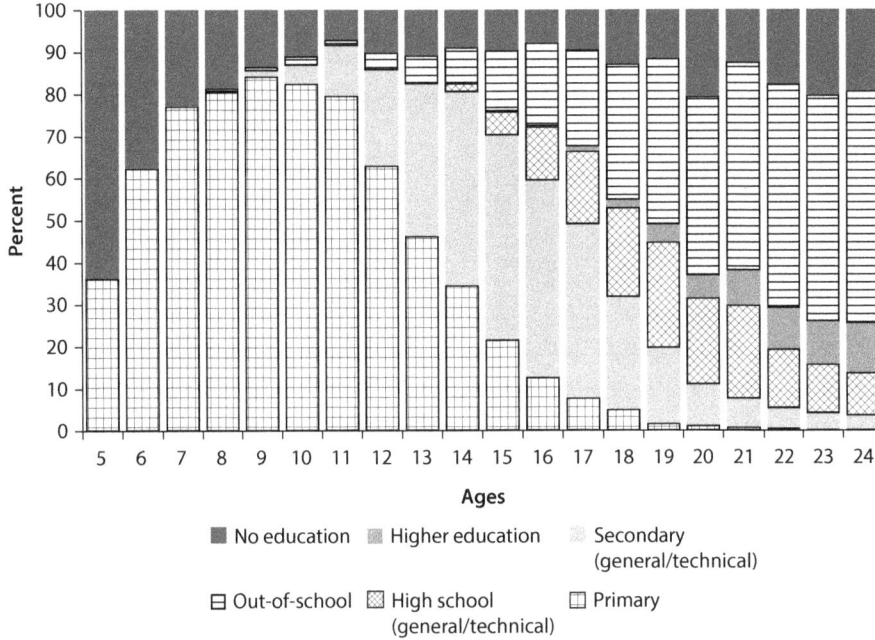

Legend:
- No education
- Higher education
- Secondary (general/technical)
- Out-of-school
- High school (general/technical)
- Primary

Source: World Bank 2013a.

secondary education, in the coming years a post-basic education crisis is likely to emerge. There is also increasing pressure from youth for diversified post-basic education (technical, vocational, and university).

Although the country's policy states that education is free, school costs are rising for households. A minimum assistance package is intended to defray the expenses of tuition and supplies. But practice does not match policy. The minimum package does not arrive on time, so households are expected to pay for expenses such as textbooks, parent-teacher association (PTA) dues, teacher salaries, and examination fees. But many households refuse to do so or are able to make only minimal payments. This is having two main effects. First, student-textbook ratios, at 12:1, are among the lowest in Sub-Saharan Africa; other learning aids are also missing; and low pay undermines incentives for teachers. Second, the quality of education is falling, especially in disadvantaged areas (urban pockets of poverty, rural areas, the ZEPs, and frontier areas). Learning levels have dropped, reflecting the deteriorating quality of education despite increased access. The government, with support from its development partners, is trying to reverse the decline in the quality of education.

Government and household spending on education and training could be considered investments. Although government spending on education rose from 1.9 percent of gross domestic product (GDP) in 2000 to 3.3 percent of GDP in 2003, it has since stagnated—remaining below the regional average of 4.3 percent (figure 5.8). Further, the distribution of these limited public resources is unequal.

Figure 5.8 Public Spending on Education, 2010
(% of gross domestic product)

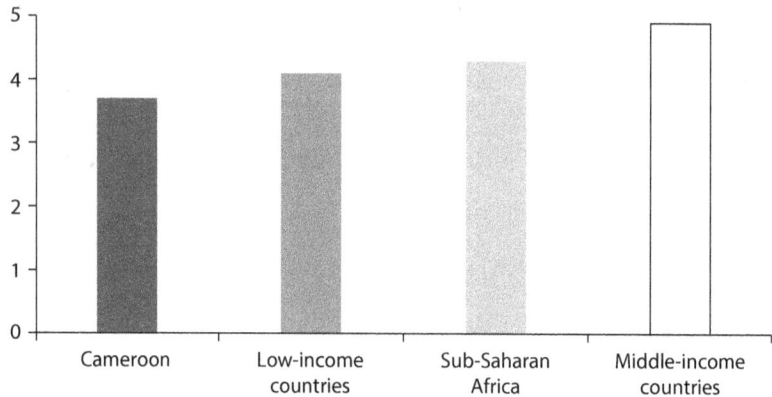

Sources: World Bank 2013b; World Bank staff estimates.

In 2011, secondary education received a disproportionately large allocation relative to primary and higher education. Most governments in Sub-Saharan Africa spend the most on primary education.

Balancing Improvements in Basic Education with Vocational, Technical, and Higher Education

Despite improvements, secondary enrollments in Cameroon are low compared with peer countries. In 2008, the gross enrollment ratio in Cameroon was similar to levels in the Democratic Republic of Congo, Eritrea, Guinea, and Liberia, but well below those in Ghana, Kenya, and South Africa. Secondary education is split into general and technical streams, but in 2008 technical secondary education accounted for less than 20 percent of total enrollment.

Vocational training is not closely linked to the needs of the labor market. Vocational institutions enroll a small number of students and focus on a few sectors, such as construction (about 25 percent of enrollment), while leaving out other important areas of the economy, such as tourism (3 percent of enrollment) and agriculture (less than 1 percent). Apprenticeships, which could be an efficient way to deliver training aligned with the needs of private employers, can only occur informally because there is no legal framework for private companies to partner with training centers. As a result, most youth do not seem to receive any professional training (especially in the Northern regions). And when they do, they tend to get it on the job (with the exception of the South-West region).

Although enrollments in higher education have increased significantly, the proposed programs might not meet the needs of the job market. Enrollments have more than doubled since 2005, mainly in public tertiary education institutions, following the creation of new universities (figure 5.9). But the allocation of students by discipline suggests that there is a gap compared with the needs of Cameroon's economy. Engineering, for instance, accounted for just 5 percent of higher education enrollments in 2010 (figure 5.10)—a level too low to support Cameroon's plans to invest in several large energy and transport projects. Health attracted just 2 percent of students.

Figure 5.9 Enrollments in Higher Education, 2010

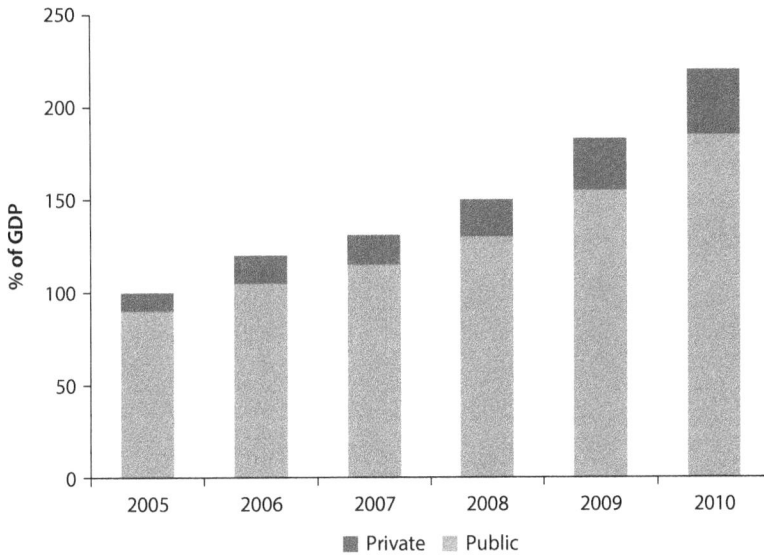

Figure 5.10 Enrollments by Discipline in Higher Education (Excluding Teacher Training), 2010

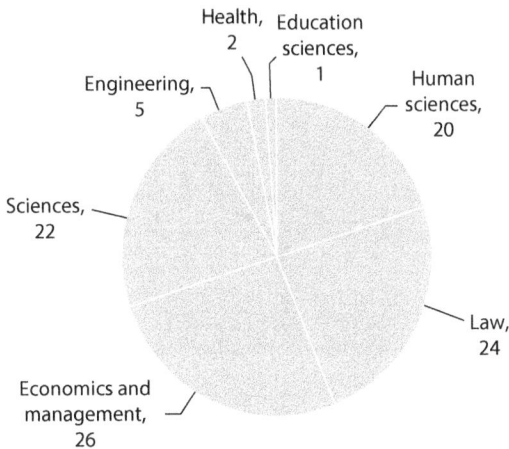

Sources: INS 2005; World Bank 2012a; World Bank staff calculations.

Returns to Education

An assessment of returns to education for Cameroon shows that youth who have completed upper secondary general or technical education have the potential to earn 40.3 percent more than youth who have completed only lower secondary general or technical education (figure 5.11). Further, youth with some higher education could earn 60.9 percent more than those who have only an upper secondary general or technical education. Thus, each additional year of schooling could generate significant private returns. Moreover, a better-educated population could contribute to GDP growth and economic competitiveness—provided it is supported by a good business environment and sound macroeconomic policies.

From the individual and collective perspectives, a well-educated and/or well-trained workforce can have significant effects on labor markets (Ndjobo 2013). Education can affect the supply of and demand for jobs as well as levels of and changes in salaries. Ndjobo used two models: discrete choice and limited dependent variable. Both approaches yielded the same result. In Cameroon, an

Figure 5.11 Rates of Return for Additional Years of Schooling by Education Level, Countries in Sub-Saharan Africa

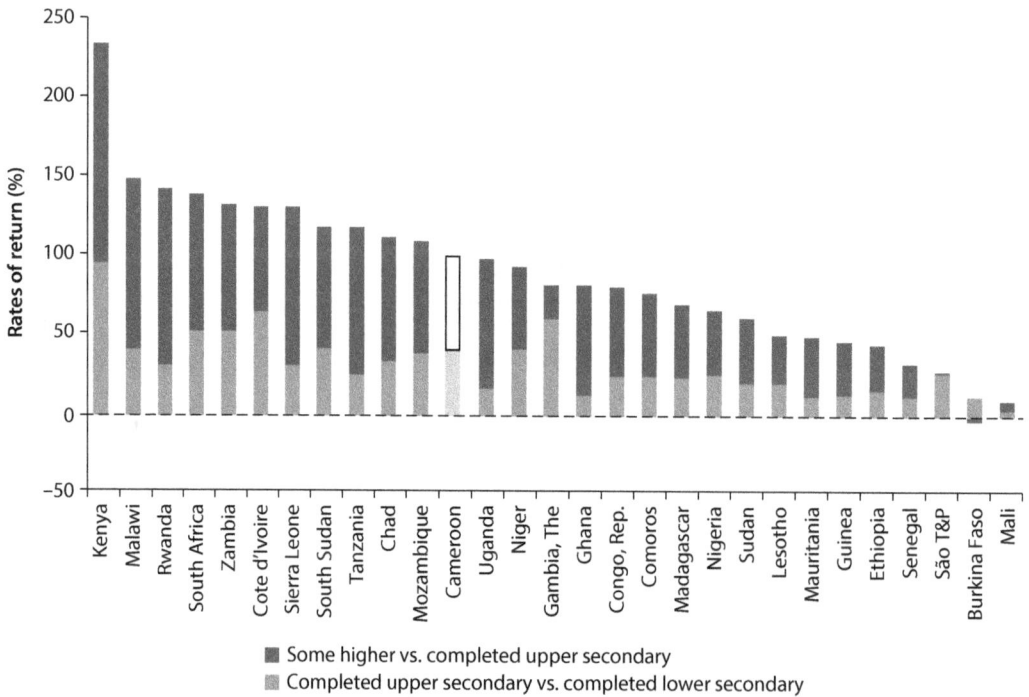

■ Some higher vs. completed upper secondary
▨ Completed upper secondary vs. completed lower secondary

Source: World Bank staff estimates using the Household Survey 2007 for Cameroon and similar household surveys for other countries: Burkina Faso (2010), Chad (2011), Comoros (2004), Côte d'Ivoire (2011), Congo Rep. (2011), Ethiopia (2011), The Gambia (2010), Ghana (2010), Guinea (2012), Kenya (2012), Lesotho (2011), Madagascar (2010), Malawi (2010), Mali (2010), Mauritania (2008), Mozambique (2009), Niger (2011), Nigeria (2010), Rwanda (2010), São Tomé and Príncipe (2010), Sierra Leone (2011), Senegal (2011), South Africa (2012), South Sudan (2009), Sudan (2009), Tanzania (2010), Uganda (2010), and Zambia (2010).

individual's education has significant influence on diverse aspects of the labor market. That is, an individual with more education has a higher propensity to exercise greater influence on their selected sector of activity than someone with less education in another sector. In other words, better-educated individuals are more likely to contribute to the productivity of their employers and command higher salaries.

However, the evolution of salary differentials is also determined by whether or not an employee is in the labor market, and for what length of time. The longer people with vocational and technical diplomas are employed, the greater is their propensity not to be declassified in the labor market. The exception is for people with a PhD degree. They have a propensity to opt out voluntarily from certain types of jobs. The result is statistically significant for university graduates seeking their first job. These results show how important it is for policy makers to take into account the knowledge and competencies of individuals with diplomas or higher-order degrees. Yet, in Cameron, individuals, enterprises, and the state are not benefiting from investments in education.

Analysis in the 2010 Survey of Employment and the Informal Sector report (Government of Cameroon 2010b) shows that one in four youths are already in a vocational training program, with four in 10 persons in urban areas (and approximately one in two in the big metropolitan areas of Yaoundé and Douala) in a vocational training program. However, only two in 10 individuals in rural areas (and only one in 20 in the Extreme North region) are enrolled in vocational programs. In the informal sector, professional vocational education and training is not marginal, as official numbers appear to indicate.

Further, over the past decade, higher education in Cameroon has gained prominence. In 1991, only about 29,000 students were enrolled. The number increased to 70,000 students in 2001, and by 2011 about 207,887 students were enrolled. That is an increase of a little more than three times over the course of 10 years, or about an average increase of 12 percent per year. Between 2008 and 2009, about 40,000 additional students were enrolled in universities.

The youth groups surveyed for this study said that knowing languages (English and French) is the most important skill for securing a job, and completion of university is the most useful training. Young people expressed concern about Cameroon's economic situation. They said that it undermines their opportunities for future employment. They also said that not enough jobs are available, which was the main reason they were unemployed or simply not looking for jobs.

Anticipated Outcomes of Reforms in Education and Training

Cameroon is taking action to upgrade the quality of education. Measures are underway to make public spending on education more efficient, reduce out-of-pocket expenses for households—especially poor and disadvantaged ones, by providing them with textbooks—reduce the numbers of PTA teachers by moving them to contract teacher status, improve literacy and numeracy in primary education, and combine primary and lower secondary education to span nine years as basic education. Cameroon will conduct a reading literacy assessment as a fundamental building block for foundational skills starting in 2016. Together these efforts will likely lead more out-of-school children to enroll in the lower grades. Over time, the primary completion rate will likely improve. If the quality of education is maintained, the combined effects would potentially benefit society, because the social rates of return would increase.

To increase schooling and offer alternate paths to general education and training, the government is preparing new strategies for TVET and higher education, with the goal of increasing investments in both. Doing so would improve the alignment of the education and training system with the labor

Figure 5.12 Simulation Results of Improvements (%) in Educational Attainment and Potential Workforce Entrants, 2015, 2020, 2025, and 2030

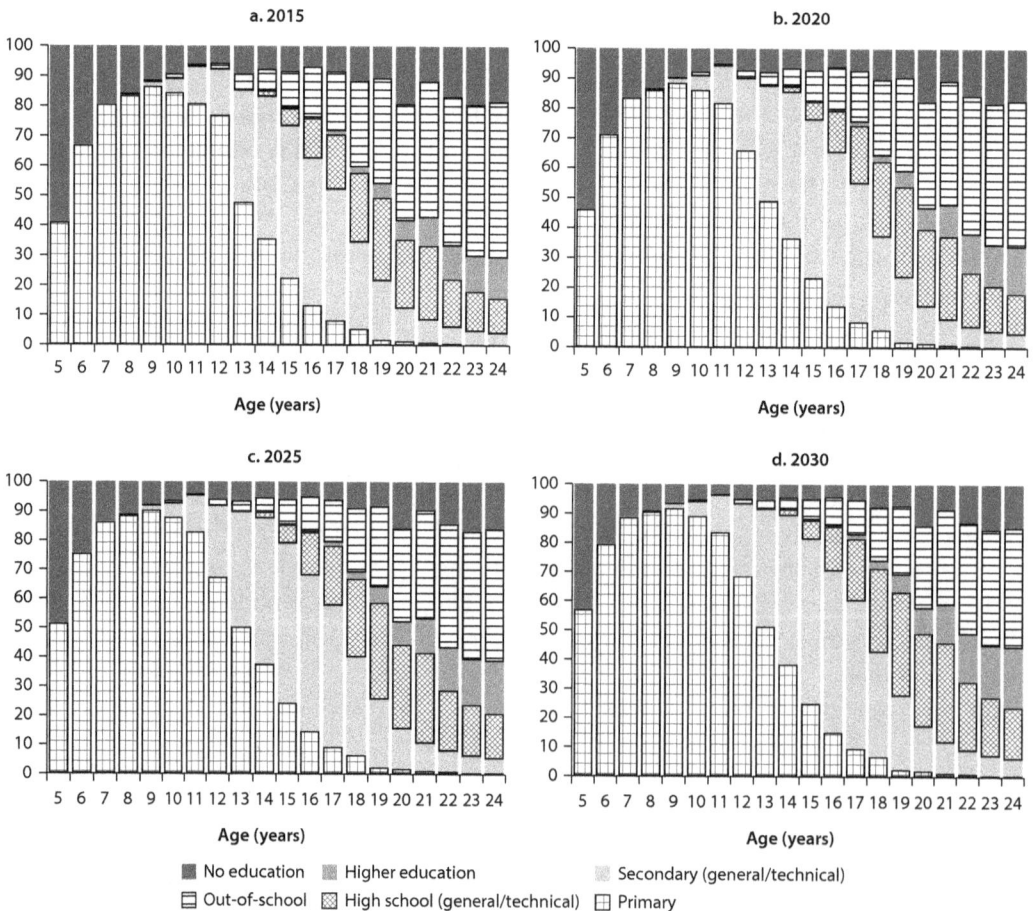

Source: World Bank 2013a.

market needs of a middle-income country. The government's ambitious targets require three key adjustments:

- Rationalizing public spending on education to boost efficiency
- Improving service delivery by ensuring, among other aspects, that a greater percentage of the education budget is decentralized to support school-based management
- Improving sector governance.

The estimated changes in educational attainment over time, factoring in the likely impacts of the ongoing and potential reforms, were simulated and the results are shown in figure 5.12. The four scenarios (2015, 2020, 2025, and 2030) are based on the base case simulation model in figure 5.7 prepared for the Cameroon Education Country Status Report (World Bank 2013a). The simulation results are provided in appendix D.

Conclusion

Economic growth in Cameroon has not been accompanied by a commensurate increase in competitiveness. This situation is partly because of the absence of structural transformation and economic diversification and an employment structure that has been increasingly skewed toward the informal tertiary services sector—where nonwage, low-return employment, relatively high poverty rates, and disguised unemployment prevail.

Education and training could contribute significantly to economic growth and the number and types of jobs in Cameroon. But that will also require aligning workforce development with key economic and social priorities, ensuring appropriate governance of the workforce development system, and managing service delivery for results.

Education and training are only one determinant—albeit an important one—of the number and types of jobs. Education and training do not constitute human capital until they are used effectively as a factor of production. The supply of and demand for workforce development (especially training) encounter labor market rigidities, such as the pricing and quantity of the workforce. Education and training systems show more structural dynamism than does the labor market, where rigidities lead to unemployment in some cases and underemployment in others (Anderson 1963 in the U.S. context, and Boudon 1973 in the French context in World Bank 2013a). For education and training to have significant influence, the skills and competencies acquired by workers need to be relevant to the labor market.

CHAPTER 6

Assessing the Workforce Development System

Introduction

What policies and institutions are involved in workforce development in Cameroon? What forces are driving the strategic direction of workforce development, and are they credible? What oversight mechanisms are in place, and are they effective? And which aspects of service delivery are working, and which are not? Based on the answers to these questions, the Systems Approach for Better Education Results (SABER) Workforce Development (WfD) tool benchmarks the country using a four-point scale—latent, emerging, established, and advanced—for each element of the WfD system.

As noted in chapter 5, skills development is costly and time consuming. But such efforts have been a long time in the making in Cameroon. With appropriate policies and institutions, the government's goal of reaching fully fledged middle-income status could become a reality if the country continues to focus on strengthening education and training, paying particular attention to skills development through technical, industrial, vocational, and entrepreneurship training and university education. Developing skills in the formal and informal sectors alike will be key to increasing competitiveness and growth.

The workforce development benchmarking conducted for this study shows that Cameroon's policies and institutions warrant adjustment to better foster workforce development. This typically takes time to achieve. To attain middle-income status by 2035, urgent action is required. The government's aspirations are set out in the Strategy Document for Growth and Employment (DSCE) (Government of Cameroon 2009). Its vision and targets for inclusive foundational skills development in basic education are described in the Education Sector Strategy 2013–20 (Government of Cameroon 2013a). However, the targets are less clear for post-basic vocational and technical education and training and higher education.

The skills development landscape in Cameroon is complex and fragmented. Spread over five ministries of education, training, and youth, as well as other ministries, the system suffers from inadequate funding, inconsistent governance, and incoherence, and is largely supply-driven. Individual ministerial programs rely on internal rationales and budgets. But the sum of the parts is not addressing Cameroon's current and emerging human development needs.

Furthermore, Cameroon has a dual education system: Francophone and Anglophone (see Appendixes B and C and chapter 5). Dual languages of instruction and dual modalities of education coexist. Schooling options are also diverse, with public education and private education, and within the latter private secular, religious schools (Catholic and Protestant), and private Muslim schools. This diversity offers choices for schooling but is challenging from the policy and institutional perspectives. Quality technical and vocational education and training better facilitates the school-to-work transition. The government recognizes the shortcomings of the system.

This chapter summarizes the study's diagnosis of workforce development policies and institutions.[1] The SABER-WfD tool was used to gather evidence and validate the findings (see appendix E). Complementary evidence from secondary sources was also used—specifically, the multiple consultations with (a) youth (appendix F); (b) with a team of experts from the Ministry of Economy, Planning, and Regional Integration (MINEPAT); Ministry of Finance; Ministries of Education and Training (Ministry of Primary Education; Ministry of Secondary Education; Ministry of Employment, Vocational Education, and Training (MINEFOP); and Ministry of Higher Education); Ministry of Youth; and Ministry of Agriculture, Mining, and Forestry (appendix G); and (c) public sector employees (appendix H); Results from a survey administered to youth groups (appendix I); And, the sources cited in the references. The data were combined, triangulated, rated, scored across the three SABER-WfD dimensions and nine policy goals, and validated through consultations.

Summary of the Benchmarking Results

The SABER-WfD assessment results rate Cameroon to have a "latent" system for all the functional dimensions of policies and institutions in the SABER-WfD analytical framework: strategic framework, system oversight, and service delivery. These findings represent an average. A deeper examination of the underlying scores for the nine policy areas reveals some confounding aspects, requiring a more nuanced approach to understanding the workforce development system.

The strategic framework is latent with respect to the policy areas of strategic direction and coordination, and being demand-led. The system is primarily characterized by centralized preparation of vision and strategy documents and action plans, although with some decentralized consultations. System oversight and service delivery are also latent. That is, there is limited collaboration and coordination across education and training ministries and other ministries that provide specialized skills. This is because of the highly fragmented approach to workforce development oversight and service delivery.

Strategic Framework: Aligning Workforce Development with Economic and Social Priorities

The SABER-WfD analytical framework for rating the strategic framework reflects the status of policies and institutions associated with three policy goals: articulating a strategic direction for workforce development, prioritizing a demand-led approach for workforce development, and fostering coordination among key stakeholders (figure 6.1).

Strategic Direction (Emerging)

With respect to setting strategic direction for WfD, Cameroon has some visible champions. However, they are only able to provide ad hoc advocacy for WfD, and have only acted on few interventions to advance strategic WfD priorities. No arrangements exist to systematically monitor and review implementation progress. The DSCE lays the groundwork and provides guidance on workforce development. The government and stakeholders conduct economic outlook assessments at the national level. Some direction on workforce development is provided by MINEFOP; the Interdepartmental Committee for the follow-up of the DSCE; meetings between the government and the multidonor group; the Ministry of Finance upstream macroeconomic budget analysis; MINEPAT reports, such as the economic policy and demographic analyses; and the Migration Division. The stakeholders have adapted a regulatory framework to promote workforce development. However, their implementation is not monitored systematically. Finally, the impact of core (literacy and mathematical skills) competencies and cognitive and noncognitive skills that the workforce must have are not evaluated systematically.

Many stakeholders are involved in workforce development efforts in Cameroon. But it is unclear whether there are any active advocates with a clear vision of how workforce development can be used to achieve the country's social and economic goals. The Association of Private Sector Employers (GICAM) is perhaps the most active nongovernment stakeholder. But it is unclear how well

Figure 6.1 Dimension 1: Scores for the Strategic Framework

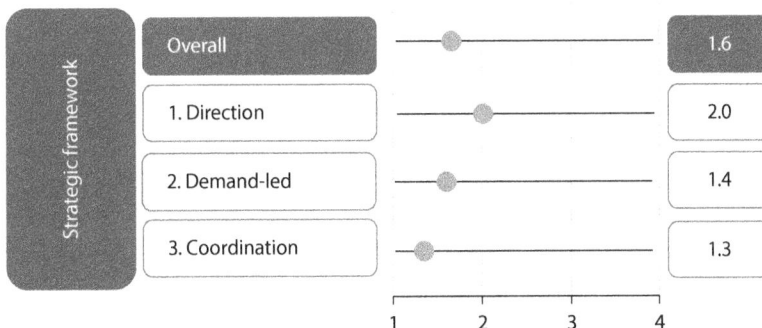

GICAM represents the informal private sector—which accounts for nearly 90 percent of the labor market. Further, it is also unclear whether government and nongovernment stakeholders have a shared strategic agenda for workforce development. Finally, the approach to workforce development is not demand-led, and there is limited coordination.

Demand-Led Approach (Latent)

With respect to fostering a demand-led approach to WfD, Cameroon has a few assessments, such as, on the topics of governance, demographics, household surveys, enterprise surveys, multi-donor reports, etc., of the country's economic prospects and their implications for skills. Further, industry and employers have a limited role in defining strategic WfD priorities. They receive limited support from the government for skills upgrading. The government conducts multi-dimensional and multi-sectoral evaluations on improving the tax environment for businesses, controlling fiscal expenditures, broadening the tax base and enhancing revenues, and assessing employment situation in the country. On the country's economic prospects under the DSCE, but it is not clear whether the studies specifically also assess the implications for workforce development. Other studies are ad hoc and only cover some economic sectors. They do not specifically address the alignment of worker skills and national economic prospects. Other assessments are donor driven. Although some constraints seem to have been identified, specifically, in the wood industry, skills shortages were identified following sponsored studies, and targeted research were conducted by development partners (Global Forest Watch 2000) and other independent researchers, it is unclear whether skills constraints have as well. It is also unclear whether steps have been taken to address these constraints.

Employers have a formal, institutionalized space to participate in policy dialogue at the Cameroon Business Forum. However, this is an unofficial and a noninstitutionalized platform. The Government Inter-Ministerial Committee, which meets twice a year, is the official platform for workforce development. Private sector and civil society organization representatives are also invited to participate. However, businesses rarely contribute to weigh in or significantly impact main strategic decisions regarding skills development. The government seems to be encouraging employers to develop the skills of their employees, in the formal and informal sectors. However, there is little evidence on the types of incentives or measures, whether they are implemented or not, and, where applicable, if their impact is assessed and how.

Coordination among Stakeholders (Latent)

With respect to strengthening critical coordination for implementation, industry/employers have a limited role in defining strategic WfD priorities. The government provides a few incentives to encourage skills upgrading by employers, but conducts no systematic reviews of such incentive programs. The mandates of government ministries and agencies with responsibilities for workforce development often overlap; no mechanism ensures coordination of strategies and programs. The legal roles and responsibilities of nongovernment stakeholders are not clear, and there is little evidence that mechanisms exist for coordination with and between government entities. There seem to be strategic workforce development measures, such as the Contract for Debt Relief and Development program, which has an implementation plan, budget, and some monitoring arrangements. However, this is not systematic in other programs.

System Oversight: Governing Workforce Development

The scores for system oversight reflect the status of policies and institutions associated with three policy goals: ensuring efficiency and equity in funding, ensuring relevant and reliable standards, and diversifying pathways for skills acquisition (figure 6.2).

Efficient and Equitable Funding (Latent)

With respect to ensuring efficiency and equity in funding, the government funds some initial or continuing vocational education and training, and active labor market programs. Some funding is also provided for on-the-job training by small and medium enterprises. The funding is based on ad hoc budgeting for a few programs. Few actions are taken to facilitate formal partnerships between training providers and employers. Finally, the impact of funding on the beneficiaries of training programs has not been reviewed recently.

The government relies on the program budget and the medium-term expenditure frameworks in line with results-based management to calculate the budget appropriations for TVET institution programs. Decisions are made by the two chambers of the Parliament, which include representatives of the people. Programs fostering on-the-job training for small and medium-size enterprises benefit from some government support. Most of the government funding for active labor market programs benefits youth and rural groups. However, support is determined through an ad hoc process involving only government officials in the implementing agencies. There are no recent formal impact evaluations of funding for training programs in initial or continuing vocational education and training or the active labor market programs. The government facilitates, for example, partnerships

Figure 6.2 Dimension 2: Scores for System Oversight

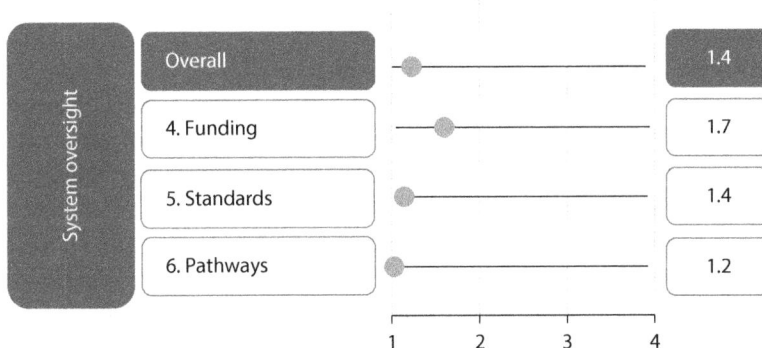

between community, regional and national levels; and in the private sector, partnership between Telcar and the organization of cocoa producers. Various ministries and institutions form partnerships with training service providers.

With respect to recurrent expenditure by cycle/type, in addition to vocational training costs, the unit costs range from CFAF 47,000 (US$94) (primary education) to CFAF 392,000 (US$784) (level 2 technical secondary education), CFAF 87,000 (US$174) (undergraduate general secondary education), CFAF 119,000 (US$238) (technical undergraduate level), and CFAF 236,000 (US$472) (general secondary). The unit cost of higher education is estimated to be about CFAF 280,000 (US$560), while pre-school is CFAF 118,000 (US$236). The structure of these costs shows that technical education is about 36 percent more expensive than the first cycle of general secondary education and 66 percent more expensive than the second cycle of general secondary education. The unit cost of pre-school is approximately 2.5 times more than that of primary education, which is likely to be detrimental for its development. General secondary is almost exactly in tandem with international norms, which indicates a level of expenditure per pupil in Cameroon identical to that of countries with the same level of gross domestic product (GDP) per capita (World Bank 2013a).

However, compared with other education subsectors, the government provides a disproportionately low allocation to vocational and technical training.

Relevant and Reliable Standards (Latent)

With respect to assuring relevant and reliable standards, policy dialogue on competency standards take place on an ad hoc basis with limited engagement of key stakeholders. However, broad-based competency standards have not yet been defined, and skills testing for major occupations is mainly theory-based and certificates awarded are recognized by public sector employers only and have little impact on employment and earnings. There are a few agencies for setting accreditation standards for institutions and training programs. However, accreditation standards are not transparent or publicly available.

Training institutions operate in a context of fierce competition from local firms and foreign companies in their respective areas of activity. The market sets the standards. Therefore, to remain competitive and ensure that their businesses are revitalized, the institutions are obliged to follow recognized and accepted standards when they develop their programs. Otherwise, they will be overturned by competition. This is in the private sector domain. In the public sector, the aspects of institutional accreditation, competencies and standards are determined differently. The National Forum on Internet Governance and the Department of Vocational Training and Guidance are the structures in charge of setting accreditation standards for institutions and training programs in their respective domains (Internet governance and general vocational education and training). Their respective roles are noteworthy. In addition, professions are organized to control admission standards at entrance, since access is mostly through competitive selection recruitment. This is strictly followed in daily practice. Moving to higher levels is largely dependent on the acquisition of diplomas or new qualifications.

Finally, in the public sector, employment and income are positively influenced by the acquisition of qualifications by category, or classification type.

Cameroon has competency standards for some occupations, but there is no framework for national qualifications. There is limited evidence on stakeholder engagement with the setting of competency standards and the extent to which training providers use standards when developing competency-based curricula. It is also unclear whether competency-based testing is used for skilled and semiskilled occupations. There is no evidence that there is skills testing for major occupations or, if there is, whether it assesses theoretical knowledge and practical skills, and whether certificates awarded have any impact on employment and earnings. There does not seem to be a transparent and well-understood system for establishing accreditation standards for training institutions and programs. Accreditation does not seem to be needed for training providers, and they have no incentives to seek and retain accreditation.

Pathways for Skills Acquisition (Latent)

With respect to diversifying pathways for skills acquisition, students in technical and vocational education have few options for further formal skills acquisition beyond the secondary level. The government takes little action to improve public perception of TVET. Certificates for technical and vocational programs have limited recognition. Qualifications certified by non-Education ministries are not recognized by formal programs under the Ministry of Education. Recognition of prior learning receives limited attention. The government provides very little support for further occupational and career development, or training programs for disadvantaged populations.

MINEFOP is responsible for the Program for the Development of Vocational Education and Training in Cameroon. A priority element for the program is the regulation of the flow of students from primary to secondary, vocational, and higher education. However, in practice, coordination of activities across the subsectors does not conform to the priority. With respect to the stock of graduates from the system, there is limited data on the programs and career paths of those who are already employed. There are many institutes of higher education that focus on vocational training. The professionalization of higher education is concretized through the subsector's medium-term expenditure framework. However, the linkages between the training programs and the labor market are at best tenuous. The government is conscious of building the skills of citizens. Some measures have been taken to encourage options for skills and career development for those who are already employed.

Service Delivery: Managing for Results

The rating for service delivery reflects the status of policies and institutions associated with the following policy goals: encouraging excellence in training programs, fostering relevant training programs, and enhancing accountability for results (figure 6.3).

Figure 6.3 Dimension 3: Scores for Service Delivery

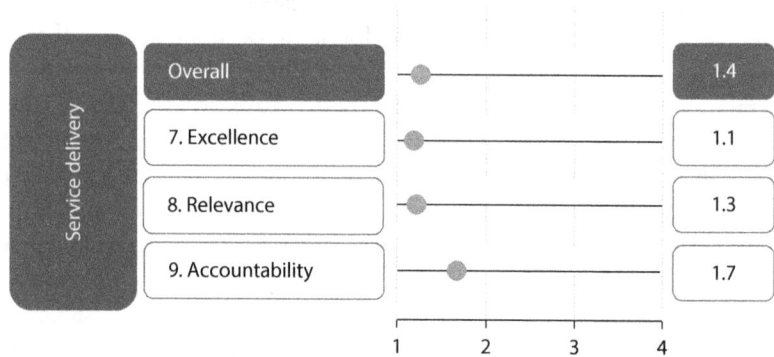

Training Excellence (Latent)

With respect to enabling diversity and excellence in training provision, there is no diversity of training provision as the system is largely comprised of public providers with limited or no autonomy. Training provision is not informed by formal assessment, stakeholder input, or performance targets.

MINEFOP approves all training institutions that can operate on Cameroonian territory. These establishments also receive some financial support in the form of grants and scholarships to achieve the strategic objectives set out for public training institutions. The government has not yet enforced the reform for rural and household artisans in the training centers for specific trades. Further, it has pursued only in a limited manner the construction and equipping of the vocational centers. To improve training, MINEFOP has recently created an enabling environment for partners to build, equip, develop, and offer programs for the National Institute of Training of Trainers. The foundation stone was laid by His Excellency the Prime Minister, Head of Government, at the beginning of 2015. This is important progress toward leading Cameroon to be among the emerging countries.

The government occasionally revises its policies relating to nonstate training institutions. However, it is unclear whether training institutions are autonomous. It appears that some of them are able to retain profits, establish boards of directors, and have some options to investigate complaints. But more information is needed to integrate these elements.

Training Relevance (Latent)

There are few attempts to foster relevance in public training programs through encouraging links between training institutions, industry and research institutions or through setting standards for the recruitment and training of heads and instructors in training institutions.

Although the government is aiming to establish formal links and encourage significant collaboration between training providers and industry, there is not enough evidence to determine whether this is being achieved. There are some tenuous links between training providers and industry, but it is not clear whether firms provide input into the design of curricula. Despite the government's stated intentions, there is no evidence that industry plays any role in specifying facility standards. There seem to be links between training and research institutions on the development of training programs and general assessments of the system. But it has not been determined whether these links are formal.

Accountability for Results (Latent)

Finally, with respect to enhancing evidence-based accountability for results, there are no specific data collection and reporting requirements, but training providers maintain their own databases. The government does not conduct or sponsor skills-related surveys or impact evaluations and rarely uses data to monitor and improve system performance.

Public sector training service providers seem to collect data and prepare reports occasionally. However, private sector training providers do not appear to be doing so, or communicating available data. More importantly, overall country-level data management procedures are imprecise. From time to time, the government conducts or finances skills surveys, but not impact evaluations. It is unclear whether the government uses the data or if information about graduates in the labor market is collected and published.

Conclusion

The overall conclusion of the SABER-WfD assessment is that Cameroon has latent potential in most domains of workforce development. This is a good springboard for policy and institutional action. The strategic framework for skills and workforce development shows promise. But in the areas of system oversight and service delivery, Cameroon faces significant challenges. The country is performing at a low equilibrium level, with significant deadweight loss, because general education drives the skills development agenda. Most workers have generalized education rather than specialized education, are in poor jobs, are underemployed, and lack incentives for increasing productivity.

Note

1. The detailed diagnostics are available in World Bank (2014d).

CHAPTER 7

Prospects, Conclusions, and Policy Recommendations

Introduction

What are the implications for Cameroon of creating a more dynamic, responsive system for developing workforce skills and competencies? And what strategies could help foster the accumulation of skills and competencies for added value in labor-intensive sectors and economic diversification and structural transformation?

Cameroon has latent potential to create an enabling environment for developing inclusive workforce skills, increasing productivity, promoting competitiveness, sustaining growth, and achieving structural transformation. But it requires a unified, action-oriented framework for skills development to promote collective action in improving system oversight and service delivery.

Framework for Action

Urgent action is required for Cameroon to catch up with global trends, address the needs of youth for skills development and job creation, increase its competitiveness and economic growth, and especially to become a middle-income country. Ten principles could guide policy making. They are optimization, concentration & assimilation, adequacy, specialization *versus* generalization, concatenation, facilitation, relevance, maximization, portability, and structural transformation. Aligned with the principles, eleven (11) prioritized actions in three areas: developing a strategic framework, improving system oversight, and strengthening service delivery could put Cameroon on an accelerated path to foster inclusive workforce development. The prioritized actions are:

- *Creating an apex authority to optimize the continuous development of skills to promote social inclusion and create jobs.* The apex authority could rationalize the system of skills development, and set up a standards, qualifications, and accreditation board to streamline programs and address inefficiencies. A public expenditure review and efficiency analysis of education and training systems would help pinpoint problems.

- *Concentrating official links among training services providers and preparing a framework on skills and qualifications.* The government has already established and continues to establish close collaboration with training service providers, businesses, and other partners through various contributions, grants, partnerships, and the promotion of collaborative networks for action. However, a framework of skills and qualifications could strongly unify the current fragmented and divided skills development system. Such a framework could be developed in close collaboration with training providers and companies in key growth sectors of the economy. Those engaged in the sectors could help to evaluate the jobs and set the required skills. Different roles played by individuals and the performance of organizations could then be directly linked to the development and reorganization of skills development programs.

- *Creating a competency framework* to help assess, maintain, and monitor the knowledge, skills, behaviors, and attributes needed for people in specific job streams to perform effectively. Making the competency framework publicly available would help guide job seekers.

    Creating a competency framework can be time consuming, but could be well worth the effort. The approach would measure current competency levels to ensure that the current workforce has the expertise needed for adding value to the economy. This would help determine the extent to which the skills of the existing workforce could be upgraded and inform decisions about curricular changes to introduce new knowledge and skills for the future workforce. Job-relevant skills, despite their limitations such as narrow specializations, are worthy of attention from job training programs. (box 7.1). The education and training system would be the ideal conveyor of new skills, competencies, and attributes, and budgets for training and development should be based on structural needs.

- *Ensuring an adequate supply of appropriate skills* would involve building foundational knowledge and skills to enable labor mobility. Such skills are needed to secure even an entry-level position in low-skill markets. One of the main goals of Cameroon's Education Sector Strategy 2013–20 is to promote foundational education and skills for all children, especially those ages 6 and 15 years.

    Other government goals include improving the quality of primary education and increasing access to education at all levels, including reaching a pre-primary enrollment rate of 50 percent by 2020. Brazil's early childhood development program is well-known (box J.2 in appendix J). Cameroon would benefit from drawing on this example.

    Second chance education for those who do not complete secondary education, because of reasons such as early marriage or pregnancy for girls or the

Box 7.1 Job-Relevant Skills and the Boundaries of Job Training Policies

Job-relevant skills are competencies and abilities valued by employers and useful for self-employment. They include technical skills relevant to specific jobs, as well as other cognitive and noncognitive skills that enhance worker productivity. These other skills include

- Problem-solving skills—the capacity for critical thinking and analysis
- Learning skills—the ability to acquire new knowledge, distill lessons from experience, and apply them in search of innovations
- Communication skills—including writing skills, collecting and using information to communicate with others, fluency in foreign languages, and use of information and communications technology
- Personal skills—for self-management, making sound judgments, and managing risks
- Social skills—for collaborating with and motivating others in a team, managing client relations, exercising leadership, resolving conflicts, and developing social networks.

Source: Banerji and others 2010.

high opportunity cost of schooling for both girls and boys, could be addressed through appropriate targeting, incentive programs, imparting relevant education and providing flexible second chance education programs would be helpful to improving the odds for completing secondary education. Incorporating life skills gradually could help streamline second chance education. Accelerated programs for highly motivated youth could be an incentive.

- *Embracing specialization versus generalization.* Specialized skills development should be embraced, as opposed to generalized education and training.

- *Facilitating economic opportunities and creating a favorable environment to develop the application of skills and using them effectively.* Economic opportunity could be created through demand-driven skills development and upgrading. For example, employers could be given tax incentives to hire interns, and the selection of interns could serve as a proxy for skills demand. School-to-work transition could be facilitated through cross-sector approaches (education, youth, labor, and planning), especially for at-risk youth.

An experiential learning approach integrates learning-by-doing and exposes trainees to real work situations. Traditional forms of experiential learning include apprenticeships and understudy. Kenya has used this approach (box 7.2). A trainee typically works with a master craftsperson or equivalent who imparts knowledge by requiring the trainee to perform tasks that have a direct bearing on commercial output. This approach might be a good fit for the agribusiness, cotton textiles, palm oil, and tourism sectors.

Box 7.2 Traditional Apprenticeship Support

Between 1996 and 1998, the nongovernmental organization Strengthening Informal Training and Enterprise managed a British-assisted project to support and develop traditional apprenticeships in Kenya. The project concentrated on metalwork, woodwork, and textiles. A total of 420 master craftspersons and 280 apprentices were trained directly, and about 1,400 apprentices received training from the project's host trainers.

The project had a positive impact. Traditional apprenticeship training became more efficient and effective, increasing productivity and earnings for the master craftspersons who received it. The number of apprentices of the master craftspersons who participated increased by 15–20 percent. The masters who received training saw increased turnover and profits as a direct result of their new skills, new products, new markets, and better workshop layouts and production organization. Some of the lessons from the project were the following:

- Master craftspersons were not interested in skills training unless it was delivered in the context of broader business improvement.
- Training for masters needs to be delivered flexibly, taking into account time constraints and opportunity costs.
- Master craftspersons provide training not necessarily to charge high training fees, but to increase income from production as a direct result of apprentices' on-the-job training.
- Training proved to be a good entry point for upgrading technology in enterprises.
- Attempts to create links between the *Jua Kali* (meaning "Under the Hot Sun") and the training institutions were disappointing. Independent trainers are more flexible and suitable.
- Collaboration with informal sector associations is crucial.
- Skills development, carefully and appropriately targeted, can be instrumental in improving the performance of informal enterprises. New skills can lead to increased growth, innovation, and productivity.

Sources: Johanson and Van Adam 2004; Haan 2006.

- *Concatenating transitions and links for skills development.* A bridges-and-ladders approach to skills development is preferable to islands of skills development. Making this change in Cameroon will require redefining the mandate of the education and training system—for example, by increasing the emphasis on science and mathematics in secondary education, aggregating the efforts of polytechnics and technical colleges to address skills deficiencies, and promoting research in science and technology and fostering innovation in universities. Education and training need to reward youth for home-grown innovations. Creating skills for adopting and adapting technologies is key for Cameroon's structural transformation.

- *Ensuring the relevance of skills by creating a qualifications and standards framework.* The qualifications and standards framework should be linked to the skills most relevant to the labor market. Sector-specific workforce forecasting would need to be developed, especially in the sectors where workforce value added is deemed greatest.

- *Maximizing the use of human resources, especially young female adults and women.* To draw on a reservoir of untapped capacity, gender-sensitive skills development could be beneficial. In Cameroon, as in other countries, there is a performance gap between male and female entrepreneurs (World Bank 2014a). Female entrepreneurs are concentrated in less productive sectors and activities. They face several constraints: initial conditions (access to finance, education, information, and networks), sector sorting (forced into sectors with low productivity or low growth potential, preferences, and managerial choices (taking the household as the unit of analysis), and institutions, legal frameworks, and the business environment.

  Female entrepreneurial decisions and activities are constrained by the complex interaction of social norms, legal institutions, and differences in subjective preferences. All these factors affect the decision to become an entrepreneur, the sector of activity, and management choices—including growth ambitions. Policies should address the challenges facing female entrepreneurs.

  Possible solutions include developing business education and networking opportunities for female entrepreneurs, addressing gaps caused by the lack of enabling initial conditions, and better diagnosing the key constraints within the socioeconomic setting. Business training for women—supported by grants— can be effective and can raise profits. There are other social spillover benefits to supporting female entrepreneurs. Women tend to plow profits back into their businesses or spend them on the education and health of their children and families.

- *Creating portable skills and competencies.* Entrepreneurship skills are portable goods, as are basic literacy and numeracy. The generalized education that most youth acquire in Cameroon is useful only up to a point. Without entrepreneurship skills and other cognitive and noncognitive skills, survival in the informal and formal sectors is hardly guaranteed.

- *Augmenting knowledge and competencies for structural transformation.* A strong workforce must be equipped with appropriate knowledge and skills to be highly productive and generate innovations. Cameroon's youth could drive structural transformation. To do so, they require knowledge of science, technology, and engineering—areas where the country's education and training system is weak. At the secondary and tertiary levels, there is inadequate emphasis on *knowledge* of science, technology, engineering, and mathematics (STEM). Skills in these areas are essential in the technology-oriented global economy. Post-basic education requires major overhauling to introduce STEM-related subjects.

  Better skills are also needed in *applied* science, engineering, and technology (ASET). ASET focuses on the continuum of skills development from the secondary through technical, industrial, vocational, and entrepreneurship training (TVET) and higher education levels. A preliminary foundational step would be to introduce sound science and mathematics curriculums in secondary education. This would make youth trainable to work in applied science, engineering, and technology areas, and prepare talented youth for university education in these areas.

Technical and vocational and higher education institutions could emphasize specific skills, such as internationally benchmarked information technology–enabled services (ITES), accompanied by skills assessment and certification programs. This sector could be a locomotive for Cameroon's economic transformation.

Finally, Cameroon needs to prepare itself to respond to the huge indirect and induced demand for skills for auxiliary trades. For example, the Kribi Port will create direct, indirect, and induced jobs, including jobs in infrastructure, hotels and hospitality, and tourism. A range of skilled and unskilled workers will be needed. Career pathways need to be identified to elevate jobs in certain sectors to the level of careers. Further, the presumption is that the workforce and skills needed in various sectors are static. But sectors change over time, and retraining and reskilling of workers become necessary. Together the focus sectors for this study could reinforce one another, creating national and regional markets, jobs, and credible careers.

Governance and Institutional Arrangements

The institutional arrangements for skill-building policies to manage the relationship between supply and demand are very important in Cameroon. The Republic of Korea and Singapore have set up governance arrangements that help articulate demand and supply in a dynamic way. The institutional context in Cameroon is considerably weaker because of the complex decision-making process, which involves multiple actors. For Cameroon to reach its full potential and become a middle-income country, the status of skills development needs to be elevated. The country needs to focus on transforming business and talent and modernizing technology.

Information Management System for Jobs

Cameroon needs to develop a management information system for jobs, including jobs forecasting. Good practice examples are available in Sub-Saharan Africa, such as the Access Nigeria Jobs Information Management System (box 7.3). In addition, job fairs would help bring together potential employers and employees and provide a venue for exchanging information and identifying talent. Cameroon also needs to move rapidly into information technology (IT) business process organization and skills development.

Curriculum review is needed to identify the skills gaps. Inputs are needed for the architecture for standards and qualifications frameworks at the TVET and higher education levels. Appropriate learning assessments are needed to examine

Box 7.3 Access Nigeria Jobs Information Management System

The ACCESS Nigeria Project, which is financed by the World Bank, supports the development of a new workforce equipped with the skills and training required by industry. The project aims to enable Nigeria to compete in fast-growing economic areas, particularly information technology–enabled services (ITES) and the services sector generally, including banking, telecommunications, business process organization services, energy, and hospitality. To empower participants and create jobs, the project uses a three-pronged approach: assessment, training, and certification. Overall, the project seeks to provide Nigerian technology and university graduates with access to employment opportunities in ITES and beyond, offer Nigerian companies access to a large pool of talented individuals seeking jobs in the services sector, and give domestic and international clients access to a global hub for ITES.

To ensure job placement upon completion of training and the overall success of the project, the World Bank and its partner, Open Data Innovations Network, have been engaged at all stages with all identified stakeholders. As part of those efforts, the project created the Access Nigeria Information Management System, an interactive electronic engagement platform. The system will connect registered stakeholders—job candidates, training providers, employers, and the ACCESS Nigeria team—and collate, store, analyze, report on, and share job-related information and data from them. It will also enable prospective employers to be fully integrated with the operations of ACCESS Nigeria, with a view to matchmaking and eventual job placement.

Source: http://www.anjims.org/?page_id=113.

outcomes more closely linked to skills areas, review learning outcomes in areas such as IT/ITES and job readiness, and determine ways to address the gaps and how they can be closed.

Public-Private Partnerships

Promoting work-based training would depend on the willingness of employers to train the potential or existing workforce (the stock) in conjunction with potential new workforce (the flow) by collaborating with government ministries involved in employment-related and productivity enhancement activities (see appendixes K and L). The approach of creating new institutions with explicit links to industry could bring positive results. This approach has been taken by Ireland, Malaysia, and Singapore (box 7.4), among others.

The Cameroon Chamber of Commerce could emulate India's National Association of Software and Services Companies model (box 7.5). The approach could make a difference to new small and medium-size enterprises in IT and ITES.

Public-private partnerships, such as the World Bank's Skills for Africa Program, could facilitate applications-based accounting and other training for youth in Cameroon (box 7.6).

Box 7.4 Singapore and Skills Development: A Strategy for Building a Pipeline of Skills for a Whole Industry

Singapore's approach of learning-by-doing to build a recognized worldwide and world-class system of technical training is instructive. In 1961, Singapore set up the Economic Development Board (EDB) as a statutory board under the Ministry of Finance, in an effort to attract foreign direct investment to the country. The key element of the strategy for skills development was to include six training-cum-production workshops run in parallel to the school system under the Engineering Industry Development Authority (EIDA), with funding from the United Nations Development Programme and technical assistance and contributions of machinery from France, Japan, and the United Kingdom.

However, the six centers turned out to be an administrative problem for EIDA. The authority underwent three management changes. The centers were not cost-effective. At the end of four years, the government had spent $12 million on EIDA, but only 86 people had graduated. The scheme was closed in 1973.

EDB experimented with worker retraining schemes. EDB worked with the Ministry of Education to offer, on the premises of existing educational facilities, retraining courses in technical subjects (such as metalwork, machine turning and fitting, radio maintenance and reports, and plumbing). The programs were remedial options for students who were performing below standards. The formal system of technical and vocational training was left untouched. Instead, the strategy adopted was one of leapfrogging and a mission-centric approach designed to operate in tandem with EDB's investment promotion and industry development effort. The strategy was to affiliate with leading international industry partners with proven training systems, to learn the training business from them, train to their needs, and adapt and improve the methods to meet local needs.

The first arrangement was with the Tata Group (India's largest engineering firm at the time, which makes trucks, excavators, locomotives, machine tools, etc.). The strategy provided a prototype for scaling up a successful model of company-affiliated training. EDB wished to attract Tata as an investor in Singapore, and set up a training facility that would produce workers trained in the way Tata required (that is, similar to the training schools that supplied Tata's workers in India). The Government of Singapore provided the land and buildings, contributed 70 percent of the operating costs of the center, and paid the stipends of the trainees, all of whom had signed a bond to serve EDB or any company as directed by the government for a period of five years. The training center opened in 1972. It trained twice the number of staff that Tata required. Tata hired the best of the graduating trainees and EDB retained the rest as a marketing asset to attract other engineering firms to Singapore.

In effect, the strategy built a pipeline of skills to grow a whole industry rather than to meet the needs of a single company. Two company-affiliated training centers were set up (Rollei-Werke and Philips). Other approaches were joint training programs through "transnational" partnership. This approach avoided the proliferation of new institutions. The practice of pooling training resources to serve companies in the industry cluster was forged.

box continues next page

Box 7.4 Singapore and Skills Development: A Strategy for Building a Pipeline of Skills for a Whole Industry *(continued)*

The approach contained key ingredients for Singapore to acquire the advanced skills for growing its new technology-intensive industries: the secondment of experts to Singapore, the training of EDB lecturers and technical staff, commitment to upgrade equipment and software, and commitment from participating companies to remain in the scheme for at least three years.

Source: Chiang 2012.

Box 7.5 India's National Association of Software and Services Companies

The National Association of Software and Services Companies (NASSCOM) is a nonprofit trade association that was created in 1988 by India's information technology and business process outsourcing industries. Its mission is to promote sustainable industry growth and harness technology to benefit society. NASSCOM is a global trade body with more than 1,500 members, more than 250 of which are companies from China, the European Union, Japan, the United Kingdom, and the United States. NASSCOM's member companies are engaged in e-commerce; information technology–enabled and business process outsourcing services; and software development, services, and products. NASSCOM facilitates business and trade in software and services and encourages the advancement of research in software technology. It sponsors a variety of activities: policy advocacy, events and international conferences, international affiliations, and skills development.

Source: http://www. NASSCOM.in.

Box 7.6 World Bank Skills for Africa Program and Skills Development in Africa

The Skills for Africa Program (SAP) (a subsidiary of SAP AG) and the World Bank planned to collaborate on skills development in Africa. This move came shortly after the launch of the SAP to provide information technology (IT) training to 2,500 students to boost access to IT education and support entrepreneurs. After announcing the collaboration, SAP Africa CEO Pfungwa Serima attended a series of meetings across the United States focused on refining synergies between SAP's African operations and the World Bank's goals for Africa.

"SAP recognizes that promoting education and training is one of the best ways to improve the problem of chronic youth unemployment, an issue affecting the technology industry as a whole," Serima said. "With growth and the scarcity of skills on the African continent a prominent issue on our minds, we anticipate that our collaboration with the

box continues next page

Box 7.6 World Bank Skills for Africa Program and Skills Development in Africa (continued)

World Bank will amplify our efforts to develop world-class IT and business skills and give Africa's youth an opportunity to play a role in contributing towards Africa's future economic growth and infrastructure development." The first phase of the joint skills development initiative was expected to be rolled out in 2013. A pilot of the SAP began in Kenya in 2012 with 100 students. Additional SAP investments in the region range from a multilateral partnership to improve Ghana's shea butter supply chain, to working with South Africa's Standard Bank Group to bring mobile banking services to people who do not have bank accounts.

Source: Triple Pundit, May 2013.

Box 7.7 Programs to Reach Smaller Employers in Chile, Malaysia, and Singapore

Chile provides an income tax rebate program for firms that train their workers, whether directly or through registered contractors. The rebate can reach a maximum of 1 percent of a firm's payroll, with a floor that benefits smaller firms. This model allows firms to choose the content and provider of their training programs according to their needs. Smaller firms that do not have the capacity to design and deliver training programs can use intermediary technical assistance institutions (OTICs) to organize training for delivery by training providers. OTICs are nonprofits established for specific sectors or regions. They are not training providers and are prohibited from delivering training directly.

Singapore's Skills Development Fund (SDF) and Malaysia's Human Resource Development Fund (HRDF) have explicit programs targeting small enterprises. The programs provide services such as vouchers to ease cash-flow constraints, grants for training needs analysis and course design, and simplification of administrative approvals. Singapore offers a training voucher to companies with fewer than 50 workers. The voucher allows firms to pay 30 to 50 percent of training costs, while the SDF supports the balance. In Malaysia, large enterprises with excess training capacity are encouraged to offer training to employees of other enterprises, particularly small and medium-size enterprises lacking the expertise and resources to do so themselves. Small enterprises that send workers to such training are eligible for grants from the HRDF.

SDF grants are also extended to enterprises to hire consultants to conduct companywide analyses of training needs, leading to the submission of worker training plans to the SDF. Subsequent financing helps smaller firms access the specialized resources needed to assess training needs and design appropriate training programs. The HRDF helps companies select the most suitable programs for the skill development of all employees. The SDF makes available a wide range of preapproved public courses for companies to subscribe to under its Approved in Principle System. This program has been effective in attracting small companies that have neither the expertise nor the critical mass to conduct such programs on their own. Malaysia's HRDF offers a similar Approved Training Program.

Sources: Galhardi 2002; Sehnbruch 2006; Hirosato 2007.

Alternative Financing Options for Skills Programs

Financing could be an effective tool for channeling the flow of students through the lifecycle stages of skills development. Given rising demand and unit costs, the Government of Cameroon should consider alternative financing options for skills programs, including the following:

- Earmarked grants for vulnerable, marginalized, and excluded populations, such as the poor, women, and the handicapped
- Secondary education bursary schemes to support the efforts of parents
- TVET bursaries
- A training levy used to shore up financing for skills development
- Incentives for major businesses to demonstrate corporate social responsibility
- Efforts to attract foreign direct investment, which would provide technical assistance, opportunities for knowledge transfer, and skills development options.

A variety of financing options could be developed and fashioned along the models of Chile, Malaysia, and Singapore (box 7.7).

Monitoring and Evaluation Systems for Skills Development Programs

Monitoring and evaluation systems for skills development programs could

- Improve data collection on day-to-day management of the program(s) with the ultimate objective of improving results
- Include as core elements identifying and tracking a good "control group"
- Provide best practice examples of skills evaluations.

Expected Outcomes

For Cameroon to become a middle-income country, a first step would be to reduce systemic inefficiencies and streamline service delivery in education and skills development. Efforts should be made in three areas: reducing systemic inefficiencies, promoting options, and boosting the contribution of the informal sector. A prioritized action plan is proposed in Appendix M.

Reducing Systemic Inefficiencies

- Addressing employer constraints by reducing the transaction costs of doing business. This would include taking steps to reduce corruption and governance challenges, reducing bureaucracy for startup firms, improving enabling infrastructure, involving the private sector in sector dialogue and decisions, improving transportation options, and guaranteeing the supply of raw materials.
- Simplifying governance and institutional arrangements by reviewing legislation, reducing the number of ministries responsible for technical and vocational training, rationalizing service delivery, and improving oversight through public-private partnerships and community involvement.

Promoting Options

- Developing a range of financing and service delivery options to respond to different demands for skills development and enhancing service delivery.
- Exploring managerial skills and micro- and small enterprises in industrial clusters, with a view toward developing industrial parks (World Bank 2009a).

Boosting the Contribution of the Informal Sector

- Addressing human development and skills constraints and needs by rationalizing the post-basic education sector. If the human dimension of skills development is not addressed, capital investments and finance alone cannot raise productivity in Cameroon. The *savoir faire* is a key element for improving productivity.
- Exploiting the synergies of knowledge and technology transfers for economic growth.

Data Sources on Employment in Cameroon[1]

Introduction

There are three main sources of data and information on employment in Cameroon: (i) the 1996, 2001, and 2007 *Household Surveys*, (ii) the *Non-Farm Enterprise Module* of the 2001 Household Survey, and (iii) the 2005 and 2010 *Employment and Informal Sector Surveys*.

Household Surveys

There have been three Household Surveys (*Enquête Camerounaise auprès des Ménages* or ECAM) undertaken in Cameroon, in 1996, 2001, and 2007. The first survey (ECAM-I) was conducted by the Ministry of Economy and Finance in 1996 over a three-month period and comprised a random sample of approximately 1,800 households across the country's 10 provinces, of which 1,731 households were actually visited.

The second survey (ECAM-II) was conducted by the National Institute of Statistics over a six-month period in 2001. It was much larger in its coverage relative to ECAM-I and comprised 11,553 households, of which 10,992 were actually visited. The format of ECAM-II was identical to that of ECAM-I in strata and territory. The National Institute of Statistics undertook a reconciliation process with support from the World Bank to render both surveys comparable (INS 2002).

The most recent survey (ECAM-III) was undertaken in 2007 (box A.1). To ensure comparability with the 2001 and 2006 surveys, the methodology of ECAM-III was the same as that for ECAM-II. ECAM-III surveyed 12,000 households across 12 regions (each province plus Douala and Yaoundé) and three strata (urban, semi-urban, and rural). A "light" survey on employment and earnings during the year involving 3,000 households was also conducted, with a view to obtain seasonal coefficients that could assist in assessing the employment situation within a year (seasonality). The results of the light survey are forthcoming.

Box A.1 Main Results of ECAM III

The ECAM-II and ECAM-III household surveys allow for a snapshot at each point in time (2001 and 2007) as well as a comparison of the evolution of individual indicators over the two time periods. The following are the main findings and trends derived from these surveys.

Employment distribution. About 85 percent of employment was self-employment or nonwage, while wage employment constituted only 15 percent. Of the 85 percent, the majority (60 percent) was self-employment on the family farm, with the remaining 25 percent being employment in nonfarm enterprises. Wage employment was principally in the private sector (9 percent), with the public sector (4 percent) and agriculture (2 percent) comprising the remainder. Although the main aggregates were broadly unchanged over the period 2001 to 2007, employment on family farms increased (from 56 percent in 2001 to 60 percent in 2007), while employment in nonfarm enterprises declined (from 29 to 25 percent).

Household enterprises by industry. Household enterprise activity was wholesale and retail trade (50 percent), manufacturing (23 percent), other services (11 percent), and transportation and communications (10 percent). Over time, the share of wholesale and retail trade declined (from 68 percent in 2001), while the shares of manufacturing and other services increased slightly. Transportation and communications increased in share by 8 percentage points during this period. Although the share of manufacturing remained constant in urban areas, it nearly doubled in importance (from 18 to 32 percent) in rural areas over this period. Other services increased in relative importance in rural areas (by 6 percentage points), while they declined in importance (by 3 percentage points) in urban areas.

Employment distribution by sex. Female employment was principally self-employment and nonwage (91 percent), and was significantly greater than male employment (78 percent) in this area. This was the case for employment on family farms (68 percent for women and 52 percent for men), with the opposite being true for women's employment in nonfarm enterprises (23 percent versus 26 percent for men). In turn, male wage employment (22 percent) was greater in importance relative to female wage employment (9 percent), which was the case for public and private wage employment. There was no significant change in these ratios for women over the period 2001 to 2007, while wage employment declined marginally in importance for males and self-employment and nonwage employment increased marginally (by 1.4 percentage points).

Employment by area. Self-employment and nonwage employment constituted the greatest share of employment in urban areas (71 percent) and rural areas (92 percent), but was relatively more important in the latter. Employment in rural areas was principally on family farms (78 percent versus 14 percent for nonfarm enterprises), while the opposite was the case in urban areas (45 percent for nonfarm enterprises versus 26 percent for family farms). Wage employment was greatest in urban areas (29 percent) versus rural areas (8 percent), with relatively larger shares for urban private and public wage employment and relatively lower shares for agricultural wage employment. Over time, the distribution of employment across activities remained relatively constant in rural areas, while there was a sharp reduction (from 38 percent in 2001 to 29 percent in 2007) in urban wage employment and an

box continues next page

equally large increase in the importance of self-employment and nonwage employment in urban areas (from 62 percent in 2001 to 71 percent in 2007).

Source of household income. Family farms constituted the most important source of income for households (64 percent) and increased in relative importance after 2001 (57 percent). In turn, nonfarm enterprises declined in relative importance (from 42 percent in 2001 to 38 percent in 2007), while the shares of wage employment remained largely unchanged.

Education distribution of the labor force. In 2007, 63 percent of wage earners had a primary education or less, down from 72 percent in 2001. The percentage of workers with primary education or below was greater in rural areas (76 percent) than in urban areas (39 percent). Over time, there was a 6 percentage point decline in rural workers with a primary education or below and a 9 percentage point decline in urban workers.

Source: Cameroon National Institute of Statistics, ECAM-II and ECAM-III.

Nonfarm Enterprise Module of the 2001 Household Survey

The 2001 ECAM included a module on the nonfarm enterprise sector. This provided a detailed perspective of the nonfarm sector at a particular point in time across a wide set of indicators (box A.2). However, since the 2007 ECAM did not include such a module, there is no scope to assess developments across these indicators since 2001. However, the module provides a useful snapshot of a single point in time (albeit a decade ago) of the composition and activities in the informal sector and/or household enterprises.

Employment and Informal Sector Surveys

There have also been two Employment and Informal Sector Surveys (EESIs), one in 2005 and the other in 2010. These followed an initial 1-2-3 survey that was focused solely on the city of Yaoundé, which was a major limitation, since the data could not be extrapolated at the national level. The EESI surveys, however, were national in coverage. They involved a two-phase statistical survey that evaluated the employment situation facing individuals (phase 1) and the economic activities of households and their members in the informal sector (phase 2). Data were provided for key informal sector employment indicators for Yaoundé, Douala, and the 10 provincial administrations, with each province subdivided into rural, semi-urban, and urban categories.

Data on enterprises were broken down by type of enterprise in the informal sector, called informal production units (UPIs). The 2005 exercise surveyed a total of 5,274 UPIs, of which 4,815 were actually interviewed. The 2010 survey expanded to 8,160 UPIs, of which 7,932 (97.2 percent) were actually surveyed. A total of 22,949 persons ages 10 years or older were captured by the survey, with a 99.2 percent success rate. The EESI-2 data allow for a comparative analysis of the performance of these key indicators over time (from 2005 to 2010). The main findings are presented in box A.3.

Box A.2 2001 Nonfarm Enterprise Module

The 2001 Nonfarm Enterprise Module provides data on household enterprises (HEs) broken down by owner and by enterprise. The main findings are summarized as follows:

Owners

- *Share of households:* 36 percent of households in Cameroon have an HE.
- *Source of employment:* HEs are the primary source of employment for over two-thirds of HE owners.
- *Gender:* largely female (56.8 percent) versus male (43.2 percent).
- *Education:* 95 percent have less than a high school education, 55 percent have less than a primary education, and 33 percent have no formal education whatsoever.
- *Age:* two-thirds of HE owners are ages 20–44 years and a quarter are age 45+.

Enterprises

- *Location:* most HEs are located in rural areas (56 percent), but HEs are also significant in urban areas (44 percent).
- *Age of enterprise:* 44 percent have been around for five years, and 17 percent are younger than one year.
- *Number of months operated per year:* about one-third of the HEs are operated only 1–3 months per year, another third only 4–6 months per year, and the remainder 7–12 months per year.
- *Sector:* over two-thirds of HEs are in wholesale and retail trade, with manufacturing (17 percent) and services (12 percent) comprising the other main sectors of activity.

Source: Cameroon National Institute of Statistics, ECAM-II, Non-Farm Enterprise Module 2001.

Box A.3 Main Findings of the 2010 Employment and Informal Sector Survey (EESI-2)

Overview

The survey involved 4,705 informal production units (UPIs) across the country and was divided into one component on the labor market and another component on the informal sector.

Size of Household

The average size of a Cameroonian household is 4.4 persons, which remained stable relative to the 2005 EESI (4.5 persons). Households are larger in rural areas (4.7 persons) than in urban areas (4.0 persons). The size is greater in the North (5.9 persons), the Extreme North (5.4 persons), and Adamaoua (4.9 persons), in contrast to the South (3.3 persons).

Head of Household

The average head of household in Cameroon is a man (74 percent), 42 years old (39 years in urban areas and 44 years in rural areas), with a primary education or less.

Structure of the Population

- Men (49.6 percent) and women (50.4 percent)
- Ages 0–14 years (43.7 percent); 15–64 years (53.1 percent); and 65+ years (3.3 percent)

box continues next page

Box A.3 Main Findings of the 2010 Employment and Informal Sector Survey (EESI-2) *(continued)*

- Migrants (67.3 percent) and non migrants (32.7 percent); the principal reasons given justifying migration were regrouping the family (53.3 percent) and job search (25.1 percent)
- Seven in 10 persons (71.2 percent) ages 15 years or older are literate
- The average age of active workers is 33 years.

Employment
- The employment rate is 66.4 percent and varies significantly between men (71.7 percent) and women (52.2 percent) and rural (74.6 percent) and urban (54.7 percent) areas.
- The proportion of salaried jobs is low (20 percent) and is higher in urban areas (41.1 percent) than in rural areas (9.4 percent), and in the towns of Yaoundé (50.5 percent) and Douala (41.9 percent).
- The breakdown by socio-professional category is as follows: Management (5 percent), workers and employees (15.2 percent), independent workers (47.2 percent), and family aids (29.7 percent).
- There are 1.41 million children ages 10–17 years engaged in employment (40 percent of people in this age group).
- The present generation is better educated than the previous one and prefers public sector jobs.
- There is a lack of awareness of public and private agencies that assist in helping people enter the job market.

Unemployment
- The unemployment rate (International Labour Organization definition) is estimated at 3.8 percent, with Yaoundé (10 percent) and Douala (9.1 percent) registering the highest unemployment rates relative to the other regions, such as the South (5.5 percent), South West (4.4 percent), and Adamaoua (4.3 percent).
- Unemployment is essentially an *urban phenomenon*, with the rate being higher in urban (8.1 percent) versus rural (1.4 percent) areas. It is highly concentrated in Douala and Yaoundé, with double-digit rates.
- Unemployment mainly affects *youth*, especially ages 15–34, where the unemployment rate is estimated at 15.5 percent.
- Women (4.5 percent) face a slightly higher unemployment rate than men (3.1 percent), and are also the most discouraged when it comes to looking for employment.
- More than half the unemployed have been looking for a salaried job for more than a year.
- The average minimum acceptable income for the unemployed is CFAF 59,800 per month (CFAF 70,900 for men and CFAF 54,000 for women), which is twice the minimum wage.

Underemployment
- The main problem in the labor market in Cameroon is not *unemployment*, but *underemployment*.
- Nearly three in four workers are *underemployed* (71 percent or 6.3 million persons), with the problem being more significant in rural areas (78.8 per cent) than in urban areas (55.7 percent).

box continues next page

Box A.3 Main Findings of the 2010 Employment and Informal Sector Survey (EESI-2) *(continued)*

- The *visible underemployment rate* (where the persons works involuntarily less than 35 hours per week) is 12.3 percent of the active population, and ranges from 10.9 percent for those unschooled to 23 percent for those with a higher level of instruction.
- The *invisible underemployment rate* (where the hourly wage is below the level fixed by the law) is 63.7 percent of the active population, or 5.7 million persons.

Source: Cameroon National Institute of Statistics.

Note

1. This appendix is based on Ames and Godang (2012).

Francophone Education and Training System

ENSEIGNEMENT SUPÉRIEUR

FORMATION PROFESSION-NELLE

FACULTÉS

Enseignement supérieur court BTS/HND/DUT

GRANDES ÉCOLES

FORMATION PROFESSIONNELLE

| BACCALAURÉAT |
| PROBATOIRE |

SECONDAIRE	2nd cycle
Général	Technique
LYCÉE	LYCÉE TECHNIQUE
Durée: 2 ans	Durée: 3 ans
2nde- Terminale	

AUTRES FORMATION PROFESSIONNELLE

ENSEIGNEMENT NORMAL	
Général	Technique
ENIEG	ENIET

BEPC	CAP
SECONDAIRE 1st cycle	
Général	Technique
CES	CET
Durée: 4 ans	Durée: 4 ans
6éme - 3éme	1ére - 3éme années

FORMATION PROFESSIONNELLE

POST PRIMAIRE SAR/SM

| CEP |
| PRIMAIRE Durée: 6 ans é Cycle: SIL-CM2 |

PRÉSCOLAIRE
Durée: 2 ans
Cycle: Petite-Grande sections

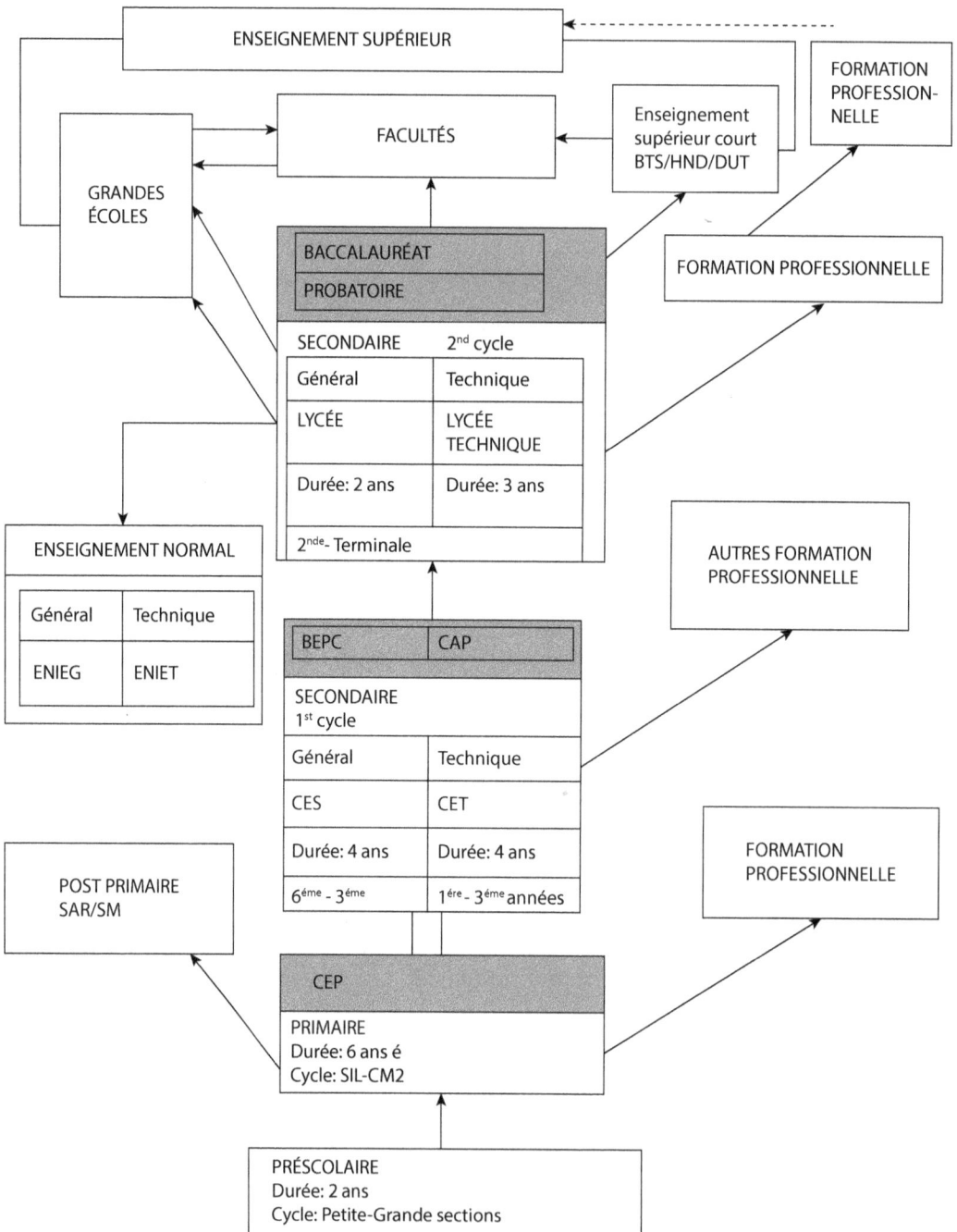

Source: Government of Cameroon 2013a.

Anglophone Education and Training System

HIGHER EDUCATION

FACULTIES

Higher professional training institutions

POST SECONDARY TRAINING

PROFESSIONAL TRAINING

PROFESSIONAL TRAINING

GCE A/L	BAC
General	Technical

SECONDARY	2nd cycle
General	Technical
HIGH SCHOOL	TECHNICAL HIGH SCHOOL
Duration: 2 years	Duration: 3 years
Lower 6 -	Form 5.16

TEACHER TRAINING COLLEGE

General	Technical
GRADE	TECHNICAL GRADE I

PROFESSIONAL TRAINING

GCE O/L	CAP
SECONDARY 1st cycle	
General	Technical
SECONDARY SCHOOL	TECHNICAL COLLEGE
Duration: 5 years	Duration: 4 years

POST PRIMARY SAR/SM

OTHER PROFESSIONAL TRAINING

FSLC
PRIMARY Duration: 6 years Cycle: Cl .1–Cl .6

PRE-PRIMARY
Duration: 2 years
Cycle: Nursery 1–2

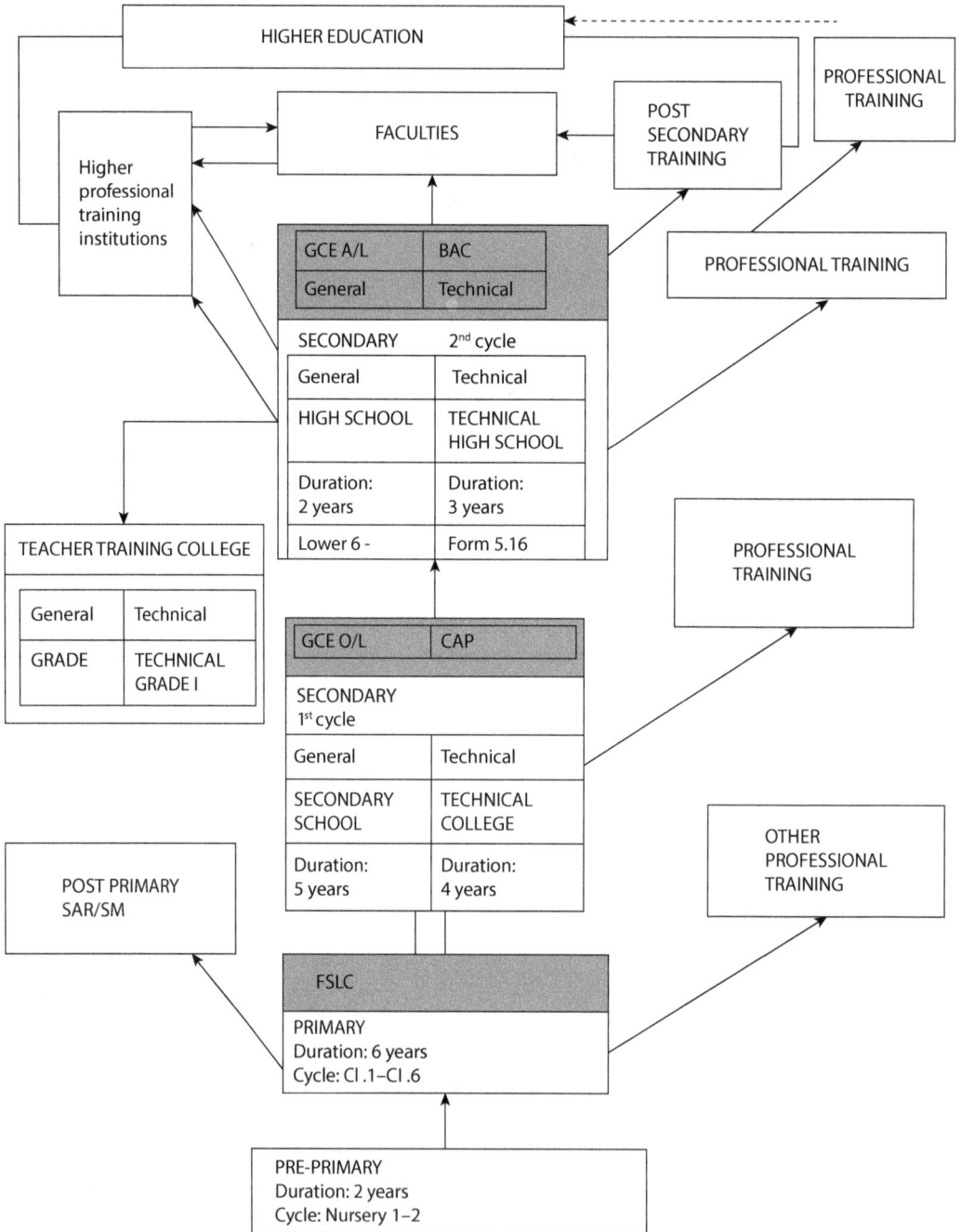

Source: Government of Cameroon 2013a.
Note: A/L = Advanced level; BAC = Bachelors; CAP = Certificate of professional competence; FSLC = First school leaving certificate; GCE = General Certification Examination; O/L = Ordinary level; SAR = Rural crafts section; SM = Household sections.

Simulation Results

Table D.1 Simulation Results for Educational Attainment

	Base case	Scenario 1	Scenario 2	Scenario 3	Scenario 4
Pre-Primary					
Gross enrollment rate	27%	40%	40%	40%	40%
% increase in the private sector		4%	4%	4%	4%
% in the Government public sector	95%	70%	70%	70%	70%
Adult Literacy					
Adult (25–45 years) illiteracy rate	41%	18%	18%	18%	18%
Young adults (15–24 years) illiteracy rate	28%	15%	15%	15%	15%
Basic Education (% admitted)	0%	0%	0%	0%	0%
Primary					
Access rate	124%	110%	110%	110%	110%
Completion rate	71%	100%	100%	100%	100%
Repetition rate	12%	5%	5%	5%	5%
Private Primary					
Share of private primary	22.2%	20%	20%	20%	20%
Subsidy to private primary as % of public	9%	9%	9%	9%	9%
Public Primary					
REM in public	54	50	50	50	50
Parent-Teacher Association (PTA) Teachers*	9,022	0	0	0	0
Target year		2020	2020	2020	2020
% of contract teachers integrated into civil-service status annually in the Zone Education Prioritaires (ZEP)	0%	6.0%	6.0%	6.0%	6.0%
% Enseignants éligibles (il y a une date de début)	0%	15%	15%	15%	15%
Year of launching		2016	2016	2016	2016
Benefits (% of average salary)		25%	25%	25%	25%

table continues next page

Table D.1 Simulation Results for Educational Attainment *(continued)*

	Base case	Scenario 1	Scenario 2	Scenario 3	Scenario 4
Tuition per student from Government (% GDP/H)**	0.3%	1.0%	1.0%	1.0%	1.0%
Primary promotion rate -1st cycle	69%	85.0%	85.0%	85.0%	85.0%
Target year		2016	2016	2016	2016
Basic Education subsector					
Year of basic education reform		2016	2016	2016	2016
Number of students by level	0.0	50	50	50	50
Number of teachers by level	0.0	1.3	1.3	1.3	1.3
General Secondary					
Number of students by level					
6th – 3rd	68.1	60.0	60.0	60.0	60.0
2nd term	65.8	60.0	60.0	60.0	60.0
Number of teachers by level					
6th – 3rd	1.8	1.4	1.4	1.4	1.4
2nd term	1.8	1.4	1.4	1.4	1.4
General secondary (new system after basic education reform)					
Number of student by level					
Orientation cycle	68.1	60.0	60.0	60.0	60.0
Second cycle-secondary	65.8	60.0	60.0	60.0	60.0
Number of teachers by level					
Orientation cycle	1.8	1.4	1.4	1.4	1.4
Second cycle-secondary	1.8	1.4	1.4	1.4	1.4
Promotion rate (1st to 2nd cycle)	60%	30%	30%	30%	30%
Distribution by level of education (%)					
General	79%	79%	79%	79%	79%
Technical and professional	21%	21%	21%	21%	21%
TVET enrollments (REM)					
TVET 1 – TVET 4 or 5	26.0	25	25	25	25
TVET 5 or 6 – TVET 7	10.6	20	20	20	20
Public sector vocational training: Quality (1 less or 2 more)					
Quality of vocational training (1 average or 2 would be better)		1	1	1	1
% exits from primary integrated system in the **SAR/SM-CFM**		10%	10%	10%	10%
% exists from secondary integrated system in the **CFPR**		20%	20%	20%	20%
Expenditure on assets and services/ learning related (CFAF '000)					
SAR/SM	129	257.4	257.4	257.4	257.4
CFPR	129	386.2	386.2	386.2	386.2
Target year		2,016	2,016	2,016	2,016

table continues next page

Table D.1 Simulation Results for Educational Attainment *(continued)*

	Base case	Scenario 1	Scenario 2	Scenario 3	Scenario 4
Higher Education (University)					
Choice (1: based on enrollments; 2:/100,000 persons)		1	1	1	2
Number of students for every 100,000 persons	1,216	2,100	2,100	2,100	2,100
% in private sector	15%	20%	20%	20%	20%
Higher education: Quality (1 at least or 2 plus)		1	1	1	1
Passing rate in baccalauréat	55%	70%	70%	70%	70%
Transition rate to upper secondary	63%	60%	60%	60%	60%
% of bachelor's level graduates going to public sector universities	85%	75%	75%	75%	75%
Share of general education programs	81%	70%	70%	70%	70%
Pupil-teacher ratio (general programs)	64	55	55	55	55
Pupil-teacher ratio (technical and professional programs)	25	35	35	35	35
Monthly salary of a teacher (Per capita GDP/population)	7.5	9	9	9	9
Unit cost per student (GDP per capita/population) general programs	0.05	0.07	0.07	0.07	0.07
Unit cost per student (GDP per capita/population) TVET programs	0.15	0.20	0.20	0.20	0.20
% of students receiving merit scholarships	36%	12%	12%	12%	12%
Per capita amount per scholarship (% GDP/population)	8%	10%	10%	10%	10%
Research allocation per teacher (GDP/population)	2.7	4	4	4	4
Unit cost of MINFI subsidies (GDP/population)	0.16	0.16	0.16	0.16	0.16
National Resources					
Fiscal impact (%): revenue (public sector/GDP)	17.5%	17.5%	20.0%	20.0%	20.0%
Education finance and expenditures and Revenue Public Sector/Revenue	18.3%	17.2%	18.0%	19.0%	20.0%
Target year for launching		**2020**	**2016**	**2016**	**2016**
Changes in salary		0%	12.3%	15.0%	15.0%

Source: World Bank 2013b.
Notes: * PTA teachers are scheduled to be phased out by 2016–17; ** reflects 'paquet minimum'.

Methodology

Transition rate:

$$TR_{h,h+1}^t = \frac{E_{h+1,1}^{t+1} - R_{h+1,1}^{t+1}}{E_{h,n}^t} * 100$$

where:

$TR_{h,h+1}^t$ = transition rate (from cycle or level of education h to $h+1$ in school year t)

$E_{h+1,1}^{t+1}$ = number of pupils enrolled in the first grade at level of education $h+1$ in school year $t+1$

$R_{h+1,1}^{t+1}$ = number of pupils repeating the first grade at level of education $h+1$ in school year $t+1$

$E_{h,n}^t$ = number of pupils enrolled in final grade n at level of education h in school year t

Gross enrollment rate:

$$GER_h^t = \frac{E_h^t}{P_{h,a}^t} * 100$$

where:

GER_h^t = gross enrollment ratio at level of education h in school year t

E_h^t = enrollment at the level of education h in school year t

$P_{h,a}^t$ = population in age group that officially corresponds to level of education h in school year t

Adult literacy:

$$LIT_{15+}^t = \frac{L_{15+}^t}{P_{15+}^t} * 100$$

where:

LIT_{15+}^t = adult literacy rate (15+) in year t

L_{15+}^t = adult literate population (15+) in year t

P_{15+}^t = adult population (15+) in year t

Promotion rate:

$$PR_i^t = \frac{NE_{i+1}^{t+1}}{E_i^t}$$

where:

PR_i^t = promotion rate at grade i in school year t

NE_{i+1}^{t+1} = new entrants to grade $i+1$, in school year $t+1$

E_i^t = number of pupils enrolled in grade i, in school year t

Repetition rate:

$$RR_i^t \quad = \quad \frac{R_i^{t+1}}{E_i^t}$$

where:

RR_i^t = repetition rate at grade i in school year t education
R_i^{t+1} = number of pupils repeating grade i, in school year $t+1$
E_i^t = number of pupils enrolled in grade i, in school year t

Pupil-teacher ratio:

$$PTR_h^t \quad = \quad \frac{E_h^t}{T_h^t}$$

where:

PTR_h^t = pupil-teacher ratio at level of h in school year t
E_h^t = total number of pupils or (students) at level of education h in school year t
T_h^t = total number of teachers at level of education h in school year t

Access rate (gross intake ratio) in the first grade of primary:

$$GIR^t \quad = \quad \frac{N^t}{P_a^t} * 100$$

where:

GIR^t = gross intake ratio in school year t
N^t = number of new entrants in the first grade of primary education, in school year t
P_a^t = population of official primary school entrance-age a, in school year t

Primary completion rate (gross intake ratio) in the last grade of primary (GIRLG):

$$GIRLG^t = \frac{NE_l^t}{P_a^t} * 100$$

where:

$GIRLG^t$ = gross intake ratio in the last grade of primary in school year t
NE_l^t = number of new entrants in the last grade l of primary education, in school year t
P_a^t = population of theoretical entrance age a in the last grade of primary, in school year t

Source: UNESCO 2009.

Table D.2 Potential New Entrants into the Workforce by Level of Education (All Scenarios)

Distribution by level of education (%)	Base	Scenario 1			Scenario 2			Scenario 3			Scenario 4		
	2010–11	2013–15	2019–20	2024–25	2013–15	2019–20	2024–25	2013–15	2019–20	2024–25	2013–15	2019–20	2024–25
Ministry of Basic Education	34.7	33.1	40.9	38.9	33.2	40.9	38.6	33.2	40.9	38.4	33.2	40.9	38.4
Pre-primary	3.2	2.8	2.3	1.9	2.9	2.3	1.9	2.9	2.4	1.9	2.9	2.4	1.9
Primary	31.3	28.0	26.0	23.7	27.9	25.5	22.9	27.9	25.4	22.6	27.9	25.4	22.6
Observation cycle	0.0	1.9	12.0	12.6	2.0	12.4	13.0	2.0	12.5	13.1	2.0	12.5	13.1
Basic nonformal education	0.0	0.0	0.0	0.0	0.0	0.0	0.0	0.0	0.0	0.0	0.0	0.0	0.0
Adult literacy	0.1	0.4	0.6	0.7	0.4	0.7	0.7	0.4	0.7	0.7	0.4	0.7	0.7
Ministry of Secondary Education	43.6	39.9	29.8	32.7	39.2	29.0	32.2	39.0	28.8	32.2	39.0	28.8	32.2
1st cycle (old cycle general secondary)	15.0	11.6	0.0	0.0	11.4	0.0	0.0	11.3	0.0	0.0	11.3	0.0	0.0
2nd cycle (old cycle, general secondary)	14.5	16.2	7.4	0.0	15.9	6.9	0.0	15.9	6.7	0.0	15.9	6.7	0.0
Orientation cycle	0.0	0.0	11.3	12.7	0.0	11.7	13.2	0.0	11.8	13.3	0.0	11.8	13.3
Secondary education, new cycle	0.0	0.0	0.0	7.0	0.0	0.0	7.3	0.0	0.0	7.3	0.0	0.0	7.3
Primary education teacher training	1.5	1.1	1.3	1.4	1.1	1.4	1.4	1.1	1.4	1.4	1.1	1.4	1.4
Technical and vocational education and training	12.6	11.0	9.7	11.5	10.7	9.0	10.3	10.7	8.9	10.2	10.7	8.9	10.2
Ministry of Technical & Professional Vocational Education	2.9	3.1	3.2	2.4	3.1	3.1	2.2	3.1	3.1	2.3	3.1	3.1	2.3
Ministry of Higher Education	18.8	23.9	26.1	26.1	24.5	27.0	27.0	24.7	27.2	27.1	24.7	27.2	27.1
Total	100.0	100.0	100.0	100.0	100.0	100.0	100.0	100.0	100.0	100.0	100.0	100.0	100.0

Source: Education & Training Simulation Model for Cameroon, World Bank 2013a.

SABER-WfD Scores and Analytical Framework

Box E.1 SABER-Workforce Development

The Systems Approach for Better Education Results–Workforce Development (SABER-WfD) is a comprehensive diagnostic of the country's WfD policies and institutions. The results are based on a new World Bank tool designed for this purpose. Known as SABER-WfD, the tool is part of the World Bank's SABER initiative,[a] whose aim is to provide systematic documentation and assessment of the policy and institutional factors that influence the performance of education and training systems. The SABER-WfD tool encompasses initial, continuing, and targeted vocational education and training that is offered through multiple channels, and focuses largely on programs at the secondary and post-secondary levels.

Analytical Framework

The tool is based on an analytical framework[b] that identifies three functional dimensions of WfD policies and institutions:

(1) *Strategic framework* refers to the praxis of high-level advocacy, partnership, and coordination, typically across traditional sector boundaries, to achieve the objective of aligning WfD in critical areas to priorities for national development.

(2) *System oversight* refers to the arrangements of governing funding, quality assurance, and learning pathways that shape the incentives and information signals affecting the choices of individuals, employers, training providers, and other stakeholders.

(3) *Service delivery* refers to the diversity, organization, and management of training provision, state and nonstate, which deliver results on the ground by enabling individuals to acquire market- and job-relevant skills.

Taken together, these three dimensions allow for systematic analysis of the functioning of the WfD system as a whole. The focus in the SABER-WfD framework is on the institutional structures and practices of public policy making and what they reveal about capacity in the system

---

box continues next page

Box E.1 SABER-Workforce Development *(continued)*

to conceptualize, design, coordinate, and implement policies to achieve results on the ground. Each dimension is composed of three policy goals that correspond to important functional aspects of WfD systems (see figure E.1.1). The policy goals are further broken down into discrete policy actions and topics that reveal more detail about the system.

Implementing the Analysis

Information for the analysis is gathered using a structured SABER-WfD data collection instrument. The instrument is designed to collect, to the extent possible, facts rather than opinions about WfD policies and institutions. For each topic, the data collection instrument poses a set of multiple choice questions that are answered based on documentary evidence and interviews with knowledgeable informants. The answers allow each topic to be scored on a four-point scale against standardized rubrics based on available knowledge on global good practice (see figure E.1.2). Topic scores are averaged to produce policy goal scores, which are

Figure E.1.1 Functional Dimensions and Policy Goals in the SABER-WfD Framework

Strategic Framework	
	1. Setting a strategic **direction** for WFD
	2. Prioritizing a **demand-led** approach to WfD
	3. Strengthening critical **coordination**

System Oversight	
	4. Ensuring efficiency and equity in **funding**
	5. Assuring relevant and reliable **standards**
	6. Diversifying **pathways** for skills acquisition

Service Delivery	
	7. Enabling **diversity and excellence** in training provision
	8. Fostering **relevance** in public training programs
	9. Enhancing evidence-based **accountability** for results

Figure E.1.2 SABER-WfD Scoring Rubrics

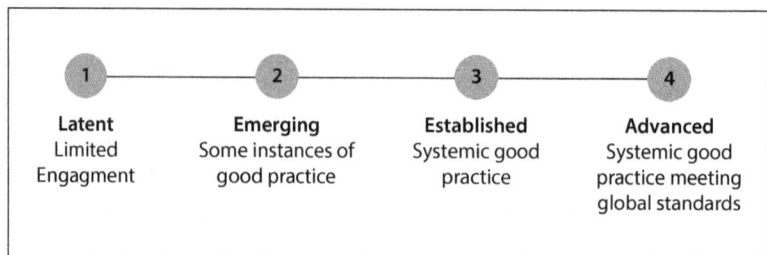

1	2	3	4
Latent	**Emerging**	**Established**	**Advanced**
Limited Engagment	Some instances of good practice	Systemic good practice	Systemic good practice meeting global standards

box continues next page

Box E.1 SABER-Workforce Development *(continued)*

then aggregated into dimension scores. The results are finalized following validation by the relevant national counterparts, including the informants themselves.

Since the composite scores are averages of the underlying scores, they are rarely whole numbers. For a given composite score, X, the conversion to the categorical rating shown is based on the following rule: $1.00 \leq X \leq 1.75$ converts to "latent;" $1.75 < X \leq 2.50$, to "emerging;" $2.50 < X \leq 3.25$, to "established;" and $3.25 < X \leq 4.00$, to "advanced."

Source: Tan and others 2013.
a. For details on SABER see http://www.worldbank.org/education/saber.
b. For an explanation of the SABER-WfD framework see Tan and others (2013).

Table E.1 Cameroon: Benchmarking Scores, 2014

Policy goal				Policy action			Topic
Dimension 1	Strategic Framework	G1	Setting a Strategic Direction	Provide sustained advocacy for WfD at the top leadership level	G1_T1	2	Advocacy for WfD to Support Economic Development
					G1_T2	2	Strategic Focus and Decisions by the WfD Champions
				Establish clarity on the demand for skills and areas of critical constraint	G2_T1	2	Overall Assessment of Economic Prospects and Skills Implications
		G2	Fostering a Demand-Led Approach		G2_T2	1	Critical Skills Constraints in Priority Economic Sectors
				Engage employers in setting WfD priorities and in enhancing skills upgrading for workers	G2_T3	1	Role of Employers and Industry
					G2_T4	2	Skills Upgrading Incentives for Employers
					G2_T5	1	Monitoring of the Incentive Programs
		G3	Strengthening Critical Coordination	Formalize key WfD roles for coordinated action on strategic priorities	G3_T1	1	Roles of Government Ministries and Agencies
					G3_T2	1	Roles of Non Government WfD Stakeholders
					G3_T3	2	Coordination for the Implementation of Strategic WfD Measures
Dimension 2	System Oversight	G4	Ensuring Efficiency and Equity in Funding	Provide stable funding for effective programs in initial, continuing, and targeted vocational education and training	G4_T1	info	Overview of Funding for WfD
					G4_T2	3	Recurrent Funding for Initial Vocational Education and Training
					G4_T3	2	Recurrent Funding for Continuing Vocational Education and Training Programs
					G4_T4	2	Recurrent Funding for Training-Related Active Labor Market Programs
				Monitor and enhance equity in funding for training	G4_T5	1	Equity in Funding for Training Programs
				Facilitate sustained partnerships between training institutions and employers	G4_T6	2	Partnerships between Training Providers and Employers

table continues next page

Table E.1 Cameroon: Benchmarking Scores, 2014 *(continued)*

	Policy goal		Policy action			Topic
	G5	Assuring Relevant and Reliable Standards	Broaden the scope of competency standards as a basis for developing qualifications frameworks	G5_T1	2	Competency Standards and National Qualifications Frameworks
				G5_T2	1	Competency Standards for Major Occupations
			Establish protocols for assuring the credibility of skills testing and certification	G5_T3	1	Occupational Skills Testing
				G5_T4	1	Skills Testing and Certification
				G5_T5	1	Skills Testing for Major Occupations
				G5_T6	info	Government Oversight of Accreditation
			Develop and enforce accreditation standards for maintaining the quality of training provision	G5_T7	2	Establishment of Accreditation Standards
				G5_T8	2	Accreditation Requirements and Enforcement of Accreditation Standards
				G5_T9	1	Incentives and Support for Accreditation
	G6	Diversifying Pathways for Skills Acquisition	Promote educational progression and permeability through multiple pathways, including for TVET students	G6_T1	1	Learning Pathways
				G6_T2	2	Public Perception of Pathways for TVET
			Facilitate life-long learning through articulation of skills certification and recognition of prior learning	G6_T3	1	Articulation of Skills Certification
				G6_T4	1	Recognition of Prior Learning
			Provide support services for skills acquisition by workers, job seekers, and the disadvantaged	G6_T5	1	Support for Further Occupational and Career Development
				G6_T6	1	Training-Related Provision of Services for the Disadvantaged
Dimension 3 Service Delivery	G7	Enabling Diversity and Excellence in Training Provision	Encourage and regulate nonstate provision of training	G7_T1	1	Scope and Formality of NonState Training Provision
				G7_T2	1	Incentives for NonState Providers
				G7_T3	1	Quality Assurance of NonState Training Provision
				G7_T4	2	Review of Policies toward NonState Training Provision

table continues next page

Table E.1 Cameroon: Benchmarking Scores, 2014 *(continued)*

Policy goal	Policy action			Topic
		G7_T5	1	Targets and Incentives for Public Training Institutions
	Combine incentives and autonomy in the management of public training institutions	G7_T6	1	Autonomy and Accountability of Public Training Institutions
		G7_T7	1	Introduction and Closure of Public Training Programs
G8 Fostering Relevance in Public Training Programs	Integrate industry and expert input into the design and delivery of public training programs	G8_T1	2	Links between Training Institutions and Industry
G8 Fostering Relevance in Public Training Programs	Integrate industry and expert input into the design and delivery of public training programs	G8_T1	1	Links between Training Institutions and Industry
		G8_T2	1	Industry Role in the Design of Program Curricula
		G8_T3	2	Industry Role in the Specification of Facility Standards
		G8_T4	2	Links between Training and Research Institutions
	Recruit and support administrators and instructors for enhancing the market-relevance of public training programs	G8_T5	1	Recruitment and In-Service Training of Heads of Public Training Institutions
		G8_T6	1	Recruitment and In-Service Training of Instructors of Public Training Institutions
G9 Enhancing Evidence-based Accountability for Results	Expand the availability and use of policy-relevant data for focusing providers' attention on training outcomes, efficiency, and innovation	G9_T1	2	Administrative Data from Training Providers
		G9_T2	2	Survey and Other Data
		G9_T3	1	Use of Data to Monitor and Improve Program and System Performance

Note: 1 = latent (limited engagement); 2 = emerging (some instances of good practice); 3 = established (systemic good practice); 4 = advanced (systemic good practice meeting global standards); TVET = technical, industrial, vocational, and entrepreneurship training.

Rubrics for Scoring the SABER-WfD Data

		Level of development		
Policy goal	Latent	Emerging	Established	Advanced
Functional Dimension 1: Strategic Framework				
G1: Setting a Strategic Direction for WfD	Visible champions for WfD are either **absent** or take **no specific action** to advance strategic WfD priorities.	**Some** visible champions provide ad hoc advocacy for WfD and have acted on **few** interventions to advance strategic WfD priorities; **no arrangements** exist to monitor and review implementation progress.	**Government leaders** exercise **sustained** advocacy for WfD with **occasional, *ad hoc*** participation from **non-government leaders;** their advocacy focuses on **selected** industries or economic sectors and manifests itself through **a range** of specific interventions implementation progress is monitored and reviewed, albeit through ad hoc reviews.	**Both government and nongovernment leaders** exercise **sustained** advocacy for WfD, and rely on **routine, institutionalized** processes to collaborate on **well-integrated** interventions to advance a **strategic, economy-wide** WfD policy agenda; implementation progress is monitored and reviewed through **routine, institutionalized** processes.
G2: Fostering a Demand-Led **Approach to WfD**	There is **no assessment** of the country's economic prospects and their implications for skills; industry and employers have a **limited or no role** in defining strategic WfD priorities and receive **limited** support from the government for skills upgrading.	**Some** ad hoc assessments exist on the country's economic prospects and their implications for skills; **some** measures are taken to address critical skills constraints (e.g., incentives for skills upgrading by employers); the government makes **limited** efforts to engage employers as strategic partners in WfD.	**Routine** assessments based on **multiple data sources** exist on the country's economic prospects and their implications for skills; a **wide range** of measures with **broad** coverage are taken to address critical skills constraints; the government recognizes employers as strategic partners in WfD, **formalizes** their role, and **provides support** for skills upgrading through incentive schemes that are **reviewed and adjusted.**	A rich array of **routine and robust** assessments by **multiple stakeholders** exists on the country's economic prospects and their implications for skills; the information provides a basis for a **wide range** of measures with **broad** coverage that address critical skills constraints; the government recognizes employers as strategic partners in WfD, **formalizes** their role, and **provides support** for skills upgrading through incentives, including some form of a **levy-grant scheme,** that are **systematically reviewed** for impact and **adjusted** accordingly.

table continues next page

119

Policy goal	Latent	Emerging	Established	Advanced
			Level of development	

Policy goal	Latent	Emerging	Established	Advanced
G3: Strengthening Critical Coordination for Implementation	Industry/employers have a **limited or no role** in defining strategic WfD priorities; the government either provides **no incentives** to encourage skills upgrading by employers or conducts **no reviews** of such incentive programs.	Industry/employers help define WfD priorities on an ad hoc basis and make **limited** contributions to address skills implications of major policy/ investment decisions; the government provides **some** incentives for skills upgrading for formal and informal sector employers; if a levy-grant scheme exists its coverage is **limited**; incentive programs are **not systematically** reviewed for impact.	Industry/employers help define WfD priorities on a **routine** basis and make **some** contributions in **selected** areas to address the skills implications of major policy/investment decisions; the government provides **a range of** incentives for skills upgrading for all employers; a levy-grant scheme with **broad** coverage of formal sector employers exists; incentive programs are **systematically** reviewed and **adjusted**; an annual report on the levy-grant scheme is published with **a time lag.**	Industry/employers help define WfD priorities on a **routine** basis and make **significant** contributions in **multiple** areas to address the skills implications of major policy/ investment decisions; the government provides **a range** of incentives for skills upgrading for all employers; a levy-grant scheme with **comprehensive** coverage of formal sector employers exists; incentive programs to encourage skills upgrading are **systematically** reviewed for **impact on skills and productivity** and are **adjusted** accordingly; an annual report on the levy-grant scheme is published in **a timely fashion.**

Functional Dimension 2: System Oversight

Policy goal	Latent	Emerging	Established	Advanced
G4: Ensuring Efficiency and Equity in Funding	The government funds IVET, CVET and ALMPs (but not OJT in SMEs) based on ad hoc budgeting processes, but takes **no action** to facilitate formal partnerships between training providers and employers; the impact of funding on the beneficiaries of training programs has **not been recently reviewed.**	The government funds IVET, CVET (including OJT in SMEs) and ALMPs; funding for IVET and CVET follows **routine** budgeting processes involving **only government officials** with allocations determined largely by the **previous year's budget;** funding for ALMPs is decided by government officials on an ad hoc basis and targets **some select** population groups through various channels; the government takes **some** action to facilitate **formal** partnerships between individual training providers	The government funds IVET, CVET (including OJT in SMEs) and ALMPs; funding for IVET is **routine** and based on **multiple** criteria, including evidence of program effectiveness; recurrent funding for CVET relies on **formal** processes with **input** from key stakeholders and annual reporting **with a lag;** funding for ALMPs is determined through a **systematic** process with **input** from key stakeholders; ALMPs target **diverse** population groups through various channels and are reviewed for impact but follow-up is **limited;** the government takes action to facilitate **formal** partnerships between training providers and employers at **multiple**	The government funds IVET, CVET (including OJT in SMEs) and ALMPs; funding for IVET is **routine** and based on **comprehensive** criteria, including evidence of program effectiveness, that are **routinely reviewed and adjusted;** recurrent funding for CVET relies on **formal** processes with **input** from key stakeholders and **timely annual reporting;** funding for ALMPs is determined through a **systematic** process with **input** from key stakeholders; ALMPs target **diverse** population groups through various channels and are reviewed for impact and **adjusted** accordingly; the government takes action to facilitate **formal** partnerships between training providers and employers at **all levels** (institutional and systemic); recent reviews

table continues next page

| Policy goal | Level of development | | | |
	Latent	Emerging	Established	Advanced
		and employers; recent reviews considered the impact of funding on only training-related indicators (e.g. enrollment, completion), which stimulated dialogue among some WfD stakeholders.	levels (institutional and systemic); recent reviews considered the impact of funding on both training-related indicators and labor market outcomes; the reviews stimulated dialogue among WfD stakeholders and some recommendations were implemented.	considered the impact of funding on a full range of training-related indicators and labor market outcomes; the reviews stimulated broad-based dialogue among WfD stakeholders and key recommendations were implemented.
G5: Assuring Relevant and Reliable Standards	Policy dialogue on competency standards and/or the NQF occurs on an ad hoc basis with limited engagement of key stakeholders; competency standards have not been defined; skills testing for major occupations is mainly theory-based and certificates awarded are recognized by public sector employers only and have little impact on employment and earnings; no system is in place to establish accreditation standards.	A few stakeholders engage in ad hoc policy dialogue on competency standards and/or the NQF; competency standards exist for a few occupations and are used by some training providers in their programs; skills testing is competency-based for a few occupations but for the most part is mainly theory-based; certificates are recognized by public and some private sector employers but have little impact on employment and earnings; the accreditation of training providers is supervised by a dedicated office in the relevant ministry; private providers are required to be accredited, however accreditation standards are not consistently publicized or enforced; providers are	Numerous stakeholders engage in policy dialogue on competency standards and/or the NQF through institutionalized processes; competency standards exist for most occupations and are used by some training providers in their programs; the NQF, if in place, covers some occupations and a range of skill levels; skills testing for most occupations follows standard procedures, is competency-based and assesses both theoretical knowledge and practical skills; certificates are recognized by both public and private sector employers and may impact employment and earnings; the accreditation of training providers is supervised by a dedicated agency in the relevant ministry; the agency is responsible for defining accreditation standards with stakeholder input; standards are reviewed on an ad hoc basis and are publicized or enforced to some	All key stakeholders engage in policy dialogue on competency standards and/or the NQF through institutionalized processes; competency standards exist for most occupations and are used by training providers in their programs; the NQF, if in place, covers most occupations and a wide range of skill levels; skills testing for most occupations follows standard procedures, is competency-based and assesses both theoretical knowledge and practical skills; robust protocols, including random audits, ensure the credibility of certification; certificates are valued by most employers and consistently improve employment prospects and earnings; the accreditation of training providers is supervised by a dedicated agency in the relevant ministry; the agency is responsible for defining accreditation standards in consultation with stakeholders; standards are reviewed following established protocols and are publicized and routinely enforced; all training providers are required as well as

table continues next page

Policy goal	Level of development			
	Latent	Emerging	Established	Advanced
		offered **some** incentives to seek and retain accreditation.	extent; all providers receiving public funding must be accredited; providers are offered **incentives and limited support** to seek and retain accreditation.	offered **incentives and support** to seek and retain accreditation.
G6: Diversifying Pathways for Skills Acquisition	Students in technical and vocational education have **few or no options** for further formal skills acquisition beyond the secondary level and the government takes **no action** to improve public perception of TVET; certificates for technical and vocational programs are **not recognized** in the NQF; qualifications certified by non-Education ministries are **not recognized** by formal programs under the Ministry of Education; recognition of prior learning receives **limited** attention; the government provides **practically no support** for further occupational and career development, or training programs for disadvantaged populations.	Students in technical and vocational education can only progress to **vocationally oriented, nonuniversity programs**; the government takes **limited** action to improve public perception of TVET (e.g. diversifying learning pathways); **some** certificates for technical and vocational programs are recognized in the NQF; **few qualifications** certified by non-Education ministries are recognized by formal programs under the Ministry of Education; policy makers pay **some** attention to the recognition of prior learning and provide the public with **some** information on the subject; the government offers **limited** services for further occupational and career development through **stand-alone local service centers** that are **not integrated** into a system; training programs for disadvantaged populations receive **ad-hoc** support.	Students in technical and vocational education can progress to **vocationally oriented programs, including at the university level**; the government takes **some** action to improve public perception of TVET (e.g. diversifying learning pathways and improving program quality) and reviews the impact of such efforts on an ad hoc basis; **most** certificates for technical and vocational programs are recognized in the NQF; **a large number of qualifications** certified by non-Education ministries are recognized by formal programs under the Ministry of Education, albeit **without the granting of credits**; policy makers give **some** attention to the recognition of prior learning and provide the public with **some** information on the subject; a **formal association of stakeholders** provides **dedicated** attention to adult learning issues; the government offers further **limited** services for further occupational and career development, which are available through an **integrated network of centers**; training programs for disadvantaged populations receive **systematic** support and are reviewed for impact on an ad hoc basis.	Students in technical and vocational education can progress to **academically or vocationally oriented programs, including at the university level**; the government takes **coherent** action on **multiple fronts** to improve public perception of TVET (e.g. diversifying learning pathways and improving program quality and relevance, with the support of a media campaign) and **routinely** reviews and **adjusts** such efforts to maximize their impact; **most** certificates for technical and vocational programs are recognized in the NQF; **a large number** of qualifications certified by non-Education ministries are recognized and **granted credits** by formal programs under the Ministry of Education; policy makers give **sustained** attention to the recognition of prior learning and provide the public with **comprehensive** information on the subject; a **national organization** of stakeholders provides **dedicated** attention to adult learning issues; the government offers a **comprehensive menu** of services for further occupational and career development, **including online resources**, which are available through an **integrated network of centers**; training programs for disadvantaged populations receive **systematic** support with **multiyear budgets** and are **routinely** reviewed for impact and **adjusted** accordingly.

table continues next page

			Level of development	
Policy goal	Latent	Emerging	Established	Advanced

Functional Dimension 3: Service Delivery

Policy goal	Latent	Emerging	Established	Advanced
G7: Enabling Diversity and Excellence in Training Provision	There is **no diversity** of training provision as the system is largely comprised of **public providers with limited or no autonomy;** training provision is **not informed** by formal assessment, stakeholder input or performance targets.	There is **some** diversity in training provision; nonstate providers **operate with limited** government incentives and **governance** over registration, licensing and quality assurance; public training is provided by institutions with **some** autonomy and informed by **some** assessment of implementation constraints, stakeholder input and basic targets.	There is **diversity** in training provision; nonstate training providers, **some** registered and licensed, operate within **a range** of government incentives, **systematic** quality assurance measures and **routine** reviews of government policies toward nonstate training providers; public providers, mostly governed by management boards, have **some** autonomy; training provision is informed by **formal analysis** of implementation constraints, stakeholder input and basic targets; lagging providers receive **support** and exemplary institutions are **rewarded.**	There is **broad** diversity in training provision; nonstate training providers, **most** registered and licensed, operate with **comprehensive** government incentives, **systematic** quality assurance measures and **routine** review and **adjustment** of government policies toward nonstate training providers; public providers, mostly governed by management boards, have **significant** autonomy; decisions about training provision are **time-bound** and informed by **formal assessment** of implementation constraints; stakeholder input and use of a **variety of measures** to incentivize performance include support, rewards and performance-based funding.
G8: Fostering Relevance in Public Training Programs	There are **few or no attempts** to foster relevance in public training programs through encouraging links between training institutions, industry and research institutions or through setting standards for the recruitment and training of heads and instructors in training institutions.	Relevance of public training is enhanced through **informal** links between **some** training institutions, industry and research institutions, including **input** into the design of curricula and facility standards; heads and instructors are recruited on the basis of **minimum academic standards** and have **limited** opportunities for professional development.	Relevance of public training is enhanced through **formal** links between **some** training institutions, industry and research institutions, leading to collaboration in **several** areas including but not limited to the design of curricula and facility standards; heads and instructors are recruited on the basis of **minimum academic and professional standards** and have **regular** access to opportunities for professional development.	Relevance of public training is enhanced through **formal** links between **most** training institutions, industry and research institutions, leading to **significant** collaboration in a **wide range** of areas; heads and instructors are recruited on the basis of **minimum academic and professional standards** and have **regular** access to **diverse** opportunities for professional development, including **industry attachments** for instructors.

table continues next page

	Level of development			
Policy goal	Latent	Emerging	Established	Advanced
G9: Enhancing Evidence-based Accountability for Results	There are **no specific** data collection and reporting requirements, but training providers maintain their **own databases;** the government **does not conduct or sponsor** skills-related surveys or impact evaluations and **rarely** uses data to monitor and improve system performance.	Training providers collect and report **administrative data** and there are **significant** gaps in reporting by nonstate providers; some public providers issue annual reports and the government **occasionally** sponsors or conducts skills-related surveys; the government **does not consolidate data** in a system wide database and uses **mostly administrative data** to monitor and improve system performance; the government publishes information on graduate labor market outcomes for **some** training programs.	Training providers collect and report **administrative and other** data (e.g., job placement statistics, earnings of graduates) and there are **some** gaps in reporting by nonstate providers; **most** public providers issue internal annual reports and the government **routinely** sponsors skills-related surveys; the government consolidates data in a **system wide database** and uses **administrative data** and information from **surveys** to monitor and improve system performance; the government publishes information on graduate labor market outcomes for **numerous** training programs.	Training providers collect and report **administrative and other** data (e.g., job placement statistics, earnings of graduates) and there are **few** gaps in reporting by nonstate providers; **most** public providers issue **publicly available** annual reports and the government **routinely** sponsors or conducts skills-related surveys and impact evaluations; the government consolidates data in a **system wide, up to date database and uses administrative data,** information from **surveys and impact evaluations** to monitor and improve system performance; the government publishes information on graduate labor market outcomes for **most** training programs **online.**

List of Organizations represented during Consultations with Youth, March 26–27, 2014

No.	Organization
1	Action Vitales pour le développement Durable (AVD)
2	GIC Tsellomar
3	ONG Développement Sans Frontières
4	African Youth Initiative on Climate Change (AYICC)
5	Association des Familles de Victimes des Accidents de la circulation (AFVAC-CAM)
6	SYNACSU
7	Jeunes Volontaires pour l'Environnement (JVE)
8	Parlement Mondial de la Jeunesse pour l'Eau (PMJE)
9	Association de Jeunes Étudiants Volontaires Humanitaires (AJEVOH)
10	Association de Lutte contre les Violences faites aux femmes (ALVF) (Centre)
11	Agence de Développement de Douala (A2D)
12	Youth Development Foundation (YDF-Cameroun)
13	Ministère de l'Emploi, de l'éducation Professionnelle et de la Formation (MINEFOP)
14	Chambre de Commerce, d'Industrie, des Mines et de l'Artisanat (CCIMA)
15	Ministère des Mines, de l'Industrie et du Développement Technologie (MINMIDT)
16	Fondation Conseil Jeune (FCJ)
17	Human Right and Freedom Movement (HRFM)
18	Association Jeunesse Verte du Cameroun (AJVC)
19	Solidarité Sans Frontière (SSF)
20	TUNZA AFRICA & JYE CAMEROUN
21	Enfant de Soleil
22	Fondation Ecolia
23	Le Groupement pour l'Éducation et l'Investissement (GEI)
24	ICES
25	APSAJE
26	Ministère de l'Agriculture et du Développement Rural (DDLC/MINADER)
27	GIC Belomar
28	Réseau des jeunes pour les forêts d'Afrique Centrale (REJEFAC)

List of Organizations represented during Consultations with Government Ministries, March 25, 2014

No.	Organization
1	Ministère des Domaines, du Cadastre et des Affaires Foncières (MINDCAF/DEPC)
2	Ministère de la Jeunesse et de l'Éducation Civique (MINJEC)
3	Ministère de l'Environnement et de la Protection de la Nature (MINEPDED)
4	Ministère de l'Autonomisation des Femmes et de la Famille (MINPROFF)
5	Ministère de l'Enseignement Secondaire (MINESEC)
6	Ministère de l'Élevage, des Pêches et des Industries Animales (MINEPIA)
7	Ministère de l'Agriculture et du Développement Rural (MINADER)
8	Ministère des Petites et Moyennes Entreprises de l'Économie Sociale et de l'Artisanat (MINPMEESA)
9	Ministère de l'Emploi, de l'éducation Professionnelle et de la Formation (IF1/Ct1/MINEFOP)
10	Ministre du Travail et de la Sécurité Sociale (CT1/MINTSS)
11	Ministère de l'Agriculture et du Développement Rural (MINADER/DEPC/CPIE)
12	Chambre de Commerce, d'Industrie, des Mines et de l'Artisanat (CCIMA)
13	Ministère de l'Emploi, de l'éducation Professionnelle et de la Formation (MINEFOP/DFOP)

List of Organizations represented during Consultations with Government Ministries (December 12–13, 2013)

No.	Organization
1	Ministère de l'Autonomisation des Femmes et de la Famille (MINPROFF)
2	Ministère de l'Emploi, de l'éducation Professionnelle et de la Formation (MINEFOP/DRMO)
3	Ministère des Finances (MINFI/DAE)
4	Ministre de la Fonction Publique et de la Réforme Administrative (MINFOPRA)
5	Ministère de l'Enseignement Secondaire (MINESEC/DPPC)
6	Ministère des Mines, de l'Industrie et du Développement Technologie (MINMIDT/DEPCO)
7	Banque mondiale

Synthesis of Consultations with Public Sector Employees

Key Findings

The goal of the consultations with public sector employees was to identify the skills public sector employees used most in their current job: written communication and language skills (English/French), and most importantly the skills they lack/need to improve to be successful in their job: language skills (English/French) and discipline-specific training. At the same time, the survey focused on the obstacles faced by public sector employees when searching for jobs. The main obstacle was skills and job market inadequacy and the amount of assistance available when searching for employment; 70 percent of respondents received little to no assistance.

Information from public sector employees was collected during a workshop and included the skills public sector employees use at their current job, the skills they need to improve to succeed in their current job, the skills they need to fulfill their career goals, the kind of training they received from their current job (if any), and who paid for the training, the type of training that would be helpful for their career, the main obstacles to finding employment, and the type of assistance they received when looking for a job.

Methodology

Eighteen public sector employees who were ages 30–60 years participated in the workshop. During the consultations, the public sector employees provided information on 36 questions, including background, current employment and experience, skills, training and education, future employment, and demographic questions.

Findings

Profile of Public Sector Employees

Eighty-nine percent of public sector employees have received a post-graduate or post-doctoral degree; 83 percent of them would pay for post-secondary education if it would help them secure another position; and all the public sector employees participated in internships during or after school. The majority of public sector employees (65 percent) would prefer to work in the private sector instead of the public sector because of higher salaries.

Current Employment

Approximately 53 percent of the public sector employees are performing administrative work, 29 percent managerial work, and 18 percent technical work. Sixty-seven percent of the public sector employees chose this area of work because they were qualified to be in that position because of their education. Public sector employees describe their current employment as decent and the main motivation for performing their job is promotion opportunities, followed by on-the-job experience, job security, training, and finally salary.

Skills

The skills that are most used by public sector employees in their current job are written communication, followed by English/French (language skills), computer literacy, and teamwork (figure H.1). The main skills public sector employees need to improve to succeed in their current job are English/French (language

Figure H.1 Which Skills Are Used Most in Your Current Job?

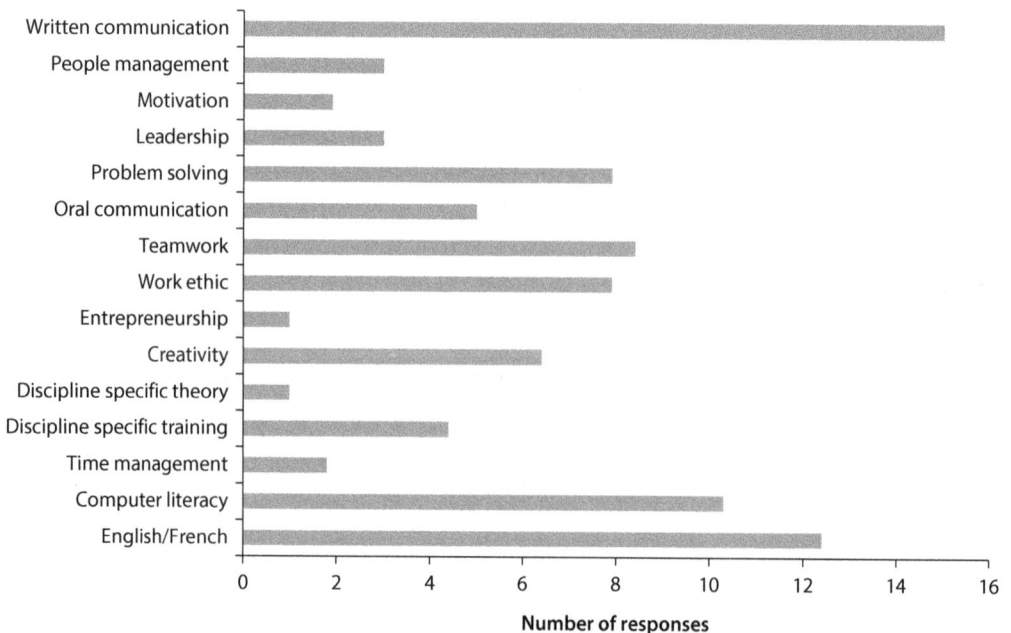

skills), discipline-specific training, computer literacy, and people management (figure H.2). The main skills they would like to improve to fulfill their career goals are discipline-specific training, English/French (language skills), creativity, and leadership skills (figure H.3).

Figure H.2 Skills That Need to Be Improved to Succeed in Current Job

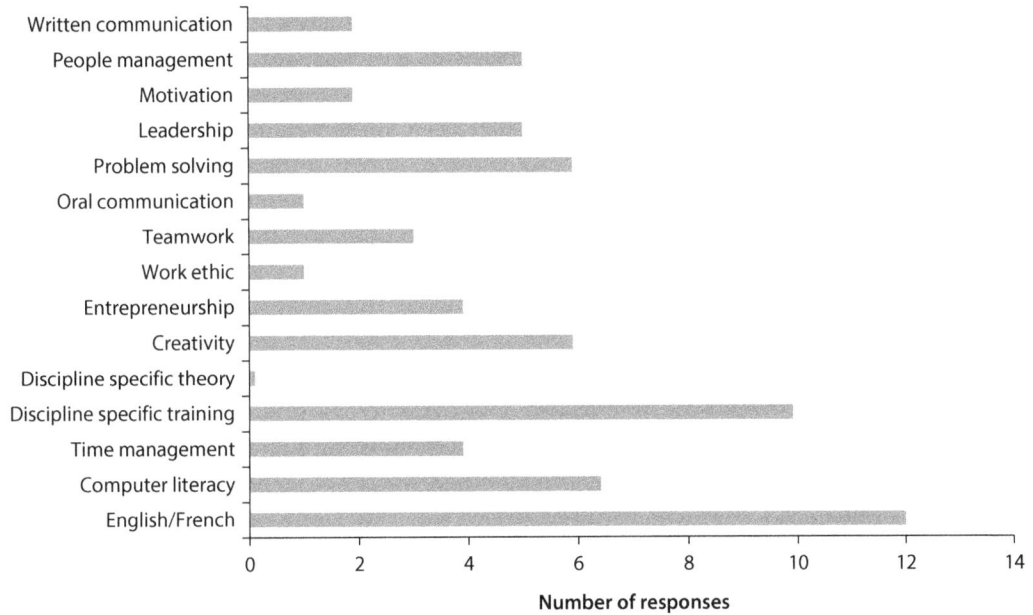

Figure H.3 Skills That Workers Need to Promote and Grow to Fulfill Career Goals

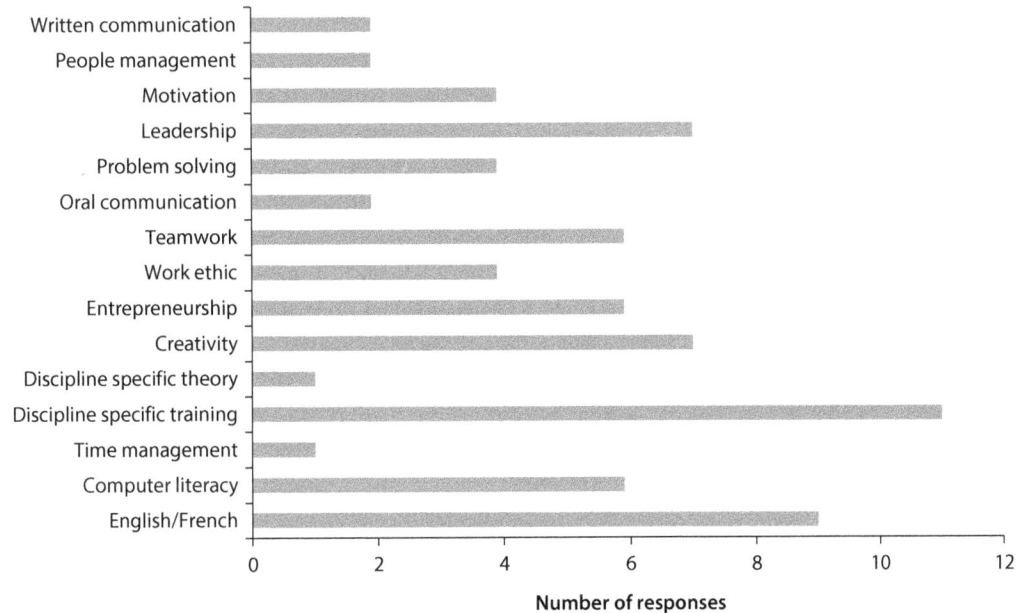

Training and Education

For 61 percent of the public sector employees, their current job offers in-service training, including administrative pre-service training for 31 percent of them and technical training for 26 percent of them. More than half the public sector employees consulted were offered training in the past 12 months; that training was offered by a government organization for the majority of them and it was either free of charge or paid by the employee. The type of training that would be helpful for public sector employees at this point in their careers is professional training, followed by entrepreneurship to start their own business and foreign language training. The education received by 67 percent of the public sector employees did not adequately prepare them for their current job.

Future Employment

The main obstacles undermining the chances of future employment are skills and job market inadequacy, according to 65 percent of the public sector employees, followed by the overall economic situation of the country. The main obstacles in finding employment include lack of available jobs and lack of work experience, followed by unsuitable vocational education, discriminatory prejudices, and poor working conditions in available jobs. Seventy percent of the public sector employees received little to no assistance while looking for a job, while 82 percent of them received no help from employment services on job search, education or training opportunities, job placement, etc.

Synthesis of Consultations with Youth Groups

Key Findings

The main goal of the consultations with youth groups was to identify the most important skills for securing a job and the skills youth think are relevant to them for securing a job in the future. Language skills (English/French) are the most important for securing a job according to the respondents, and completion of university is the most useful training. Young people expressed concern about the economic situation of the country, which undermines their opportunities for future employment. Similarly, according to the respondents, there are not enough jobs in the market, which was identified as the main reason they are unemployed or not looking for jobs.

Methodology

The information was collected during consultations with various youth groups in Cameroon to elicit their concerns. The number of youth consulted was 96 people between the ages of 21 and 50, including group leaders and their constituents. Members of youth groups were asked to give their views on 35 questions, including background, current employment and experience, skills, training and education, future employment, and demographic questions.

Findings

Profile of Youths Consulted

Thirty-three percent of the young people are available for work and actively looking for employment, 20 percent are students, 16 percent are self-employed, and 12 percent are engaged in training. More than half of them have finished post-graduate school and 40 percent of them have finished university or vocational school. Nearly all the respondents would pay for post-secondary education if it would help them secure another position in the future and 87 percent of them participated in internships during or after school.

Current Employment and Experience

Two-thirds of the young people worked while studying, and more than half of those who worked were paid for their work. The main motivation for working while studying was to gain experience, followed by making connections to help them with future employment. The majority of respondents are employed in the private/informal sector, followed by those who are self-employed. Thirty percent are doing professional work in their current job, followed by 22 percent who are doing managerial work and 19 percent who are doing technical work.

The main reason members of the youth groups decided to follow this area of work was primarily because they were qualified, but also many of them could not get their dream job. In describing their current job, most of the respondents said it was a survival job, followed by their job being decent. For 61 percent of the young people, their current job guarantees growth opportunities and for 14 percent of them it guarantees job security. The main motivation, according to the respondents, for being in their current job is on-the-job experience, followed by training, job security, and promotion.

Skills, Training, and Education

The main skills identified as the most important for securing a job are English/French (language skills), followed by computer literacy, disciplined scientific training, motivation, creativity, and teamwork (figure I.1). For two-thirds of the respondents, their education prepared them adequately for their current job. The type of training most useful for young people at this point is completion of

Figure I.1 Most Important Skills for Securing a Job

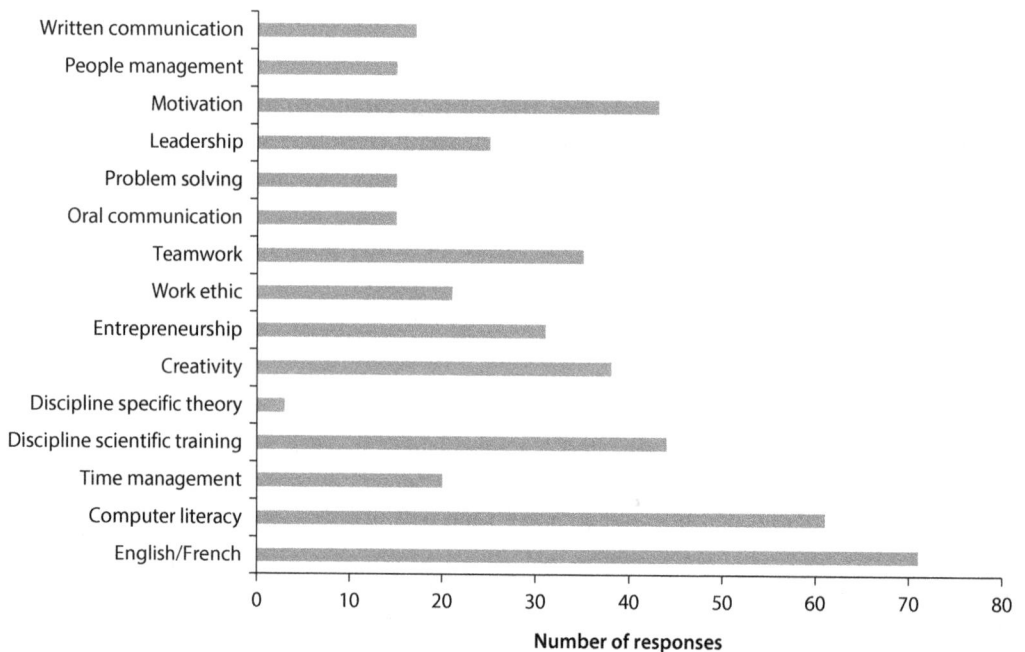

university, followed by professional training, foreign language training, and entrepreneurship training to start their own business (figure I.2).

Future Employment

The main obstacle that could undermine future employment opportunities, according to the respondents, is the overall economic situation in the country, followed by skills and job market inadequacy. The majority of people received little or no help when searching for a job; 62 percent of the youth consulted received no assistance or advice from employment services when searching for employment. The main obstacle in finding a job is the lack of jobs available in the market, followed by the lack of work experience, unsuitable general education, poor working conditions in available jobs, and discriminatory prejudices. The main reasons why respondents are not working or are currently not looking for employment are they do not meet the employers' requirements for the positions and they are not able to find suitable work.

Self-Employment

More than half the respondents were self-employed. Being more independent when working was identified as the main reason they chose to be self-employed. Likewise, a number of people chose to be self-employed because they could not find a wage or salary job, followed by more flexible work hours. Forty-three percent of those who are self-employed received no help and used their personal savings to start their business. The two most important problems that self-employed youths face are problems with Internet service and insufficient training to prepare them for their jobs.

Figure I.2 Most Helpful Training at This Point

Number of responses

Youth Skills Survey

Coopération Banque mondiale/Cameroun	World Bank/Cameroon Cooperation
Enquête auprès de la Jeunesse	Youth Skills Survey

Disclaimer:
- This survey has a restricted distribution and may be used by recipients only to provide information.
- This survey is not intended for employment. Your response to this survey is voluntary.
- This survey is not authorized for further distribution.
- Please contribute to its effectiveness by responding only once.

Avertissement:
- Ce questionnaire est soumis à politique de <u>restriction dans sa distribution</u> et ne peut être utilisé par les répondants que dans le but de fournir des informations.
- Ce questionnaire n'offre <u>aucune garantie d'emploi.</u> Les réponses sont soumises de façon exclusivement volontaire.
- Ce questionnaire n'est pas autorisé à une <u>distribution ultérieure.</u>
- Veuillez s'il vous plaît contribuer à l'effectivité de cette enquête en ne répondant <u>qu'une seule fois</u>

Directions/Consigne: Please read each question carefully and respond accordingly/Merci de lire attentivement chacune des questions et entourer la lettre correspondant à votre choix

I. Background information/Information de Base

1. Current status/Situation actuelle
   a. Employed/Employé
   b. Work for wage/salary w/employer (full or part-time)/Salarié(e) à temps plein ou partiel
   c. Self-employed/own-account worker/travailleur indépendant
   d. Available and actively looking for work/Disponible et activement à la recherche d'un emploi
   e. Engaged in training/En formation
   f. Engaged in home duties/Engagé(e) dans un travail à domicile
   g. Did not work or seek work for other reasons/N'a pas travaillé ou cherché du travail pour d'autres raisons
   h. Student/Etudiant
   i. Just graduated/Jeune diplomé(e)

2. Most recent educational activity/Activité scolaire la plus récente
   a. I have never studied/Je n'ai jamais été à l'école
   b. I left before graduating from secondary/J'ai arrêté les études sans être diplomé(e) du secondaire
   c. I have completed primary and secondary/J'ai achevé les cycles primaire et secondaire

Coopération Banque mondiale/Cameroun	World Bank/Cameroon Cooperation
Enquête auprès de la Jeunesse	Youth Skills Survey

d. I have completed primary, secondary, and vocational/J'ai achevé les cycles: primaire secondaire et professionnel

e. I have completed primary, secondary, and university/J'ai achevé les cycles: primaire, secondaire et universitaire

f. I am currently studying/Je suis encore scolarisé(e)

    a. Primary level/Niveau de l'enseignement primaire

    b. Vocational school/En formation professionnelle

    c. Secondary level/Niveau de l'Enseignement secondaire

    d. Higher education level/= Niveau Licence de l'Enseignement supérieur

    e. Post-graduate, post-doctoral level Post-graduate, post-doctoral level/ Niveau Maîtrise, Doctorat ou post-doctorat

3. What is the highest level of education/training you have attained?/Quel est votre niveau de formation le plus élevé?

    a. Elementary education/Cycle Primaire et Élémentaire

    b. Secondary education/Education secondaire

    c. Vocational education/Formation professionnelle

    d. University/Premier cycle universitaire

    e. Post-graduate studies/Second cycle universitaire (Maîtrise, Doctorat, Post-Doctorat)

    f. Other/Autre: _____

4. Would you pay for post-secondary education if it would help you to secure another position?/Investiriez-vous de l'argent dans des études universitaires si cela vous aidait à trouver un nouvel emploi?

    a. Yes/Oui

    b. No/Non

5. Field of study/Filière d'étude

    a. Education and humanities/Éducation et Sciences humaines

    b. Social sciences/Sciences sociales

    c. Medicine/Médecine

    d. Scientific, technical, and engineering/Science technique, et ingénierie

    e. Tourism/Tourisme

    f. Other/Autre: _____

6. Did you participate in any of the following, post or during school?/Avez-vous pris part aux activités suivantes pendant ou après vos études?

    a. Internships/Stages

    b. Mentoring/Parainnage

    c. None of the above/Aucun des sus-mentionnés

Coopération Banque mondiale/Cameroun	World Bank/Cameroon Cooperation
Enquête auprès de la Jeunesse	Youth Skills Survey

7. What is the highest level of education/training you hope to attain? Quel le niveau d'étude souhaitez-vous atteindre?
   a. Elementary education/Formation primaire _____
   b. Vocational education/Formation professionnelle: Level/Niveau _____
   c. Secondary educaiton/Niveau de l'enseignement secondaire

   _____
   d. University/Premier Cycle Universitaire: level/Niveau: _____
   e. Post- graduate studies/studies: Maîtrise/Doctorat/Post-doctorat _____
   f. Other/Autre _____

II. Employment/Experience professionnelle

8. Did you work while you studied?/Avez-vous travaillé durant vos études?
   a. Yes/Oui
   b. No/Non

9. If so, was the work paid?/Si oui, cet emploi était-il remunéré?
   a. Yes/Oui
   b. No/Non

10. What was your primary motivation in working while studying?/Qu'elle était votre motivation première à combiner travail et études?
    a. Earn money/Gagner de l'argent?
    b. Gain experience/Accumuler de l'expérience professionnelle?
    c. Make connections that could help with future employment/Se constituer un réseau de connaissances nécessaires à un emploi futur?
    d. Other/Autre: _____

11. In what sector are you currently employed?/Dans quel secteur êtes-vous actuellement employé(e)?
    a. Public sector/Fonction publique
    b. Private/informal sector/Secteur privé/informel
    c. Self-employed/Indépendant
    d. Other/Autre: _____

12. Which of the following describes the type of work you do in your current job?/Comment décririez-vous votre travail actuel?
    a. Manual work/Manutention
    b. Clerical work/Assistance
    c. Technical work/Intervention technique
    d. Administrative work/Travail administratif
    e. Managerial work/Coordination
    f. Professionnal work/Travail lié à une formation professionnelle
    g. Other/Autre: _____

Coopération Banque mondiale/Cameroun	World Bank/Cameroon Cooperation
Enquête auprès de la Jeunesse	Youth Skills Survey

13. Why have you decided to choose this area of work?/Qu'est-ce qui vous a poussé à choisir cette profession/ce secteur d'activité?
    a. I was qualified because of my education/Mon parcours scolaire
    b. I couldn't get my dream job/Je n'arrivais pas à décrocher l'emploi souhaité
    c. Lack of education/Manque d'éducation
    d. Other/Autre: _____

14. How would you describe your current employment?/Comment qualifierez-vous votre emploi actuel
    a. Decent/Acceptable
    b. Dream job/Emploi souhaité
    c. Survival job/emploi de survie
    d. Other/autre: _____

15. Which of the following does your current job guarantee? Que vous garantit votre emploi actuel?
    a. Job security/Sécurité d'emploi
    b. Growth opportunities/Possibilités d'évolution
    c. Other/Autre: _____

16. Which of the following motivates you most for your job (please rate your preference)/Qu'est-ce qui vous motive le plus dans votre position actuelle? Veuillez marquer votre niveau de motivation selon une échelle de 1 à 5
    1 = Peu ou pas motivé du tout; 5 = Très motivé
    a. Salary _____ Le salaire
    b. Promotion _____ Possibilité de promotion
    c. Job security _____ Sécurité de l'emploi
    d. Training _____ Opportunité de formation
    e. On-the-job experience _____ Accumulation de l'expérience professionnelle

17. Which of the following skills are most important for securing a job (please select up to 5)? Lesquelles de ces compétences sont les plus importantes pour garantir un emploi (merci de choisir au plus 5)
    a. English/French/Français- Anglais
    b. Computer literacy/Connaissances en informatique
    c. Time management/Gestion du temps
    d. Discipline specific training/Formation spécifique
    e. Discipline specific theory/Théorie spécifique
    f. Creativity/Créativité
    g. Entrepreneurship/Entrepenariat
    h. Work ethic/Éthique de travail

Coopération Banque mondiale/Cameroun	World Bank/Cameroon Cooperation
Enquête auprès de la Jeunesse	Youth Skills Survey

i. Teamwork/Travail en équipe
j. Oral communication/Communication orale
k. Problem solving/Résolution de problème
l. Leadership/Leadership
m. Motivation/Motivation
n. People management/Gestion du personnel
o. Written communication/Communication écrite

18. **Do you feel your education adequately prepared you for a job? Avez-vous le sentiment que votre formation vous a préparé de façon adéquate à votre emploi?**
    a. Yes/Oui
    b. No/Non

19. **What do you think could undermine your chances of future employment opportunities?/Qu'est ce qui selon vous pourrait réduire vos chances d'employabilité future?**
    a. Long-term studies/De longues études
    b. Skills and job market inadequacy/Incompatibilité entre les compétences et le marché du travail
    c. Overall economic situation of the country/Situation économique générale
    d. Other/Autres: _____

20. **How much help/assistance have you received when looking for a job?/Quel degré d'assistance avez-vous reçu pendant votre recherche d'emploi?**
    a. Little to no help/Peu ou aucune assistance du tout
    b. Some help/Une certaine assistance
    c. A lot of help/Une grande assistance

21. **Which of these professions are exciting and fulfilling for you?/Lesquelles des professions ci-dessous jugez-vous passisonnante et enrichissante**
    a. Engineer/Ingénieur
    b. Doctor/surgeon/Médecin/Chirurgien
    c. Accountant/Comptable
    d. Financial analyst/Analyste financier
    e. School teacher/Enseignant
    f. IT technician/Informaticien
    g. Web developer/Developpeur site Web
    h. Lodging manager/Agent immobilier
    i. Police officer/Officier de police
    j. Graphic designer/Plasticien
    k. Teacher assistance/Professeur/Maître assistant

Coopération Banque mondiale/Cameroun	World Bank/Cameroon Cooperation
Enquête auprès de la Jeunesse	Youth Skills Survey

    l. Customer service/Service client

    m. Medical assistant/Assistant(e) medical(e)

    n. Desk clerk/reception/Réceptionniste

    o. Secretary/Secrétaire

    p. Fire-fighter/Sapeur pompier

    q. Recruiting specialist/Agent de recrutement

    r. Health care technician/Technicien de la santé

    s. Sales representative/Représentant Commercial

    t. Social worker/Travailleur social

    u. Marketing agent/Commercial

    v. Child care worker/Assistante Maternelle/Puéricultrice

    w. Real estate agent/Agent immobilier

    x. Auto mechanic/Mécanicien

    y. Electrician/Électricien

22. **How much do you expect to earn per month?/Combien vous attendiez-vous à gagner par mois?**

    a. Below/Moins de 75,000 CFA

    b. Between/Entre 75,000 CFA - 175,000 CFA

    c. Between/Entre 175,000 CFA - 250,000 CFA

    d. Above/250,000 CFA et plus

23. **What kind of training do you think would be most helpful for you at this point?/quelle formation pensez-vous être le plus utile pour vous à votre niveau actuel?**

    a. Completion of vocational training/Achèvement de la formation professionnelle

    b. Completion of secondary education/Achèvement des études secondaires

    c. Completion of university/Achèvement des études Universitaires

    d. Apprenticeship with an employer/Apprentissage chez un employeur

    e. Entrepreneurship training to start own business/formation en entrepreneuriat pour se lancer dans les affaires

    f. Computer and IT training/Informatique

    g. Foreign language/Langue étrangère

    h. Professional training/Formation professionnelle

24. **Have you ever received any advice/help/assistance from employment services? Avez-vous reçu des conseils, de l'aide ou de l'assistance des services d'aide à l'emploi?**

    a. None/Aucun

    b. Advice on how to search for a job/Conseils relatifs à la recherche d'emploi

Coopération Banque mondiale/Cameroun	World Bank/Cameroon Cooperation
Enquête auprès de la Jeunesse	Youth Skills Survey

c. Information on vacancies/Information sur des postes vacants

d. Guidance on education and training opportunities/Orientations sur des opportunités d'étude ou de formation

e. Placecement in education or training programs/Placement dans une école ou un dans un programme de formation

f. Other/Autre: _____

25. **What would you say has been an obstacle in finding a job?/Qu'est ce qui selon vous a constitué un obstacle à trouver du travail?**

a. No education/Aucune éducation

b. Unsuitable general education/Éducation générale inadéquate

c. Unsuitable vocational education/Formation technique inadéquate

d. No suitable training opportunities/Aucune opportunité de formation adéquate

e. Requirements for job higher than education/training received/Nécessité d'une éducation de plus haut niveau

f. No work experience/Aucune experience professionnelle

g. Not enough jobs available/Pas assez d'opportunités d'emploi

h. Considered too young/Considéré très jeune

i. Being male/female/Genre (Homme/Femme)

j. Discriminatory prejudices/Discrimination

k. Low wages in available jobs/Salaire bas pour les positions disponibles

l. Poor working conditions in available jobs/Mauvaises conditions de travail

m. Other/Autres: _____

26. **If you are not currently employed, what has been your main reason for not working or looking for work? Si vous n'êtes pas actuellement employé(e), quelles sont les principales raisons de votre situation de chercheur d'emploi ou de chômeur?**

a. Own illness, injury, pregnancy/maladie, accident, grossesse

b. Personal family responsibilities/Responsabilités familiales

c. Education leave or training/Arrêt scolaire ou de formation

d. Arrangements for self-employment to start at later date/préparation pour un travail indépendant à une date ultérieure

e. Slow hiring period/Période de basse activité pour le recrutement

f. Belief in no suitable work available (in area of relevance to one's skills, capacities)/Aucun emploi adapté dans le domaine de compétences

g. Lack employers' requirements (qualifications, training, experience, age, etc.)/Ne réponds pas aux critères des Employeurs (qualifications, formation, expérience, âge, etc...)

Coopération Banque mondiale/Cameroun	World Bank/Cameroon Cooperation
Enquête auprès de la Jeunesse	Youth Skills Survey

    h. Could not find suitable work/N'a pas trouvé un travail adapté

    i. Do not know how or where to seek work/Ne sais pas comment et où chercher du travail

    j. Not yet started to seek work/N'a pas encore commencé des recherches d' emploi

    k. No reason given/Pas de raison

III. Self-Employed/Entrepreneurs

27. **Why did you choose to be self-employed or an own-account worker rather than work for someone else (as a wage and salaried worker)? Pourquoi avez-vous choisi d'être à votre propre compte au lieu de travailler pour une entreprise ou quelqu'un d'autre comme salarié?**

    a. Could not find a wage or salary job/Je n'ai pas trouvé d'emploi salarié

    b. Greater independence as self-employed/own-account worker/Grande indépendance en tant que travailleur indépendant

    c. More flexible hours of work/heures de travail plus souples

    d. Higher income level/revenus plus élevés

    e. Other/autres: _____

28. **Do you have anyone helping you in your business/economic activity?/ Recevez--vous de l'assistance dans votre activité?**

    a. Paid employees/Un salarié

    b. Family members/Un membre de votre famille

    c. No help, working alone/aucune aide, travaille seul(e)

29. **Where did you get the money to start your current business? Comment avez-vous eu l'argent qui vous a permis de demarrer votre affaire personnel? Comment avez-vous financé votre activité?**

    a. No money needed/pas eu besoin d'argent

    b. Personal savings/épargnes personnelles

    c. Savings from other family members/Fonds d'appuis reçus de la famille

    d. Loan from family or friends/Prêts effectués auprès de la famille et des amis

    e. Loan from bank or commercial institution/Prêts effectués auprès d'une Banque

    f. Loan from private money lender/Fonds reçus d'un organisme de crédit privé

    g. Loan/assistance from government institution/Prêt reçus d'un organisme gouvernemental

    h. Loan/assistance from NGO, donor project, etc./Prêt reçus d'un organisme non gouvernemental/Projet, etc.

Coopération Banque mondiale/Cameroun	World Bank/Cameroon Cooperation
Enquête auprès de la Jeunesse	Youth Skills Survey

i. Funds from savings and credit/group/Fonds d'un groupe d'épargnes ou de crédits

j. Credit from customer/middleman/agent/supplier/Fonds d'un groupe d'épargne ou de crédit

k. Other sources/Autre sources: _____

30. **What are the two most important problems you face in running your business? Quels sont les 2 problèmes les plus importants auxquels vous faites face dans la gestion de votre activité?**

a. Business information/Information sur l'activité

b. Marketing services/Services de marketing

c. Financial services/Services financiers

d. Accounting/Comptabilité

e. Legal services/Services juridiques

f. Counseling/advice/Conseil

g. Business training/Formation en gestion d'entreprise

h. Language training/Formation en linguistique Langue

i. Skills training/Formation professionelle

j. Internet service/Accès/Service d'accès Internet

k. Access to technology/Accès au matériel technologique

l. Product development/Développment de produit

m. Other/Autre: _____

IV. **Demographic information/Informations démographiques**

31. **Age/âge**

a. Moins de 20 ans

b. 21–30 ans

c. 31–40ans

d. 41–50 ans

e. 51 ans et plus

32. **Sex/Sexe**

a. Male

b. Female

33. **Quelle est votre province d'origine?**

a. Adamaoua

b. Centre

c. Est

d. Extreme-Nord

e. Littoral

f. Nord

Coopération Banque mondiale/Cameroun	World Bank/Cameroon Cooperation
Enquête auprès de la Jeunesse	Youth Skills Survey

    g. Nord-Ouest

    h. Ouest

    i. Sud

    j. Sud-Ouest

34. What is your language of expression?/Quelle est votre langue d'expression?

    a. English/Anglais

    b. French/Français

35. What is your marital status? Quel votre statut d'état civil

    a. Single - Célibataire

    b. Married- Marié (e)

    c. Separated- Séparé (e)

    d. Widowed- Veuf (ve)

    e. Co-habitation – En cohabitation

Skills Development Solutions in Vietnam and Brazil

Box J.1 Skilling Up Vietnam: Preparing the Workforce for a Modern Market Economy

Education has played an important role in making Vietnam a development success story over the past 20 years. Vietnam's rapid economic growth in the 1990s was driven predominantly by productivity increases that came in the wake of a rapid shift of employment out of low productivity agriculture and into higher productivity nonfarm jobs. Vietnam's economy began to industrialize and modernize. Poverty fell dramatically. And education played an enabling role.

Vietnam's committed effort to promote access to primary education for all and to ensure its quality through centrally setting minimum quality standards has contributed to its reputation for having a well-educated, young workforce. Literacy and numeracy among Vietnam's adult workforce is widespread and more so than in other countries, including wealthier ones. Recognizing that capital investment is one of the main sources of economic growth, Vietnam has also recognized that making its workforce more productive and alleviating skills barriers to labor mobility is central to the country's economic modernization. Economic modernization will involve a shift in labor demand from predominantly manual and elementary jobs, toward more skill-intensive nonmanual jobs; from jobs that largely involve routine tasks, to those with nonroutine tasks; and from old jobs, to "new" jobs.

And "new" jobs will require new skills. Despite impressive literacy and numeracy achievements among Vietnamese workers, many Vietnamese firms report a shortage of workers with adequate skills as a significant obstacle to their activity. Employers identify job-specific technical skills as the most important skill they are looking for when hiring white collar and blue collar workers. Employers are equally looking for *cognitive skills* and *behavioral skills*. Job-specific technical skills, working well in teams, and being able to solve problems are considered important behavioral and cognitive skills for blue collar workers. Employers expect white collar workers to be able to think critically, solve problems, and present their work in a convincing manner to clients and colleagues.

---

box continues next page

Box J.1 Skilling Up Vietnam: Preparing the Workforce for a Modern Market Economy *(continued)*

Vietnam's new jobs require that workers have good foundational skills, such as good reading ability. Workers also need more advanced skills that help them to be responsive to changes in workplace demands. Vietnam's focused investments over the past decades in universalizing primary education completion and expanding access to all levels of education have paid off. This has allowed increasing shares of the population to take advantage of the expanding economic opportunities. Strengthening the skills development system is an important element of Vietnam's restructuring needs to ensure that the structural transformation proceeds apace and Vietnam succeeds as a middle-income country.

The Systems Approach for Better Education Results (SABER) analytical framework for workforce development (WfD) benchmarking results show that already in 2011 Vietnam had a strongly *emerging* system of policies and institutions. That is, the country has (i) a strategic framework that clarifies the direction for WfD, prioritizes a demand-led approach, and has a strong critical coordination mechanism fit for a solid middle-income country; (ii) system oversight that provides diverse pathways for skills acquisition, and ensures relevant and reliable standards; and (iii) in the area of service delivery, the system fosters relevance in training programs, and provides incentives for excellence in training provision. In the areas of ensuring efficiency and equity in funding and enhancing accountability for results, more efforts are required in Vietnam.

Source: World Bank 2012c, 2014b.

Box J.2 Brazil's Better Early Childhood Development Program

Brazil's Better Early Childhood Development Program (PIM), headed by the State Department of Health, coordinates efforts by the State Departments of Education, Culture, Justice, and Social Development. The program's concept and implementation reflects a deep recognition of the relevance and complexity of child development and is fully committed to promoting it through the articulation of the necessary sectors and resources. The program's basic premise is that child development is a complex process that comprises several dimensions: neurological, affective, cognitive, and social. It cannot be decontextualized; rather, a child's environment, family, and community play core roles.

PIM was strongly based on lessons learned from the Cuban program "Educa a Tu Hijo" (Ministry of Education of Cuba 2002). Defined as a nonformal, noninstitutional, community-based, family-oriented early childhood development program, of an intersector nature, the program has operated under the responsibility of the Ministry of Education in Cuba since its implementation in 1992–94.

Like Educa a Tu Hijo, PIM is organized around a structural troika: *family*, *community*, and *sectors*. The *family* is viewed as the most important primary human group in the early years of an individual's life. It is an affective unit of relationship, care, protection, and education, not necessarily based on blood or legal ties. The importance of family becomes even more critical

box continues next page

Box J.2 Brazil's Better Early Childhood Development Program *(continued)*

in light of the fact that almost 75.28 percent of the population ages 0 to 6 years has no access to early childhood education facilities in Rio Grande do Sul. (Instituto Brasileiro de Geografia e Estatísca (IBGE) (Brazilian Institute for Geography and Statistics) 2007; Ministry of Education/ Ministry of Education, Instituto Nacional de Estudos e Pesquisas (INEP) (National Institute for Educational Studies and Research) 2007). The program views the *community* as a central space for potentialities and human, material, and institutional resources. Its customs, traditions, and cultural production are key elements for the education, health, and development of children. *Sectors* are considered a key element for the success of PIM. Integration among government departments of health, education, social services, and culture, as well as the full commitment of administrators in all spheres, are gradually converting PIM into a reality that is not only feasible, but also increasingly promising. Moreover, the program's articulation with the second and third sectors has also contributed to positive results.

PIM provides assisted families with two modalities of care: *individual* and *group* care, complemented by a community-based approach. All parental guidance and child stimulation activities are planned and carried out in a playful way, appropriate to children's ages or women's stages of pregnancy, and take into consideration the developmental dimensions targeted by the program, its theoretical framework, and the local context and cultural aspects.

The *Individual Care Modality* is designed for families with children ages 0 to 2 years and 11 months, and pregnant women assisted by the program. Children are seen once a week and pregnant women are seen once every two weeks in home visits lasting approximately one hour. Each visit has three distinct stages: a review of the previous visit and an exploration of the present topic (during which the home visitor explains the benefits of the proposed activities for the various developmental aspects of the child and/or for the mother-baby dyad); the actual activity, observed and supported by the family visitor; and the final assessment stage.

The *Group Care Modality* is designed for families with children ages 3 to 6 years and/or pregnant women, in weekly and monthly schedules, respectively. Meetings can happen in community centers, church halls, parks, and homes big enough to accommodate all the participants. The meetings include games and playful educational activities planned by the home visitors under the supervision of the PIM technical coordination team. The main goal of the group modality for pregnant women is to provide relevant information on topics such as child delivery and the importance of breastfeeding, as well as to promote socialization and the exchange of experiences.

As a result of the program's consolidation and effectiveness, a state law has been passed (State Law #12544) to guarantee the continuity of investments in early childhood development at the local level. This law establishes PIM as a public policy that aims at promoting the holistic development of children from pregnancy to age six years as a complement to family and community actions.

Source: Schneider and others 2009.

Synthesis of Employment-Related and Productivity Enhancement Activities[1]

Introduction

Seventeen government ministries are involved in the areas of job creation and productivity enhancement (box K.1). Four ministries focus on the formal education of the general population and workforce development; nine focus on the promotion of employment, including informal employment; and four others focus on "second chance" skills development for the vulnerable and excluded. The National Employment Fund is the main implementing agency for national employment policy. Each of these agencies manages several programs, the Ministry of Agriculture and Rural Development running, for instance, 17 programs. Many programs even within the same agency have similar objectives.

This environment leads to a confused and untargeted approach to employment, where efforts and financial resources are spread very thin. Education is a case in point. Four ministries are involved in delivering education and vocational training, which complicates the government's ability to have a coherent, comprehensive, and consistent sector wide approach.

Similar to other developing countries, Cameroon has seven main traditional partners that provide support in the areas of job creation and productivity enhancement:

- African Development Bank (AfDB)
- European Union (EU)
- Food and Agriculture Organization (FAO)
- French Development Agency (AFD)
- International Fund for Agriculture Development (IFAD)
- Japanese International Cooperation Agency (JICA)
- World Bank Group (WBG), including the International Finance Corporation (IFC).

Box K.1 Government Ministries Involved in Employment-Related and Productivity Enhancement Activities

Ministries focused on formal education of the general population and work force:

- Ministry of Primary Education (MINEDUB)
- Ministry of Secondary Education (MINESEC)
- Ministry of Higher Education (MINESUP)
- Ministry of Employment and Vocational Training (MINEFOP).

Ministries focused on promotion of employment, including informal employment:

- Ministry of Employment and Vocational Training (MINEFOP)
- Ministry of Youth (MINJEUN)
- Ministry of Labor and Social Security (MINTSS)
- Ministry of Women's Empowerment and Family (MINPROFF)
- Ministry of Agriculture and Rural Development (MINADER)
- Ministry of Urban Development and Housing (MINDUH)
- Ministry of Small and Medium Size Enterprises, Social Economy and Handicrafts (MINPMEESA)
- Ministry of Industry, Mines, and Technological Development (MINMIDT)
- Ministry of Livestock, Fisheries and Animal Industry (MINEPIA).

Ministries focused on "second chances" for the vulnerable and excluded:

- Ministry of Social Affairs (MINAS)
- Ministry of Women's Empowerment and Family (MINPROFF)
- Ministry of Employment and Vocational Training (MINEFOP)
- Ministry of Small and Medium Size Enterprises, Social Economy and Handicrafts (MINPMEESA).

Lack of coordination could also be here a source of concern with very similar programs run by different donors. AFD, for instance, manages support programs for the competitiveness of agricultural farms, while the EU runs a program for the improvement of agricultural productivity. Both programs cover similar zones and include similar interventions.[2]

Limited Explicit Targeting of the Informal Sector

With the exception the Integrated Support Program for Actors in the Informal Sector (PIAASI), the informal sector has not been the object of any explicit program, despite its importance as a job provider. The government seems to have preferred handling this sector through programs covering issues closely related to it rather than dealing head-on with the constraints faced by this sector. Furthermore, efforts seem to have been focused on ways to lure operators away from the informal sector and attract them to formality, although survey results would tend to indicate that most of them are satisfied with the greater flexibility informality provides them. Furthermore, although the stock-taking uncovered various interventions at the local level aimed at facilitating nonfarm informal businesses, many municipalities are still trying to contain or repress these activities.

Even when a program explicitly targets the informal sector, as in the case of PIAASI, the results are mixed. Launched in 2005, the program aimed at facilitating migration from the informal to the formal sector. The priorities were youth and women, and the main objectives were to: (i) organize activities into professional groups, (ii) provide training, and (iii) provide financial assistance. The program tried to reach as many people as possible, was rolled out in all the regions, and covered all activities, without proper targeting. As a result, the program overextended itself rapidly. Not being able to deal with the specificities of each activity, its portfolio remained mostly urban. Financial resources were spread thin, and were not able to provide enough of an incentive to operators to become formal. Increases in investment were limited. Furthermore, the repayment rate on the loans was low (40 percent).

World Bank Focus on the Formal Sector

The World Bank's involvement has primarily been in the formal sector (table K.1). In coverage by institution, government projects in support of employment are mainly for the farm sector (18 projects), informal nonfarm sector (18), and youth (13 projects). Similarly, the majority of development partner projects outside the World Bank Group are for the farm sector (10 projects), the informal nonfarm sector (three projects), youth (two projects), and women (one project). In stark contrast, the majority of the World Bank Group activities with implications for employment are for the formal sector (19 projects), with the World Bank also supporting the farm sector to a lesser degree (one project) and the IFC aiding the nonfarm informal sector (three activities).

Table K.1 Coverage of Government and Development Partner
Employment-Related programs and projects

Area	Government	Development partners	World Bank/International Finance Corporation
Formal sector	0	0	14/5
Farm sector	18	10	1/0
Informal sector:			
Household enterprises	0	0	0/0
Other enterprises	18	3	0/3
Youth employment	13	2	0/0
Women employment	0	1	0/0

Notes

1. This appendix is based on Ames and Godang (2012).

2. There are also various private, nongovernmental, or faith-based groups involved in employment-related activities. However, most of these are small interventions and, hence, are beyond the scope of the present exercise.

Training and Employment Promotion Schemes and Initiatives in the Formal Sector in Cameroon

Providers	Type of training/employment promotion intervention	Target groups/target labor market	Qualifications achieved	Knowledge about relevance/effectiveness
Government				
Multifunctional Center for Youth Development (MINJEUN-MINEFOP/CMPJ)	Support and assistance Counseling	Youths	Vocational Qualification Certificate (CQP) in projects implementation	72 operating centers 1,500 youths in training
Referral Program for Micro-Enterprises (MINJEUN-MINEFOP/MICROPAR)	Technical support Financing	Small business owners Entrepreneurs Youths	Skills transfer	
MINADER (Agricultural Education Cooperative and Community Division (DEFACC) - Regional Centers for Agriculture (CRA)/Technical Schools of Agriculture (ETA))	Capacity building in Agriculture Continuous training in forestry	Youths unemployed	CQP in forestry/agriculture	1,000 people trained in 2009
Rural Training Centers (MINADER-CFR)	Forestry Agriculture	Forest operators Agricultural specialists	CQP in agriculture	
Training School for Rural Development Specialists (MINADER-EFSEAR)	Infrastructure, water management, rural equipment	College students	CQP in natural resource management	
Support Programme for Youths Inclusion in Agriculture (MINADER-PAIJA)	Capacity building	Young landowners		
School of Geology and Mining (MINESUP-EGEM)	Mining	Students Professionals	Higher education Recognition in mining	Well renowned school
Academic and Technological Institute-Wood (MINESUP-UIT)	Wood processing	Graduates	Specialized vocational training certificate	Well-functioning school
Craft and Rural Department (MINESEC: SAR)/Household Department (SM)	Functional literacy Vocational training	Illiterates Primary school: dropouts/graduates High school: dropouts/graduates	CQP in chosen training	

table continues next page

Providers	Type of training/employment promotion intervention	Target groups/target labor market	Qualifications achieved	Knowledge about relevance/ effectiveness
MINJEUN/MINEFOP (Rural and Urban Youth Support Program, FNE–PAJERU)	Job placement Counseling Project funding	Underprivileged youths, ages 15–35 years	Job readiness	2,390 projects funded
MINEFOP (Retirement and Youth Employment Program, FNE–PREJ)	Skills transfer	Youths Retirees to be	On the job training	
MINEFOP	Carpentry Woodwork	Youths Graduates Professionals	Relevant vocational training recognition	4,500 students in 2010
Mining Vocational Training Center (MINEFOP-CFPM)	Mining	Unemployed Youths Professionals	CQP in mining	
Support Program for Rural Jobs (MINEFOP-FNE-PADER)	Training and placement Project funding	Youths in rural areas	Self-employment Qualification	36,000 people trained and self-employed
National School of Forestry and Water Resources (MINFOF-ENEF)	Agronomist engineers Forest managers Forest operators	Professionals Graduates	Specialized certificate in forestry	Well renowned school
Graduate Employment Program (PED)	Internship placement	Youths Local enterprises	On the job training	1,000 youths enrolled in 2010
National Civic Service for Participation in Development (MINJEUN–SCNPD)	Project design, monitoring, and management	Youths	CQP in project development/ implementation	6,000 youths trained CFAF 129,000 funding for each project
Interprofessional Group for Craftsmen (MINPMEESA-GIPA)	Capacity building for entrepreneurs Apprenticeship	Craftsmen	CQP in craftsmanship	
Partnerships				
MINEFOP-South Korean government (Vocational Training Centers of Excellence, CFPE)	Advanced technical training (electricity, auto mechanics, carpentry, design, etc.)	Youths (unemployed and graduates)	CQP in chosen discipline	Training centers in a building process
MINEFOP-AFD (Vocational Sectoral Training Centers, CFPS)	Initial and continuing training in industrial maintenance, food processing, transport, logistics	Unemployed Graduates	CQP in relevant domains	Operating training centers

table continues next page

Providers	Type of training/employment promotion intervention	Target groups/target labor market	Qualifications achieved	Knowledge about relevance/effectiveness
MINADER-MINEPIA-AFD (AFOP1&2)	Agriculture Stock rearing	Young high school graduates	CQP in agriculture	42 operating public centers More than 2,260 post-primary students and 441 high school graduates trained
AFD-GICAM (Vocational Training Center, CFM)	Agro-processing, capacity building, construction, electricity, accounting, and information technology	Jobseekers Private sector professionals Youths Business owners	CQP in the agro-industry	Ongoing program
Development partners				
French cooperation-Support Cluster for Professionalization of Higher Education in Central Africa (PAPESAC)	Capacity building Higher education Support for training facilities and universities	Government University administrators University lecturers Researchers Students	Program management	Ongoing program
AFD-ARIZ (Monitoring Financial Risk) CONFEJES-FIJ	Entrepreneurship Self-employment	Microfinance institutions Youths (younger than age 30)		322 companies assisted in 2012 37 youths trained in 2012
Technological Excellence Cluster (UNESCO-PETU)	Technology Research Engineering	College graduates Scholars Researchers Professionals	Master's degree PhD in relevant fields	Operating institutions under the supervision of MINESUP Internationally renowned
The World Bank-Africa Centers of Excellence (ACE)	Research ICT STEM	College graduates Scholars Researchers Professionals	Master's degree PhD in relevant fields	Operating institutions
Private investors				
National Electric Company (AES-SONEL)/Group 4 Securicor (G4S)	Security	Youths (riparian)	(CQP) security agent qualification	500 youths trained and hired
AES-SONEL/SCADA	Training and job placement Control, supervision	Riparian	Capacity building in electricity	40 people hired in the community
AES-SONEL/T-Line Watchers	Training and job placement Surveillance	Riparian	Capacity building in electricity	108 watchers recruited (coming from 54 villages) in 2012 550 T-lines secured

Note: The formal sector is defined as those sectors that provide assured employment and salary to employees.

Proposed Action Plan

Policy goal	Workforce development domain/issues/findings	Strategic directions for reforms and policy actions	Responsibility	Timing
1. Setting Strategic Direction				
Functional Dimension 1. Strategic Framework		**Principle of Optimization: Provide sustained advocacy for WfD at the top leadership level**		
		Topic 1. Advocacy for WfD to support economic development		
	Some **visible champions advocate for WfD** to support economic development on an ad hoc and limited basis. They have taken a few specific measures to adjust the regulatory framework for WfD. However, the implementation of the adjustments is not systematically monitored. Based on multiple data sources, the government and other WfD stakeholders appear to conduct routine assessments of the country's economic prospects and skills implications only for key growth sectors. They do not assess the implications of foundational (literacy and numeracy), cognitive, and noncognitive skills that are necessary albeit not sufficient conditions.	Government leaders **exercise sustained advocacy for WfD** with support from nongovernment leaders, and collaborate on the WfD policy agenda for selected industries or economic sectors	PRIMATURE with MINEPAT Secretariat	Short-term
		Advocate for workforce development as a priority for economic growth: bring together strategic sectors that contribute to or have the potential to contribute to growth; outline systematic demand-led criteria; build in well-defined coordination, roles, and responsibilities; and build the capacity of those in charge of advocacy	Cameroon Inter-Ministerial Steering Group for Workforce Development (CIMSGWD) comprising membership of MINFI, MINEPAT, MINEFOP, MINESUP, GICAM, MINEJEUN, INS, sector skills committees/councils, association of informal sector actors, representation from youth groups, development partners focusing on education & training and skills development, CIEP, Technical Secretariat, Technical Monitoring Committee of the implementation of DSCE (CTSE), MINESEC, and MINADER	Short-term then ongoing
	There is an absence of **active advocates** with a clear vision on how WfD could be a tool to achieve the country's social and economic goals.			
	There is no evidence of the government taking actions to improve public perception of TVET.	Adopt strategic communications about the importance of workforce development for competitiveness and economic growth		

table continues next page

Policy goal	Workforce development domain/issues/findings	Strategic directions for reforms and policy actions	Responsibility	Timing
	Cameroon's DSCE provides a basis and some direction for workforce development.	**Topic 2. Strategic focus and decisions by WfD champions** Develop a strategic agenda and mechanism for inclusive workforce development, evaluate economic prospects and its implications for skills, and commission studies on the country's economic prospects under the DSCE with clear assessment of the implications for skills	Cameroon Inter-Ministerial Steering Group for Workforce Development (CIMSGWD) Working Groups, INS, development partners, CIEP, CTSE, MINEFOP and MINTSS	Short-term, then periodic and regular
	WfD champions have taken specific action on strategic WfD priorities through a few interventions, but no arrangements exist to monitor and review implementation progress.	Conduct systematic monitoring and review of implementation progress with the public and private sectors by making a clear distinction in the 6187 budget line (stock internship training)		
2. Fostering a Demand-Led Approach				
Functional Dimension 1. Strategic Framework		**Principle of specialization versus generalization: Establish clarity on the demand for skills and areas of critical constraint: promote a demand-driven approach** **Topic 3. Overall assessment of economic prospects and skills implications**		
	Insufficient strategic direction for WfD that is demand led and well coordinated. There are some indications that the government provides incentives for skills development and upgrading for employees in the formal and informal sectors, but not enough evidence to confirm the nature of these programs and whether they are implemented.	Toward addressing demand-led workforce development, conduct regular labor market surveys and studies to review/assess the demand for skills, *activate* and develop a labor market information system (LMIS)	Cameroon Inter-Ministerial Steering Group for Workforce Development (CIMSGWD), INS, development partners, MINEFOP	Medium-term, then periodic and regular

table continues next page

Policy goal	Workforce development domain/issues/findings	Strategic directions for reforms and policy actions	Responsibility	Timing
	Although incentive programs to encourage skills upgrading by employers seem to exist, it is not clear what they consist of and whether they are reviewed for impact.	Conduct periodic reviews and assess the impact of skills upgrading programs by employers		
		Engage employers in setting WfD priorities and in enhancing skills upgrading for workers		
	Employers seem to have a formal institutionalized space to participate in policy dialogue at the CBF. However, it is not clear whether this mechanism is currently active and working, and if WfD-specific discussions take place in this scenario.	Engage employers in setting WfD priorities and in enhancing skills upgrading for workers; strengthen firms' demand for skills to improve productivity through active involvement of employers using the CBF platform for policy dialogue	Cameroon Inter-Ministerial Steering Group for Workforce Development (CIMSGWD)	Ongoing
		Principle of Adequacy: Address critical challenges on the future supply of skills		
		Topic 4. Critical skills constraints in priority economic sectors		
	Insufficient systematic assessment (monitoring and evaluation) of foundational skills (literacy and numeracy), cognitive and noncognitive skills that are necessary conditions for workforce development, diffusion of findings, and targeted programs for the disadvantaged and vulnerable (girls, women, children with disabilities).	Improve access to, quality, and monitoring for the following areas:		
		Foundational skills—early childhood development (ECD); ECCD	MINEDUB, development partners	Medium through long-term
		Formative skills: literacy and numeracy	MINEDUB, MINESEC, development partners	Medium through long-term

table continues next page

Policy goal	Workforce development domain/issues/findings	Strategic directions for reforms and policy actions	Responsibility	Timing
		Introduce career guidance in curricula (areas where students can use the knowledge they acquire)		
		Demand-driven TVET programs in various trades linked to the key growth sectors		
		Revise curricula to make programs more responsive to labor market needs; incorporate soft skills, problem-solving skills and critical thinking skills		
		Strengthen public sector training institutions		
		Specify targets for public training institutions		
		Foster private sector training institutions	MINEFOP, GICAM, development partners	Medium through long-term
		Involve the private sector in institutional management		
		Develop labor market responsive curricula incorporating soft and critical skills (communications, writing, problem solving, critical thinking)		
		Introduce career guidance in the curricula		
		Recruit teachers with industry experience		
		Provide support for teachers to acquire further occupational and career development		
		Provide targeted support for training programs targeted to disadvantaged populations on a systematic basis	CIMSGWD, development partners	Ongoing

table continues next page

Policy goal	Workforce development domain/issues/findings	Strategic directions for reforms and policy actions	Responsibility	Timing
	Absence of national level data on skills supply.	Higher education	MINESUP, development partners	Medium through long-term
		Coordinate the regular collection of quality data on key indicators (enrollments, programs, staffing, financial data, data from graduate tracer studies) to assess skills supply	INS with MINEDUB, MINESEC, MINEFOP, MINESUP, MINEJEUN, development partners	Ongoing
		Principle of Facilitation: Engage employers in setting WfD priorities and in enhancing skills-upgrading of workers		
		Topic 5. Role of employers and industry		
	Many small enterprises are not registered and operate illegally.	Require all enterprises (small/medium/large) to be registered	Cameroon Inter-Ministerial Steering Group for Workforce Development (CIMSGWD), sector skills councils, development partners, INS	Medium-term, followed by periodic evaluations
		Provide tax incentives for enterprises to enhance option for firms to be registered		
	There is no sufficient incubation for innovations.	Patent innovations, establish incentives by promoting innovation		
		Topic 6. Skills-upgrading incentives for employers		
	Enterprises do not invest in training employees, fearing poaching of human resources and knowledge.	Provide measure incentives for enterprises to enhance options for employers skills' upgrading	MINFI, MINEPAT, GICAM, MINJUSTICE, MINPMEESA, MINTSS, CBF, employer organizations (GICAM)	Medium-term, followed by periodic revisions to calibrate incentives and regulations to evolving economic circumstances

table continues next page

Policy goal	Workforce development domain/issues/findings	Strategic directions for reforms and policy actions	Responsibility	Timing
	Enterprises do not invest in training employees fearing poaching of industry intellectual property	Develop regulations for intellectual property to help protect small entrepreneurs		
		Topic 7. Monitoring of the incentive programs		
		Periodic assessment of the incentive programs to determine efficacy and efficiency	CIMSGWD, CTSE	
3. Strengthening Critical Coordination				
Functional Dimension 1. Strategic Framework		**Principle of concentration and assimilation: Formalize key WfD roles for coordinated action on strategic priorities**		
		Topic 8. Roles of government ministries and agencies		
	Absence of unified vision regarding workforce development.	Ensure coherence of key strategic workforce development priorities	CIMSGWD, INS, Development Partners	Ongoing
		Topic 9. Roles of nongovernment WfD stakeholders		
	Evidence about the existence of coordination mechanisms with government entities is rather weak.	Prepare terms of reference setting out key WfD roles for coordinated action on strategic priorities	CIMSGWD, INS, Development Partners, Civil Society Organization (ROJAC, DMJ)	Medium-term
	The mandates of government ministries and agencies with responsibility for WfD overlap in multiple areas; no mechanism exists to ensure coordination of WfD strategies and programs. The legally defined roles and responsibilities of nongovernment stakeholders are not clear.	Institutionalize the structure of workforce development roles and responsibilities by prioritizing the establishment of the Cameroon Inter-Ministerial Steering Group for Workforce Development (CIMSGWD) comprising membership of MINFI, MINEPAT, MINEFOP, MINESUP, GICAM, MINJEC, MINEJEUN, MINPMEESA, Sector Skills Committees/ Councils, Association of Informal Sector Actors, representatives of youth groups, and development partners	MINEPAT and key growth sector ministries	Medium-term

table continues next page

Policy goal	Workforce development domain/issues/findings	Strategic directions for reforms and policy actions	Responsibility	Timing
		Topic 10. Coordination for the implementation of strategic WfD measures		
	Absence of communication on workforce development.	Facilitate communication and interaction among all workforce development stakeholders through the regular publication of a newsletter on workforce development	Cameroon Inter-Ministerial Steering Group for Workforce Development (CIMSGWD)	Medium-term, then periodic and regular
	Absence of concerted planning and strategizing for workforce development.	Ensure semi-annual planning, review of action plan, stocktaking of actions, review of impact evaluation results, and development of priorities at workforce development fora	Nongovernmental platform	
5. Ensuring Efficiency and Equity in Funding				
Functional Dimension 2. System Oversight		**Principle of facilitation: Provide stable funding for effective programs in initial, continuing, and targeted vocational education and training**		
		Topic 11. Overview of funding for WfD		
		Articulate funding strategy		
	The government relies on routine historical budgeting processes to determine funding for technical vocational education and training (TVET) institutions and programs.	Institute performance-based funding for public sector training institutions	MINFI, MINEPAT, CIMSGWD, development partners, CIEP, CCIMA, and others	Medium-term, then periodic and regular

table continues next page

Policy goal	Workforce development domain/issues/findings	Strategic directions for reforms and policy actions	Responsibility	Timing
	The government determines recurrent funding for TVET through a formal process involving only government officials and produces an annual report on TVET for internal purposes.	**Topic 12. Recurrent funding for initial vocational education and training (TVET)** Institute recurrent funding for TVET through a formal process involving government officials and private sector employers; produce annual report to inform the public	MINFI, MINEPAT, CIMSGWD, development partners, MINEFOP, and MINPMEESA	Medium-term, then regular with periodic assessment
		Topic 13. Recurrent funding for continuing vocational education and training (TVET) Institute recurrent funding for continuing TVET through a formal process involving both government officials and private sector employers; produce annual report to inform the public		
	Programs fostering on-the-job training in small and medium enterprises (SMEs) benefit from government support. Government funding for targeted ALMPs benefits mainly youth and rural groups. Support is determined through an ad hoc process involving only government officials in the corresponding implementing agencies.	**Topic 14. Recurrent funding for Training-related Active Labor Market Programs (ALMPs)** Formalize and systematize funding for targeted ALMPs benefiting youth and rural groups and make the process transparent	MINADER, MINJEC	
		Setting up the program management planning of employment and skills at territorial level (GPECT-CAM)	**MINEFOP GICAM CCIMA**	**Short-term**

table continues next page

Policy goal	Workforce development domain/issues/findings	Strategic directions for reforms and policy actions	Responsibility	Timing
		Monitor and enhance equity in funding for training		
		Topic 15. Equity in funding for training programs		
		Allocate funds to achieve efficient results		
	It is unclear if multiple criteria are used to determine funding for the institutions and programs, and whether the criteria are reviewed periodically and consistently.	Clarify criteria applied to determine funding for public sector training institutions	MINFI, MINEPAT, CIMSGWD, development partners	Medium-term, then ongoing
		Clarify criteria for and periodicity of review of funding for public sector training institutions		
	There are no recent formal impact evaluations of funding for beneficiaries of training programs either at the IVET, CVET, levels or under the ALMPs.	Introduce tracer studies to track the beneficiaries of training programs funded by the government	MINEFOP, GICAM, INS, development partners, ministries in charge of education and training	Medium-term, then periodic and regular
		Facilitate sustained partnerships between training institutions and employers		
		Topic 16. Partnerships between training providers and employers		
	Government facilitates formal partnerships between training providers and employers. But there is no information as to whether these take place at the national, regional, or institutional level. Benefits for each party are also unclear.	Promote partnerships between training providers and employers to maximize synergies and learning	MINEFOP, GICAM, MINPMEESA, development partners	Medium-term

table continues next page

Policy goal	Workforce development domain/issues/findings	Strategic directions for reforms and policy actions	Responsibility	Timing
6. Assuring Relevant and Reliable Standards				
Functional Dimension 2. System Oversight		**Broaden the scope of competency standards as a basis for developing qualifications frameworks**		
		Topic 17. Competency standards and National Qualifications Frameworks		
	There are competency standards for some occupations, but there is no National Qualifications Framework (NQF).	Specify accreditation standards by developing and instituting a National Qualifications Framework (NQF) to address accreditation standards for programs, ensure quality assurance, and an NQF certification process	CIMSGWD, GICAM, development partners, key growth sector ministries, ANOR	Medium-term
	There is limited evidence regarding stakeholder engagement with setting competency standards and the extent to which these are used by training providers when developing competency-based curricula			
		Topic 18. Competency standards for major occupations		
	There are competency standards for some occupations, but not for all occupations	Develop and institute competency standards for major occupations in collaboration with the private sector	CIMSGWD, GICAM, development partners, key growth sector ministries, ANOR	Medium-term
	There is limited evidence regarding stakeholder engagement with setting competency standards and the extent to which these are used by training providers when developing competency-based curricula.			

table continues next page

Policy goal	Workforce development domain/issues/findings	Strategic directions for reforms and policy actions	Responsibility	Timing
		Establish protocols for assuring the credibility of skills testing and certification		
		Topic 19. Occupational skills testing		
	Unclear whether competency-based testing is used for skilled and semi-skilled occupations. There is no evidence that there are skills testing for major occupations, whether it assesses theoretical knowledge and practical skills, and whether certificates awarded have any impact on employment and earnings.	Develop protocols for assessing the credibility of public and private sector skills programs	CIMSGWD, INS, development partners	Short-term
		Develop competency-based testing for skills and semi-skilled occupations	MINEDUB, MINESEC, MINEFOP, MINESUP, MINJEC, sector skills committees/councils, INS, development partners	Medium-term
		Topic 20. Skills testing and certification		
	Qualifications certified by noneducation ministers are not recognized for admission into formal programs under the Ministry of Education.	Assess qualifications certified by noneducation ministers against national accreditation standards for equivalency		
		Outline threshold conditions and entry level guidelines for recognition of noneducation ministers certified qualifications and admission into formal programs under the Ministry of Education	MINEDUB, MINESEC, MINEFOP, MINESUP, MINJEC, development partners, CCIMA	Medium-term

table continues next page

Policy goal	Workforce development domain/issues/findings	Strategic directions for reforms and policy actions	Responsibility	Timing
	Recognition of prior learning is just now receiving some attention, reflected in the development of a regulatory framework with the support of donors.	Develop regulatory framework (threshold conditions, guidelines) for recognition of prior learning for continuing education programs		
		Topic 21. Skills testing for major occupations		
	Unclear whether competency-based testing is used for skilled and semi-skilled occupations. There is no evidence that there are skills testing for major occupations, whether it assesses theoretical knowledge and practical skills, and whether certificates awarded have any impact on employment and earnings.	Develop protocols for major occupations	CIMSGWD, INS, development partners	Short-term
		Develop competency-based testing for the major occupations	MINEDUB, MINESEC, MINEFOP, MINESUP, MINJEC, sector skills committees/councils, INS, development partners	Medium-term
		Develop and enforce accreditation standards for maintaining the quality of training provision		
		Topic 22. Government oversight of accreditation		
	Absence of central oversight for the accreditation of training institutions.	Terms of reference and action to establish government working group for oversight of accreditation	CIMSGWD	Short-term

table continues next page

171

Policy goal	Workforce development domain/issues/findings	Strategic directions for reforms and policy actions	Responsibility	Timing
		Topic 23. Establishment of accreditation standards		
	There is no National Accreditation Framework (NQF). There is limited evidence regarding stakeholder engagement with setting accreditation standards and the extent to which these are used by potential training providers.	Specify accreditation standards by developing and instituting a National Accreditation Framework (NAF) to address accreditation standards for programs, renewal of accreditation by training institutions, and a NAF certification process	CIMSGWD working group on accreditation, CCIMA, key growth sector ministries, MINEFO	Medium-term
		Topic 25. Incentives and support for accreditation		
	Absence of evidence of incentives and support for training institutions to become accredited.	Outline incentives and support for training institutions to seek accreditation		Medium-term
		Provide for the regulation and give redeployment opportunities at the MINFOPRA and MINTSS	**MINFOPRA, MINTSS**	**Medium-term**
4. Diversifying Pathways for Skills Acquisition				
Functional Dimension 2. System Oversight		**Principle of concatenation:** promote educational progression and permeability through multiple pathways, including for TVET students		
		Topic 26. Develop learning pathways and foster articulation across levels and programs		
	Weak pathways for learning, gathering credits, and building credentials.	Build bridges and ladders in the education and training system and facilitate credit transfers, credit portability	MINEDUB, MINESEC, MINEFOP, MINESUP, MINJEC, MINFOF, MINADER, MINEPIA, MINPROFF	Medium-term

table continues next page

Policy goal	Workforce development domain/issues/findings	Strategic directions for reforms and policy actions	Responsibility	Timing
	There is no evidence as to whether students in technical and vocational education have options for further formal skills acquisition beyond the secondary level.	**Topic 27. Public perception of pathways for TVET** Launch strategic communications to improve information dissemination regarding learning and career pathways beyond secondary education **Facilitate lifelong learning through articulation of skills certification and recognition of prior learning**	CIMSGWD, MINESEC, MINEFOP, MINJEC	Medium-term
	Infrastructure for lifelong learning largely absent. There are limited opportunities for lifelong learning. Limited evidence regarding demand for TVET programs.	Develop the infrastructure for lifelong learning through pathways for formal adult education programs and other forms of learning, including setting up public venues for knowledge dissemination (museums, learning centers, public libraries) **Topic 28. Articulation of skills certification** Refer to topic 20 on Skills Testing and Certification **Topic 29. Recognition of prior learning** Refer to topic 20 and Topic 27	Ministry of Culture, Ministry of Commerce, Ministry of Tourism, GICAM, CCIMA	Medium through long-term
	Recognition of prior learning is just now receiving some attention, reflected in the development of a regulatory framework with the support of donors.	**Provide support services for skills acquisition by workers, job-seekers and the disadvantaged**		

table continues next page

Policy goal	Workforce development domain/issues/findings	Strategic directions for reforms and policy actions	Responsibility	Timing
		Topic 30. Support for further occupational and career development		
		Set policies and procedures to renew programs		
	Limited number of registered private sector training institutions.	Create a market for learning by leveraging the private sector for pre-employment and on-the-job training	Ministry of Commerce, GICAM	Medium through long-term
		Review and updates for existing programs	CIMSGWD, INS, development partners	Periodic and regular
		Topic 31. Training-related provision of services for the disadvantaged		
	Absence of targeted policies for training services for minority groups.	Develop policies for training services for disadvantaged and vulnerable groups	CIMSGWD working group	Medium-term
7. Enabling Diversity and Excellence in Training Provision				
Functional Dimension 3. Service Delivery		**Encourage and regulate nonstate provision of training**		
		Topic 32. Scope and formality of nonstate training provision		
	There seem to be limited measures for quality assurance, but there is no information on what these are.	Promote diversity in training provision by encouraging formal private sector training provision	CIMSGWD, development partners, CCIMA	Short-term
		Develop quality assurance measures for nonformal training		Medium-term

table continues next page

Policy goal	Workforce development domain/issues/findings	Strategic directions for reforms and policy actions	Responsibility	Timing
		Topic 33. Incentives for nonstate providers		
		Refer to related topics 3, 5, 6, 25, & 45		
		Topic 34. Quality assurance of nonstate training provision		
		Refer to topic 17		
		Topic 35. Review of policies toward nonstate training provision	CIMSGWD working groups, MINEFOP, CCIMA	Medium-term
		Refer to related topics 3, 5, 6, 17, 25, 38, 45		
		Combine incentives and autonomy in the management of public training institutions		
		Topic 36. Targets and incentives for public training institutions		
		Refer to topics 4 and 38		
		Motivate public training institutions to respond to demand for skills		
		Topic 37. Autonomy and accountability of public training institutions		
	It is unclear if public training providers have autonomy. Some seem to be able to generate and retain revenues, and have a management board and limited channels to address complaints.	Provide autonomy to public sector training institutions enabling them to generate and retain revenues, establish a management board comprising public sector employees, Sector Skills Committees/Council members, and GICAM members	CIMSGWD, MINEFOP, CCIMA, and key growth sector ministries	Medium-term, then ongoing
		Create a complaints redressal mechanism		

table continues next page

Policy goal	Workforce development domain/issues/findings	Strategic directions for reforms and policy actions	Responsibility	Timing
	It is unclear if approvals and closures of training programs are well informed and follow a rigorous process.	Specify norms and rigorous processes for assessing the validity and external efficiency (labor market outcomes) of training programs	CIMSGWD, development partners	Medium-term
		Topic 38. Introduction and closure of public training programs		
	Public providers seem to offer training, but there is not enough evidence regarding the conditions under which public institutions are set up and the conditions under which they are closed.	Incentivize public providers to meet workforce development standards by publicly recognizing and rewarding public providers who do adhere consistently to established standards	Cameroon Inter-Ministerial Steering Group for Workforce Development (CIMSGWD) and sector skills councils	Medium-term
		Develop regulations for intellectual property to help protect public sector employees		
		Patent innovations		
8. Fostering Relevance in Training Programs				
Functional Dimension 3. Service Delivery		**Principle of relevance: integrate industry and expert input into the design and delivery of public training programs**		
		Topic 39. Links between training institutions and industry		
		Link training industry and research institutions		
	There seem to be some informal links between training and research institutions around the development of training programs and general assessment of the system.	Specify and develop systematic formal links between training and research institutions through annual seminars/conferences	CIMSGWD, MINRESI	Medium-term, then ongoing

table continues next page

Policy goal	Workforce development domain/issues/findings	Strategic directions for reforms and policy actions	Responsibility	Timing
		Establish formal links between training providers and industry through annual WfD congresses	MINEFOP, GICAM, sector skills committees/councils, development partners	Ongoing
		Integrate industry and expert input into the design and delivery of public training programs		
		Topic 40. Links between training institutions and industry		
	There is limited evidence of the extent to which government is successful in establishing formal links and encouraging significant collaboration between training providers and industry.	Refer to topics 4, 5, 6, 16, 32, 33, 34, 35, 36, & 39	MINEFOP, GICAM, MINFI MINEPAT CCIMA sector skills committees/councils, development partners	Medium-term, then on an ongoing basis
		Topic 41. Industry role in the design of program curricula		
		Refer to topic 4		
		Topic 42. Industry role in the specification of facility standards		
		Refer to topics 17, 18, 19, 20, 21, 22, 23 & 25		
		Topic 43. Links between training and research institutions		
		Recruit and support administrators and instructors for enhancing the market-relevance of public training programs		
		Topic 44. Recruitment and in-service training of heads of public training institutions		

table continues next page

Policy goal	Workforce development domain/issues/findings	Strategic directions for reforms and policy actions	Responsibility	Timing
	Institutional setup exists; extant public training institutions have heads of institutions.	Review of management competencies, assessment of competency levels, development of in-service training programs, administration of training programs, and certification of programs		
		Topic 45. Recruitment and in-service training of instructors of public training institutions		
	Institutional setup exists; extant public training institutions have instructors of institutions.	Review of competencies required for instructors, assessment of competency levels, development of in-service training programs, administration of training programs, and certification of programs		
	Although there are some links between training providers and industry in some sectors, it is unclear whether firms provide input into the design of curricula. Further, despite the government's stated intentions, there is not enough evidence that industry has any role in specifying facility standards.	Design training with industry inputs	MINEFOP, GICAM, sector skills committees/councils, development partners, key growth sector ministries	Medium-term
		Establish sector skills councils for the key growth sectors to advise the government on sector skill needs, standards (minimum requirements), qualification frameworks, governance, and financing options	CIMSGWD, key growth sector ministries	Short-term
		Improve competence of WfD administrators and instructors	Key growth sector ministries	
	Limited data and information are available to verify the competence of WfD administrators and instructors.	Provide incentives for periodic participation of WfD administrators and instructors in conferences to improve their understanding of subject matter, develop networks to exchange knowledge, and foster peer learning	CIMSGWD, development partners key growth sector ministries	Ongoing

table continues next page

Policy goal	Workforce development domain/issues/findings	Strategic directions for reforms and policy actions	Responsibility	Timing
9. Enhancing Evidence-Based Accountability for Results				
Functional Dimension 3. Service Delivery		**Expand the availability and use of policy-relevant data for focusing providers' attention on training outcomes, efficiency, and innovation**		
		Topic 46. Administrative data from training providers		
	There is insufficient national-level data on skills supply.	Coordinate the regular collection of quality data on key indicators (enrollment, programs, staffing, financial data, data from graduate tracer studies) to assess the skills supply	INS with MINEDUB, MINESEC, MINEFOP, MINESUP, MINJEC, development partners, **GICAM, key growth sector ministries**	Ongoing
	Public training providers seem to collect some data and occasionally produce reports; private training providers are not required to collect and report data.	Specify reporting requirements by training institutions, including the periodicity of reports to be produced and made available to the public	CIMSGWD	Short-term
	The government occasionally conducts or sponsors skills-related surveys in a limited number of sectors, but not impact evaluations of existing programs to determine their efficacy.	Strengthen workforce development monitoring and evaluation	Sector skills committees/councils, **MINEFOP, MINESUP, INS,** development partners	Short to medium-term, then periodic and regular
		Conduct periodic impact evaluations of existing programs to determine efficacy vis-à-vis the labor market, program quality, uptake/ enrollment, numbers graduating, numbers dropping out		
		Topic 47. Survey and other data		
		Conduct periodic labor and workforce development surveys to assess the demand and supply of skills		

table continues next page

Policy goal	Workforce development domain/issues/findings	Strategic directions for reforms and policy actions	Responsibility	Timing
		Topic 48. Use of data to monitor and improve program and system performance		
	Government does not use the available data, and does not emphasize the need for data collection and publication of labor market outcomes of graduates.	Increase focus on outcomes, efficiency, and innovation by linking labor market reports with training providers' reports to assess achievement of outcomes, efficiency of the programs, and whether innovations can be fostered	CIMSGWD, INS, development partners	Ongoing

Note: ALMPs = Active Labor Market Programs; ANOR = Standards and Quality Agency; CBF = Cameroon Business Forum; CCIMA = Chamber of Commerce, Industry, Mines, and Crafts; CIEP =International Center for Education Studies of Paris; CIMSGWD = Cameroon Inter-Ministerial Steering Group for Workforce Development; CTSE = Technical Committee of Monitoring and Evaluation; CVET = Continuing Vocational Education and Training; DWJ = Dynamic World Youth; DSCE = Strategy Document for Growth and Employment; ECCD = early childhood care and development; ECD = early childhood development; GPECT= Provisional Management of Jobs and Skills; GICAM = Association of Private Sector Employers; INS = National Institute of Statistics; IVET = Initial Vocational Education and Training; LMIS = labor market information system; MINADER = Ministry of Agriculture and Rural Development; MINEDUB = Ministry of Primary Education; MINEFOP = Ministry of Employment, Vocational Education and Training; MINEJEUN = Ministry of Youth; MINEPAT = Ministry of Economy, Planning and Regional Integration; MINEPIA = Ministry of Livestock, Fisheries and Animal Industry; MINESEC = Ministry of Secondary Education; MINESUP = Ministry of Higher Education; MINFI = Ministry of Finance; MINFOF = Ministry of Forests and Wildlife; MINFOPRA = Ministry of Public Service and Administrative Reform; MINJEC = Ministry of Youth and Civic Education; MINJUSTICE = Ministry of Justice; MINPMEESA = Ministry of Small and Medium Size Enterprises, Social Economy and Handicrafts; MINPROFF = Ministry of Women's Empowerment and Family; MINRESI = Ministry of Scientific Research and Innovation; MINTSS = Ministry of Labor and Social Security; NAF = National Accreditation Framework; NQF = National Qualifications Framework; PRIMATURE = Prime Minister's Office; ROJAC= Network of Youth Organizations for Citizen Action; SMEs = small and medium enterprises; TVET = technical, industrial, vocational, and entrepreneurship training; WfD = Workforce Development.

References

Almeida, Rita, Jere Behrman, and David Robalino, eds. 2012. *The Right Skills for the Job? Rethinking Training Policies for Workers*. Washington, DC: World Bank.

Ames and Godang. 2012. "Employment in Cameroon: Stock Take of Studies and Programs, Assessment of Existing Gaps and Opportunities and Proposed Next Steps." World Bank, Washington, DC.

Anderson, Arnold C., 1963. *The Impact of the Educational System on Technological Change and Modernization*. First Edition in Industrialization and Society. Edited by Bert F. Hoslitz and Wilbert E. Moore. 1963. UNESCO. Mouton. Second Edition in 1970.

Ansu, Yaw, and Jee-Peng Tan. 2012. "Skills Development for Economic Growth in Sub-Saharan Africa: A Pragmatic Perspective." In *Good Growth and Governance in Africa: Rethinking Development Strategies*, edited by Akbar Noman, Kwesi Botchwey, Howard Stein, and Joseph E. Stiglitz. Oxford Scholarship Online: May 2012. doi:10.1093/acp rof:oso/9780199698561.001.0001.

Banerji, Arup, Wendy Cunningham, Ariel Fiszbein, Elizabeth King, Harry Patrinos, David Robalino, and Jee-Peng Tan. 2010. *Stepping Up Skills for More Jobs and Higher Productivity*. Washington, DC: World Bank.

Barro, R. J., and J. W. Lee. 2010. "A New Data Set of Educational Attainment in the World, 1950–2010." NBER Working Paper 15902, National Bureau of Economic Research, Cambridge, MA.

Bem, Justin, Pierre Joubert Nguetse Tegoum, Tatiana Morel Samo Tcheeko, and Jackson Essoh. 2013. *Efficience de production du secteur informel non-agricole et réduction de la pauvreté au Cameroun*. Working Paper 2013–06, Partnership for Economic Policy, Nairobi, Kenya.

Boudon, Raymond. 1973. *L'inégalité des chances, la mobilité sociale dans les sociétés industrielles*. Colin A. Paris, 1973. p.237. Série Sociologie.

Brazilian Institute of Geography and Statistics. 2006. *Pesquisa Nacional por Amostra de Domicílios (National Household Survey)—PNAD*. In Schneider et al. 2009.

Charlier, Florence, and Charles N'çho-Oguie. 2009. *Sustaining Reforms for Inclusive Growth in Cameroon: A Development Policy Review*. Washington, DC: World Bank.

Chiang 1998 in Ansu and Tan, May 2012.

Cunningham, Wendy, Marcia Laura Sanchez-Puerta, and Alice Wuermli. November 2010. *World Bank: Employment Policy Primer: Active Labor Market Programs for Youth*. No. 16. World Bank. Washington, DC.

Dinh, Hinh T., V. Palmade, V. Chandra, and F. Cossar. 2012. *Light Manufacturing in Africa: Targeted Policies to Enhance Private Investment and Create Jobs.* Africa Development Forum, World Bank, Washington, DC.

Elder, Sara, and Koko Siaka Koné. 2014. "Labour Market Transitions of Young Women and Men in Sub-Saharan Africa." International Labour Organization, Geneva.

Filmer, Deon, and Louise Fox, with Karen Brooks, Aparijita Goyal, Taye Mengistae, Patrick Premand, Dena Ringold, Siddharth Sharma, and Sergiy Zorya. 2014. *Youth Employment in Sub-Saharan Africa.* Washington, DC: World Bank and Agence Française de Développement.

Ghura, Dhaneshwar. 1997. "Private Investment and Endogenous Growth: Evidence from Cameroon." IMF Working Paper No. WP/97/165, International Monetary Fund, Washington, DC.

Government of Cameroon. 2005. "Survey of Employment and the Informal Sector in Cameroon" [Productivité dans le secteur informel à Cameroun]. National Institute of Statistics, Yaoundé, Cameroon.

———. 2009. "Strategy Document for Growth and Employment." Yaoundé, Cameroon.

———. 2010a. *Recensement général des entreprises (RGE 2009): Rapport principal des résultats.* National Institute of Statistics, Yaoundé, Cameroon.

———. 2010b. "Survey of Employment and the Informal Sector in Cameroon" [Productivité dans le secteur informel à Cameroun]. National Institute of Statistics, Yaoundé, Cameroon.

———. 2011. "La population du Cameroun en 2010." National Institute of Statistics, Yaoundé, Cameroon.

———. 2012a. *Deuxième enquête sur l'emploi et le secteur informel au Cameroun (ESSI 2): Distorsions et mobilité sur le marché du travail.* National Institute of Statistics, Yaoundé, Cameroon.

———. 2012b. *Deuxième enquête sur l'emploi et le secteur informel au Cameroun (ESSI 2): Insertion sur le marché du travail.* National Institute of Statistics, Yaoundé, Cameroon.

———. 2012c. "Second Survey of Employment and the Informal Sector in Cameroon" [Productivité dans le secteur informel à Cameroun]. National Institute of Statistics, Yaoundé, Cameroon.

———. 2013a. "Document de Stratégie du Secteur de l'Éducation et de la Formation: 2013–2020." (Education and Training Sector Strategy 2013–2020). Yaoundé, Cameroon.

———. 2013b. *Évaluation de la pertinence des filières de formation préparant à l'industrie minérale.* By Serge Again Godong. Rapport Intermediaire No.1. Projet de Renforcement des Capacités du Secteur Minier (PRECASEM). Yaoundé, Cameroon.

———. 2014. *Diagnostique de la formation technique et professionnelle et la présentation d'un plan d'action dans les métiers du Bois au Cameroun.* Government of Cameroon, Yaoundé, Cameroon.

Government of Cameroon. Ministry of Forestry and Wildlife (MINFOF). 2012. Decision No.2637/D/MINFOF of December 6, 2012. Yaoundé, Cameroon.

Himelein, Kristen. 2014. "Growth Inclusiveness and the Impact of Fiscal and Budget Decisions in Cameroon." Mimeo. Africa Region, World Bank, Washington, DC.

IFC (International Finance Corporation). 2011. "Education for Employment." IFC, Washington, DC. http://www.e4earabyouth.com/pdf/MGLPDF136022536640.pdf.

IFC (International Finance Corporation) and Islamic Development Bank. 2011. "Education for Employment: Realizing Arab Youth Potential." IFC, Washington, DC.

ILO (International Labour Organization). 2009a. Étude sur la filière porteuse d'emploi "Palmier à Huile" [Study on the Carrier Industry Job "Palm Oil"]. Ministry of Employment and Professional Training, Yaoundé, Cameroon.

ILO (International Labour Organization). 2009b. "School to Work Transition Survey." ILO, Geneva. http://www.ilo.org/wcmsp5/groups/public/---ed_emp/documents /instructionalmaterial/wcms_140858.pdf.

ILO (International Labour Organization). 2010. "Global Employment Trends for Youth." Special Issue on the Impact of the Global Economic Crisis on Youth. ILO, Geneva.

IMF (International Monetary Fund). *World Economic Outlook*, October 2013. Washington, DC: IMF.

INS (National Institute of Statistics). 1996. "Cameroon Household Survey." INS, Yaoundé, Cameroon.

———. 2001. "Second Cameroon Household Survey." INS, Yaoundé, Cameroon.

———. 2002. "Deuxième enquête camerounaise auprès des ménages. Pauvreté et éducation au Cameroun en 2001" [Second Cameroon Household Survey: Poverty and Education in Cameroon in 2001]. INS, Yaoundé, Cameroon.

———. 2005. "Employment and Informal Sector Surveys." INS, Yaoundé, Cameroon.

———. 2006 "Note de synthése de principaux résultats de l'enquéte Nationale sur l'emploi au Cameroun. (Atelier du 31 mai 2006 a Yaoundé)" [Synthesis Note on the Results of the National Survey on Employment in Cameroon]. INS, Yaoundé, Cameroon.

———. 2007. "Third Cameroon Household Survey." INS, Yaoundé, Cameroon.

———. 2009a. "Demographic and Health Surveys 2009." INS, Yaoundé, Cameroon.

———. 2009b. *Recensement Général des Entreprises*. Yaoundé, Cameroon: INS.

———. 2012. "Productivity in the Informal Sector in Cameroon: A Comprehensive Analysis of the National Statistical Institute, Employment, and Informal Sector Surveys." EESI II Dataset. INS, Yaoundé, Cameroon.

Kwemo, Stéphanie. 2012. *L'OHADA et le secteur informel, l'exemple du Cameroun*. Brussels: Éditions Larcier.

McKinsey Global Institute. 2012. "Africa at Work: Job Creation and Inclusive Growth." McKinsey Global Institute.

MINEFOP (Ministry of Employment, Vocational Education, and Training) and ILO (International Labour Organization). 2009a. "Étude sur la filière porteuse d'emploi 'Palmier à Huile.'" MINEFOP, Yaoundé, Cameroon.

———. 2009b. *Projet d'Appui à la Promotion de l'Emploi et à la Réduction de la Pauvreté: Étude sur le filière porteuses d'emploi* "Le Tourisme." Onana, Zacharie Ewolo. MINEFOP, Yaoundé, Cameroon.

MINEFOP (Ministry of Employment, Vocational Education, and Training), ILO (International Labour Organization) Bureau Sous Régional pour l'Afrique centrale avec Ministère de l'Enseignement de la Formation et Professionnelle, and BIT/BSR. 2009. *Étude sur la filière porteuse d'Emploi* "Le Tourisme." Projet d'Appui à la Promotion de l'Emploi et à la Réduction de la Pauvreté. Rapport définitif par Zacharie Ewolo Onana. Yaoundé, Cameroon.

MINEPAT (Ministry of Economy, Planning, and Regional Integration). 2014. "PCFC Value Chain Report." Diagnostic commissioned for the Projet Compétitivité des Filières de Croissance. MINEPAT, Yaoundé, Cameroon.

Ministère de l'Emploi et de la Formation Professionnelle et Organisation Internationale du Travail—Bureau Sous Régional pour l'Afrique centrale. 2009a. *Étude de la filière Bois au Camero un: Identification des interventions porteuses d'emplois.* Rapport Final. By Ed Perry and Kolokosso A. Bediang. Yaoundé, Cameroon.

———. 2009b. *Etude sur la filière porteuse d'Emploi* "Palmier à Huile." Rapport Final. By Lebailly Philippe and Tentchou Jean. Yaoundé, Cameroon.

Ministry of Education. 2013. "Education Sector Strategy 2013–2020." Ministry of Education, Government of Cameroon, Yaoundé.

Ministry of Education, Cuba. 2002. *Educa a tu hijo (Educate your Child).* Havana. MINED. United Nations Children's Fund (UNICEF). Latin American Reference Center for Preschool Education (CELEP) in Schneider et al. 2009.

Ministry of Education & National Institute of Education Studies, Anisio, Teixeira, Brazil. 2007. *Censo escolar: sinopse estatística da educação básica (School census: statistical synopsis of basic education).* Brasília: MEC/INEP. In Schneider et al. 2009.

Ndjobo, Patrick Marie Nga. 2013. "Analyse des impacts de l'éducation sur le fonctionnement du marché du travail au Cameroun". PhD dissertation. University of Yaoundé 2, Cameroon.

OIT (Organisation International du Travail). 2009. *Étude sur le potentiel d'emploi dans le secteur des infrastructures au Cameroun.* By Samuel Yemene, Martine Ekoue Niyabi, Donnat Takuete, and Francis Teubissi, with Vincent Kouete and Angélique Matene Sob. OIT, Yaoundé, Cameroon.

Pro-Invest. 2014. World Bank financed IDA-47800 CM. Report prepared by Pro-Invest. January 2014. "Technical Assistance for the Realization of a Diagnostic Study of the Technical and Vocational Training and the Presentation of an Action Plan in the Trade of Wood in Cameroon." Pro-Invest.

Republic of Cameroon. Ministry of Planning, Economy and Regional Development. February 2009. Cameroon Vision 2035. Working Paper. Yaoundé, Cameroon.

Schneider, Alessandra, Vera Regina Ramires, Maria da Graça Gomes Paiva, and Leila Almeida. 2009. *The Better Early Childhood Development Program: An Innovative Brazilian Public Policy.* United Nations Educational, Scientific, and Cultural Organization, Paris.

Tan, Jee-Peng, Kiong Hock Lee, Alexandria Valerio, Joy Yoo-Jeung Nam. 2013. *What Matters in Workforce Development: A Framework and Tool for Analysis. Systems Approach for Better Education (SABER)—Workforce Development (WfD).* World Bank. Washington, DC.

Tegoum, Pierre Ngueste. 2013. "Poverty Maps of Cameroon." In *Cameroon Poverty Assessment.* National Institute of Statistics and Central Bureau of Census and Population Studies, Yaoundé, Cameroon.

UNESCO (United Nations Education Scientific, and Cultural Organization). 2009. *Education Indicators, Technical Guidelines.* Institute for Statistics, UNESCO, Paris.

World Bank. 2003. "Education Sector Status Report." Yaoundé, Cameroon.

———. 2005. "Pro-poor Growth in the 1990s: Lessons and Insights from 14 Countries." World Bank, Washington, D.C.

————. 2008. "Cameroun: Étude de compétitivité de la chaîne de valeur du secteur agricole." Report No. AAA25-CM. Agriculture and Rural Development Department, Africa Region, World Bank, Washington, DC.

————. 2009a. *Cluster Initiatives for Competitiveness: A Practical Guide and Toolkit.* Washington, DC: World Bank.

————. 2009b. "Enterprise Surveys: Cameroon Country Profile." World Bank, Washington, DC.

————. 2012a. "Cameroon Economic Update: Unlocking the Labor Force: An Economic Update on Cameroon, with a Focus on Employment." Cameroon Country Office, World Bank, Yaoundé, Cameroon.

————. 2012b. "Education for All-Fast Track Initiative: Support to the Education Sector. Implementation Completion and Results Report." Report No: ICR00002369. World Bank, Washington, DC.

————. 2012c. *SABER Workforce Development Country Report: Vietnam 2012. Systems Approach for Better Education Results.* Washington, DC: World Bank.

————. 2013a. *Human Development in Africa: Strategic Directions.* Washington, DC: Africa Region, World Bank.

————. 2013b. "Le système d'éducation et de formation du Cameroun dans la perspective de l'émergence." Cameroon Country Status Report on Education. World Bank, Washington, DC.

————. 2014a. "Cameroon SABER-Workforce Development and Country Report 2014." World Bank, Washington, DC.

————. 2014b. *Skilling Up Vietnam: Preparing the Workforce for a Modern Market Economy.* Vietnam Development Report 2014. Washington, DC: World Bank.

————. 2014c. "Some Facts on Cameroon's Growth and Poverty Dynamics." Presentation for the Cameroon Country Economic Memorandum. World Bank, Washington, DC.

————. 2014d. *World Development Indicators.* Washington, DC: World Bank.

World Bank and IFC (International Finance Corporation). 2014. *Doing Business 2014: Understanding Regulations for Small and Medium-Size Enterprises.* Washington, DC: World Bank.

Environmental Benefits Statement

The World Bank Group is committed to reducing its environmental footprint. In support of this commitment, the Publishing and Knowledge Division leverages electronic publishing options and print-on-demand technology, which is located in regional hubs worldwide. Together, these initiatives enable print runs to be lowered and shipping distances decreased, resulting in reduced paper consumption, chemical use, greenhouse gas emissions, and waste.

The Publishing and Knowledge Division follows the recommended standards for paper use set by the Green Press Initiative. The majority of our books are printed on Forest Stewardship Council (FSC)–certified paper, with nearly all containing 50–100 percent recycled content. The recycled fiber in our book paper is either unbleached or bleached using totally chlorine-free (TCF), processed chlorine-free (PCF), or enhanced elemental chlorine-free (EECF) processes.

More information about the Bank's environmental philosophy can be found at http://www.worldbank.org/corporateresponsibility.

www.ingramcontent.com/pod-product-compliance
Lightning Source LLC
Chambersburg PA
CBHW082354270326
41935CB00013B/1623